Remaking Mul

TRANSLANGUAGING IN THEORY AND PRACTICE
Series Editors: Li Wei, *University College London*, Angel Lin, *Simon Fraser University*, Yuen Yi Lo, *The University of Hong Kong* and Saskia Van Viegen, *York University*.

Translanguaging in Theory and Practice aims to publish work that highlights the dynamic use of an individual's linguistic repertoire and challenges the socially and politically defined boundaries of languages and their hierarchy. We invite research from across disciplines by both established and emergent researchers in multifarious settings, including everyday use, educational, digital and workplace contexts. We also actively welcome and solicit studies on translanguaging in contexts where English is not the mainstream language and where other modalities and semiotic resources take prominence over speech and writing. The series is transdisciplinary and encourages scholars to publish empirical research on translanguaging, especially that which aims to disrupt power relations, to create new identities and communities, to engage in the discussion of translanguaging theories and pedagogies, and/or to help the field of translanguaging consolidate its scholarship.

Topics to be covered by the series include:

- Theoretical underpinnings of Translanguaging.
- Translanguaging Pedagogies.
- Translanguaging in Assessment.
- Translanguaging and Language Policy.
- Translanguaging in Everyday Social Practices in Different Contexts and Communities, including Digital/ Social/ Media.

All books in this series are externally peer-reviewed.

Full details of all the books in this series and of all our other publications can be found on http://www.multilingual-matters.com, or by writing to Multilingual Matters, St Nicholas House, 31-34 High Street, Bristol, BS1 2AW, UK.

TRANSLANGUAGING IN THEORY AND PRACTICE: 2

Remaking Multilingualism

A Translanguaging Approach

Edited by
Bahar Otcu-Grillman and Maryam Borjian

MULTILINGUAL MATTERS
Bristol • Jackson

DOI https://doi.org/10.21832/OTCU0848

Library of Congress Cataloging in Publication Data

A catalog record for this book is available from the Library of Congress.

Names: Otcu-Grillman, Bahar, editor. | Borjian, Maryam, editor. | García, Ofelia, honouree.

Title: Remaking Multilingualism: A Translanguaging Approach/Edited by Bahar Otcu-Grillman, Maryam Borjian.

Description: Bristol, UK; Blue Ridge Summit, PA: Multilingual Matters, 2022. | Series: Translanguaging in Theory and Practice: 2 | Includes bibliographical references and index. | Summary: 'This book is both a collection of cutting-edge research in the areas of multilingualism, translanguaging and bilingual education, and a tribute to the research and influence of Ofelia García. It recognizes Ofelia García's contribution as both a scholar and friend, and her place at the centre of a movement dedicated to equality and inclusion' – Provided by publisher.

Identifiers: LCCN 2021043145 (print) | LCCN 2021043146 (ebook) | ISBN 9781800410831 (paperback) | ISBN 9781800410848 (hardback) | ISBN 9781800410855 (pdf) | ISBN 9781800410862 (epub)

Subjects: LCSH: Multilingualism. | Bilingual education. | Translanguaging (Linguistics) | LCGFT: Essays. | Festschriften.

Classification: LCC P118 .R44 20221 (print) | LCC P118 (ebook) | DDC 404/.2 – dc23/eng/20211101 LC record available at https://lccn.loc.gov/2021043145 LC ebook record available at https://lccn.loc.gov/2021043146

British Library Cataloguing in Publication Data

A catalogue entry for this book is available from the British Library.

ISBN-13: 978-1-80041-084-8 (hbk)
ISBN-13: 978-1-80041-083-1 (pbk)

Multilingual Matters
UK: St Nicholas House, 31-34 High Street, Bristol, BS1 2AW, UK.
USA: Ingram, Jackson, TN, USA.

Website: www.multilingual-matters.com
Twitter: Multi_Ling_Mat
Facebook: https://www.facebook.com/multilingualmatters
Blog: www.channelviewpublications.wordpress.com

The policy of Multilingual Matters/Channel View Publications is to use papers that are natural, renewable and recyclable products, made from wood grown in sustainable forests. In the manufacturing process of our books, and to further support our policy, preference is given to printers that have FSC and PEFC Chain of Custody certification. The FSC and/or PEFC logos will appear on those books where full certification has been granted to the printer concerned.

Typeset by Riverside Publishing Solutions.

*Dedicated to Ofelia García for her lifetime
commitment to the cause of bilingual education,
multilingualism and educational linguistics*

Contents

Contributors   xi

Foreword
A Note on Ofelia García   xvii
Bernard Spolsky

Preface
The Genesis of this Book   xxiii
Maryam Borjian and Bahar Otcu-Grillman

Introduction
Part One: The Local Roots and Global Reach
of Ofelia García's Multilingualism   1
Maryam Borjian

Part Two: A Tribute to Ofelia García: A Translanguaging
Approach   7
Bahar Otcu-Grillman

Part 1: Remaking Multilingualism

1   Imagining Multilingualism with Ofelia: Translanguaging and
the Continua of Biliteracy   19
Nancy H. Hornberger

2   A Mentor from Afar   32
Suresh Canagarajah

3   Ofelia García's Global Classroom   35
Bahar Otcu-Grillman

4   A Letter for Ofelia García   38
Lesley Bartlett

Part 2: Bilingual Pedagogies and Teacher Education

5   Emergent Bilinguals and Trans-Semiotic Practices in the
    New Media Age   43
    Jo Anne Kleifgen

6   Using 'Transfeaturing' to Explore Differentiation in the
    Pursuit of Translanguaging Pedagogical Goals   66
    Marianne Turner and Angel M.Y. Lin

7   Translanguaging in an Urban Social Justice Teacher
    Education Program   80
    Anel V. Suriel and Mary E. Curran

8   Where the Banyan Tree Grows: Nurturing Teachers'
    Translanguaging Pedagogy through A Study Group   97
    Ivana Espinet and Karen Zaino

9   Bilingual Teachers Engage: Poetic Inquiry as a Site for
    Languaging Dilemmas   110
    Carmina Makar

Part 3: Bilingual Community Education

10 Parental Voices in Bilingual Education   129
    Li Wei and Zhu Hua

11 Translanguaging in Bilingual Community Education   141
    Bahar Otcu-Grillman

12 Bilingual Education: Making a U-Turn with Parents and
    Communities   158
    Fabrice Jaumont

Part 4: Language Policy and Language Ideologies

13 Translanguaging: An Ideological Perspective   167
    Angela Creese and Adrian Blackledge

14 Multiple Actors and Interactions Are at Work: English
    Language Policies in Post-Revolutionary Iran   180
    Maryam Borjian

15 Reimagining Language Policy through the Lived Realities
    of Bilingual Youth   195
    Sarah Hesson

16 American Jewish Summer Camps as Translanguaging Thirdspaces   212
    Sharon Avni

Part 5: Epilogue

Afterword
A Brief History of Work and Play with Ofelia García   229
Jo Anne Kleifgen

Appendix
Ofelia García's Publications with Multilingual Matters   233
Bahar Otcu-Grillman

Index   236

Contributors

Sharon Avni is Professor of Academic Literacy and Linguistics at BMCC at the City University of New York (CUNY). Her work uses ethnographic and discourse analytic approaches to address the discursive, ideological, historical and policy perspectives of Hebrew learning and usage in formal and experiential contexts in the United States. She is the co-author of *Hebrew Infusion: Language and Community and American Jewish Summer Camps*, a research affiliate at the Jack, Joseph and Morton Mandel Center for Studies in Jewish Education at Brandeis and a Research Associate at the Research Institute for the Study of Language in Urban Society (RISLUS) at CUNY Graduate Center. She is the recipient of numerous fellowships, including the Advanced Research Collaborative Distinguished Fellowship/CUNY Graduate Center, Spencer Foundation Small Grant and Mellon/ACLS Community College Faculty Fellowship, and won the Distinguished Teaching Award at BMCC/CUNY (2018–2019). Her publications appear in a wide range of academic journals and edited volumes.

Lesley Bartlett is a Professor in Educational Policy Studies. She is also affiliated with Anthropology, Curriculum and Instruction, and Latin American, Caribbean, and Iberian Studies (LACIS). An anthropologist by training who works in the field of International and Comparative Education, Professor Bartlett does research in literacy studies (including multilingual literacies), migration and educator professional development. In 2019, Professor Bartlett was named Faculty Director of the Institute for Regional and International Studies at University of Wisconsin-Madison. She currently co-edits the Anthropology and Education Quarterly with her colleague, Professor Stacey Lee.

Adrian Blackledge is Professor of Sociolinguistics at University of Stirling. He conducts ethnographic research in the fields of multilingualism and translanguaging in education and society. His most recent study was funded by the Arts and Humanities Research Council, 'Translation and Translanguaging: Investigating Linguistic and Cultural Transformations in Superdiverse Wards in Four UK Cities'. His publications include *Voices* *of a City Market* (with Angela Creese, 2019), *The Routledge Handbook of Language and Superdiversity* (with Angela Creese, 2018), *Heteroglossia as Practice and Pedagogy* (with Angela Creese, 2014), *The Routledge Handbook of Multilingualism* (with Marilyn Martin-Jones and Angela Creese, 2012) and *Multilingualism, A Critical Perspective* (with Angela Creese, 2010). He was Poet Laureate for the city of Birmingham, 2014–2016.

Maryam Borjian is Associate Professor of Sociolinguistics and Director of African, Middle Eastern and South Asian Language Programs at Rutgers, the State University of New Jersey. She is the author of *English in Post-Revolutionary Iran: From Indigenization to Internationalization* (Multilingual Matters, 2013), editor of *Language and Globalization: An Autoethnographic Approach* (Routledge, 2017) and the co-editor (with Charles Häberl) of 'Middle Eastern Languages in Diasporic USA Community' a special issue of *International Journal of the Sociology of Language* (Mouton de Gruyter, 2016).

Suresh Canagarajah is the Edwin Erle Sparks Professor of Applied Linguistics, English, and Asian Studies at Penn State University. He teaches multilingual writing, World Englishes, and postcolonial studies. He edited the Routledge Handbook on Migration and Language which won AAAL's 2020 best book award.

Angela Creese is Professor of Linguistic Ethnography in the Faculty of Social Sciences at the University of Stirling. Her research interests are in sociolinguistics, multilingualism and interaction in everyday life. She has co-written on linguistic ethnography (with Fiona Copland, 2014), and multilingualism (with Adrian Blackledge, 2010). She has edited several large handbook collections on superdiversity (with Blackledge, 2017), multilingualism (with Martin-Jones and Blackledge) and heteroglossia (with Blackledge, 2010). She has also published on collaborative teaching in linguistically diverse classrooms (2008). She is a Fellow of the Academy of Social Science. In 2010 she received the Helen C Bailey Award (Alumni) for 'Outstanding contribution to educational linguistics', from the University of Pennsylvania.

Mary E. Curran is a Professor of Professional Practice in Language Education at Rutgers Graduate School of Education. For more than 20 years, she has prepared future world language, English as a second language and bilingual educators. She directs the Rutgers GSE Office of Local-Global Partnerships. Her scholarship focuses on community-engaged language education, language teacher education and local-global partnerships.

Ivana Espinet is an Assistant Professor at Kingsborough Community College. She holds a PhD in Urban Education from the CUNY Graduate

Center and an MA in Instructional Technology and Education from Teachers College, Columbia University. She is a former project director for CUNY New York State Initiative on Emergent Bilinguals. She is interested in the use of multimodal and collaborative methodologies to learn about emergent bilinguals in school and in out of school programs.

Sarah Hesson is an Associate Professor in the Educational Studies Department and the Co-Director of the TESOL Program at Rhode Island College. She earned her doctorate in Urban Education at the CUNY Graduate Center. Some of her current research interests include the school experiences of Latinx adolescent youth, translanguaging as social justice pedagogy and the possibilities of Youth Participatory Action Research (YPAR) with emergent bilingual adolescent youth. She previously worked as an adjunct professor at Hunter College as well as a Research Assistant with the City University of New York – New York State Initiative on Emergent Bilinguals (CUNY-NYSIEB). Sarah received her BA in Comparative Literature from Bryn Mawr College, and earned her Master's in Bilingual Childhood Education from Fordham University through the NYC Teaching Fellows Program. She previously worked at the NYC Department of Education as a bilingual elementary and middle school teacher, and has taught in various educational settings PK-Adult as well.

Nancy H. Hornberger is Professor Emerita at the University of Pennsylvania, USA. She is an educational linguist/anthropologist researching on multilingual education policy and practice in immigrant/ refugee and Indigenous communities. With sustained commitment and work with Quechua speakers and Indigenous bilingual intercultural education in the Andes beginning in 1974, she has also taught, lectured, collaborated and advised internationally. A prolific author and editor, her books include *Indigenous Literacies in the Americas: Language Planning from the Bottom Up* (1997), *Continua of Biliteracy* (2003), *Can Schools Save Indigenous Languages? Policy and Practice on Four Continents* (2008) and *Honoring Richard Ruiz and his Work on Language Planning and Bilingual Education* (2017). Her enduring interests are in how best to support Indigenous and raciolinguistically minoritized learners in education policy and practice and in ongoing collaboration with Indigenous and raciolinguistically minoritized researchers and communities in reclamation and development of their languages.

Fabrice Jaumont is a French educator and researcher based in New York. He currently serves as Education Attaché for the Embassy of France to the United States, a Research Fellow at Fondation Maison des Sciences de l'Homme in Paris and an adjunct professor at New York University. He is President of the Center for the Advancement of Languages, Education, and Communities, a nonprofit publishing organization with a focus on multilingualism, cross-cultural understanding and the empowerment of linguistic communities. An award-winning author, he has published five books, including *The Bilingual Revolution: The Future of Education is in Two Languages*, which provides guidance and advice for parents and educators who want to create a dual-language program in their own school. Jaumont holds a PhD in Comparative and International Education from New York University.

Jo Anne Kleifgen is Professor Emerita of Linguistics and Education and a founder of the Center for Multiple Languages and Literacies at Teachers College, Columbia University. Her research has focused on multilingual/multimodal practices in school and the workplace. She has authored and edited several books, and her work is widely published in language journals and book chapters. She directed funded research projects on using new media to support Latinx adolescents' language and literacy development. Recently, she supervised the evaluation of a program bringing classrooms in the United States and Middle-East/ North Africa together for online collaborative learning. She has been a member of the Executive Committee of the International Linguistic Association since 1991, has served twice as president, and is its current vice president. She serves on several editorial boards and has been a visiting scholar at universities in the United States and abroad.

Angel M.Y. Lin is well respected for her interdisciplinary research on critical literacies, plurilingual education, Content and Language Integrated Learning (CLIL) and language policy and planning in postcolonial contexts. She has published six research books and over 100 research articles. She serves on the editorial boards of international research journals including *Applied Linguistics, International Journal of Bilingual Education and Bilingualism, Critical Inquiry in Language Studies, Language and Education*. In 2018 Angel Lin moved from the University of Hong Kong to Simon Fraser University to take up the position of Tier 1 Canada Research Chair in Plurilingual and Intercultural Education. She is one of the pioneering researchers in translanguaging, trans-semiotizing and plurilingual approaches to pedagogies and literacy assessment.

Carmina Makar was born and raised in Guadalajara, Mexico. She received her BA in Communication Studies from ITESO University, and then as a Fulbright Fellow, earned her MA in International Education Development with focus on Bilingual and Bicultural Education from Teachers College, Columbia University and a doctoral degree in International Development from the same institution. Her research and teaching interests focus on education for diverse populations; bilingual education, critical education; sociocultural approaches to language and literacy and transnational approaches to education and teacher training. Carmina has worked around activating critical education practices across formal and non-formal education spaces, working with schools and grassroots organizations to serve the needs of linguistically diverse learners and their families. As part of her work with childhood, space and community development, Carmina has served as a consultant for UNESCO and UNDP in issues regarding education and development of children in urban environments. She currently serves as faculty for the programs of Bilingual Education and TESOL at the City College of New York.

Bahar Otcu-Grillman is a Professor of TESOL/Bilingual Education in the Literacy and Multilingual Studies Department at Mercy College, New York. She is also the Director of Clinically Rich Intensive Teacher Institute in ESOL (CR-ITI ESOL) grant program within the same department. She teaches bilingual education, ESL teaching methods, clinical practices and linguistics. She earned her doctorate from the program in International Educational Development with a focus on Language, Literacy and Technology at Teachers College Columbia University. Dr Otcu-Grillman's dissertation was published as a book entitled *Language Maintenance and Cultural Identity Construction* (2010) and is the first case study of a Turkish community school in the United States. Among other publications, she co-edited *Bilingual Community Education and Multilingualism: Beyond Heritage Languages in a Global City* (2013) within Multilingual Matters' Bilingual Education and Bilingualism series.

Bernard Spolsky was born and educated in New Zealand and has taught in New Zealand, Australia, England, Canada and Israel. His main publications are in the fields of educational linguistics and language policy. He retired from Bar-Ilan University as Professor Emeritus in 2000 and has published half a dozen books since then.

Anel V. Suriel is a doctoral student at the Rutgers Graduate School of Education. Her research interests broadly include language education policy practices, language teacher education and the identity formation of multilingual students in American classrooms. She was a Bilingual Literacy Instructor for grades 3–8 in New York City and in New Jersey for thirteen years, and she currently serves as the Graduate Student Representative for NJTESOL/NJBE.

Marianne Turner is a Senior Lecturer in Bilingual Education and TESOL at Monash University, Australia. She researches context-sensitive approaches to the integration of language and content in English as an additional language (EAL), foreign and heritage language contexts and her work has been published widely in both language-focused and general education journals. Her interests include the leveraging of students' linguistic and cultural resources for learning, the oral language production of students from different language backgrounds in bilingual programs and teacher collaboration. She has recently written a book entitled *Multilingualism as a Resource and a Goal: Using and Learning Languages in Mainstream Schools* (2019, Palgrave).

Li Wei is Chair of Applied Linguistics at the UCL Institute of Education, University College London (UCL), and Fellow of the Academy of Social Sciences, UK. His research covers various aspects of bilingualism and multilingualism. He is currently Editor of the *International Journal of Bilingual Education and Bilingualism*. His book, co-authored with Ofelia García, *Translanguaging: Language, Bilingualism and Education* (2014, Palgrave) won the 2015 British Association of Applied Linguistics Book Prize.

Karen Zaino is a doctoral student in Urban Education at the CUNY Graduate Center and a Teaching Fellow in the Queens College English Education Department. She studies how teachers make sense of their roles in student-teacher research collaborations. Prior to graduate study, Karen was a high school English teacher for 12 years, and she has also worked for the CUNY Initiative on Immigration and Education, the CUNY-New York State Initiative on Emergent Bilinguals and the College Access: Research and Action Center.

Zhu Hua is Professor of Educational Linguistics and Director of the MOSAIC Research Group for Multilingualism in the School of Education, University of Birmingham. She is Fellow of Academy of Social Sciences, UK. Her research is centered around multilingual and intercultural communication. She has also studied child language development and language learning. She is book series co-editor for Routledge Studies in Language and Intercultural Communication and Cambridge Key Topics in Applied Linguistics, and Forum and Book Reviews Editor of *Applied Linguistics* (Oxford University Press).

Foreword: A Note on Ofelia García

In the days when international travel was still possible (and when I was younger), I would regularly spice up my trips to New York by visiting the Graduate Center of the City University of New York to see Ofelia García and give a talk to her students. I was impressed not just by her and her work, but also by the colleagues and students who shared her enthusiasm for and knowledge about minority language education. I soon learned that this was explained in part by her close association with Joshua Fishman;[1] in her long career, she shared with him exceptionally high productivity, a concern for linguistic minorities and a willingness to innovate. Like Fishman, she was a strong advocate for bilingualism and the recognition of the significance of non-dominant languages and their speakers.

Starting with a jointly written paper in the *International Journal of the Sociology of Language* (García *et al.*, 1985), they collaborated on over a score of papers and books, the last being an issue of the IJSL on Fishmanian sociolinguistics (issue 213); she also co-edited with him a number of highly significant books, including (Fishman & García, 2010; García & Fishman, 2002), and edited a festschrift in his honor (García, 1991). And in his last years, she continued to meet with him when his illness led to his virtual isolation. It was fitting that she served as associate editor of IJSL from 2009 to 2015 and succeeded him as editor from 2015 to 2019.

For many years, García was the leading US advocate for bilingualism. Her first paper, published in IJSL, dealt with the Bilingual Education Act, which she criticized because she thought it was concerned with the assimilation of Hispanics rather than with the language rights of minorities (García, 1983). Her publications and teaching dealt with bilingual education and the rights and problems of Spanish speakers in the United States. Later, she became an expert on translanguaging, a concept developed by Cen Williams in his doctoral thesis (Williams, 1994) and adopted by Colin Baker (Baker, 2001), and first discussed by García in a paper on social justice (García, 2009).

When I first came across the new word, I wondered whether it was another fad adding to the list of language teaching methods (Spolsky, 1979, 1990), but reading García's recent papers, I am now starting to appreciate the value and applicability of the concept. The term is important for making what had been seen as a technical interest in code switching, normally considered by language educators to be a sign of limited proficiency, into a normal practice for those growing up with the complex linguistic repertoires encouraged by multilingual environments such as New York which (García & Fishman, 2002) is celebrated as the multilingual apple. Recognizing the need to replace a goal of producing native-like speakers of authorized named languages with the encouragement of rich multilingual repertoires, she showed her independence of Fishman's favoring of purity (Fishman, 2006a) by approving of the normal language mixing of those growing up with several varieties, making unashamed use of several parts of their language repertoire. By validating this acceptance of multilingual repertoires, she has had a major influence on the freeing of educational linguistics from the chains of the teaching of dead classical languages and allowing for the freedom of living vernacular speech.

In an interview with colleagues from Brazil (Lorenzetti & da Silva, 2020), García expresses concern about what happens to the concept of translanguaging when it institutionally adopted: it was a notion intended initially to disrupt the 'way of looking at bilingual minoritized populations as having a language that is inferior and a language that is dominant, and as having to make sure that [children] followed the norm in both languages, [which] therefore excluded most of these children' (2020: 171). Thus, it is a political act, which leads to feelings of discomfort when one realizes one is working against the state. She confesses that she started with the theories of her mentor Joshua Fishman, but she 'moved because I had a different experience than he had – I had a different life, I was of a different generation...'. She also rejects the notions of Canagarajah [or 'maybe it was Makoni'] who wanted her to talk about 'languaging' because her concern is with 'bilingual minoritized groups'. Named languages are important – 'I want the students that we work with to be able to be successful in standardized English only exams' – but these bilinguals are not shifting from one language to another: she rejected code switching because there were no structural constraints in the bilingual speech she witnessed. She insists on 'trans' because translanguaging is transit, involving one step at a time.

Sitting at home in isolation, García (2020b) questions two beliefs that she believes work to damage Latin American bilingual students, the notion that they have linguistic deficiencies especially in English, and the idea that the deficiencies extend to Spanish because they lack 'academic language'. These myths lead to comparison with monolingual

English speakers learning Spanish, and miss the implication of their translanguaging repertoires, the result of colonialism and global capitalism. By recognizing this, and teaching 'with difficult loving care', she believes that a way can be found to help these minority children 'resignify their lives and education with dignity'. How this might work in practice is suggested in García (2020a: 558) which discusses how Latinx (male and female Latin American) bilingual pupils learn to read: they do not learn in either of their languages but 'use their entire linguistic/multimodal repertoire' and 'leverage all of their meaning-making resources and all of themselves as they engage with text'. A translanguaging approach that encourages them to use all their resources, linguistic in both varieties and non-linguistic, will free them from the restrictions that condemn them to poorer performance. It 'has the potential to also reposition them socially and politically' (2020a: 562), reminding us that García is concerned not just about reading and education but the social and political status of minority groups. What happens in the normal school situation in the United States is the creation of language borders that labels Mexican-Americans (and other Spanish bilinguals) as 'English language learners' and thus minoritizes them, denying them access to advanced coursework and further education, and 'producing an opportunity gap that will result in producing another generation of miseducated, low-wage workers' (Valdés, 2020). By acknowledging the relevance of developing language repertoires rather than proficiency in named languages, translanguaging offers a much better way of dealing with the problems of minority pupils. Liu and Fang (2020) also show how translanguaging can be used as a basis for change in language teaching.

It was García's concern for the pupils rather than for the fate of the named languages that they spoke that helps account for her breaking with the ideology of her mentor, Joshua Fishman. Although Fishman was rightly acclaimed by speakers of endangered languages for his support of the process he called reversing language shift (Fishman, 1990, 1991), his original motivation was to try to understand why other languages besides his own beloved Yiddish were under threat (Fishman, 2006b); although more a sociologist than a linguist, he shared with most linguists other than Labov (2008) a concern for preserving named languages rather than for solving the social and political problems of minorities. Although García's doctorate was in Hispanic and Luso-Brazilian literatures and language, her first job was as a bilingual and ESL teacher and her career has been in education. Translanguaging provided her with the ideological stance to tackle the problems of minority pupils and not to focus on language revival and maintenance. It was this recognition of the political meaning of language issues and the colonialist and racist import of much language teaching that separates her from most applied linguists, who set out to correct the weaknesses of minority pupils just as colonial powers set out to civilize those they had conquered and enslaved (García & Alvis, 2019).

Translanguaging becomes more than a new term for code switching, and goes beyond the ideological claim of those who talk about languaging. It is rather a call for attention to the complex but regular development of bilingual (and presumably multilingual or plurilingual) individual linguistic repertoires and the recognition of the nature of the repertoires of modern societies.

Bernard Spolsky,
Bar-Ilan University, Professor Emeritus

Note

(1) For five years after completing her PhD, she was associated with Yeshiva University.

References

Baker, C. (2001) *Foundations of Bilingual Education and Bilingualism* (3rd edn). Clevedon: Multilingual Matters.

Fishman, J.A. (1990) What is reversing language shift (RLS) and how can it succeed? *Journal of Multilingual and Multicultural Development* 11 (1&2), 5−36.

Fishman, J.A. (1991) *Reversing Language Shift*. Clevedon: Multilingual Matters.

Fishman, J.A. (2006a) *Do Not Leave Your Language Alone: The Hidden Status Agendas Within Corpus Planning in Language Policy*. Mahwah, NJ: Lawrence Erlbaum.

Fishman, J.A. (2006b) A week in the life of a man from the moon. In O. García, R. Peltz, H. Schiffman and G.S. Fishman (eds) *Language Loyalty, Continuity and Change: Joshua A. Fishman's Contributions to International Sociolinguistics* (pp. 111−121). Clevedon: Multilingual Matters.

Fishman, J.A. and García, O. (eds) (2010) *Handbook of Language and Ethnic Identity: Disciplinary and Regional Perspectives* (3rd edn). New York and Oxford: Oxford University Press.

García, O. (1983) Sociolinguistics and language planning in bilingual education for Hispanics in the United States. *International Journal of the Sociology of Language* (44), 43−54.

García, O. (ed.) (1991) *Focus on Bilingual Education: Essays in honor of Joshua A. Fishman* (Vol. I). Amsterdam & Philadelphia: John Benjamins.

García, O. (2009) Education, multilingualism and translanguaging in the 21st century. In T. Skutnabb-Kangas, R. Phillipson, A.K. Mohanty and M. Panda (eds) *Social Justice Through Multilingual Education* (pp. 140−158). Bristol: Multilingual Matters.

García, O. (2020a) Translanguaging and Latinx bilingual readers. *The Reading Teacher* 73 (5), 557−562.

García, O. (2020b) The education of Latinx bilingual children in times of isolation: Unlearning and relearning. *MinneTESOLJournal* 36 (1).

García, O. and Alvis, J. (2019) The decoloniality of language and translanguaging: Latinx knowledge-production. *Journal of Postcolonial Linguistics* 1, 26−40.

García, O. and Fishman, J.A. (eds) (2002) *The Multilingual Apple: Languages in New York* (2nd edn). Berlin: Mouton de Gruyter.

García, O., Fishman, J.A., Gertner, M. and Burunat, S. (1985) Written Spanish in the United States: an analysis of the Spanish of the ethnic press. *International Journal of the Sociology of Language* 1985 (56), 85−98.

Labov, W. (2008) Unendangered dialects, endangered people. In K.A. King, N. Schilling-Estes, L. Fogle, J. L. Lia and B. Soukup (eds) *Sustaining Linguistic Diversity: Endangered and Minority Languages and Language Varieties (Georgetown University Round Table on Languages and Linguistics)* (pp. 219–238). Washington DC: Georgetown University Press.

Liu, Y. and Fang, F. (2020) Translanguaging theory and practice: How stakeholders perceive translanguaging as a practical theory of language. *RELC Journal.* doi:10.1177/0033688220939222.

Lorenzetti, A.N. and da Silva, J.E. (2020) If we don't name ourselves, who's gonna name us?: Hablando de tudo um pouco con Ofelia García. *Revista Interfaces* 11 (01), 170–181.

Spolsky, B. (1979) Contrastive analysis, error analysis, interlanguage and other useful fads. *Modern Language Journal* 62, 250–257.

Spolsky, B. (1990, 8 October) *Language teaching: myths, fairy-tales and politics*, 17th Annual Conference of the Israeli Association of Applied Linguistics, Tel Aviv.

Valdés, G. (2020) (Mis)educating the children of Mexican-origin people in the United States: the challenge of internal language borders. *Intercultural Education.* doi:10.108 0/14675986.2020.1794122.

Williams, C. (1994) Arfarniad o ddulliau dysgu ac addysgu yng nghyd-destun addysg uwchradd ddwyieithog [An evaluation of teaching and learning methods in the context of bilingual secondary education] (PhD). University of Wales, Bangor.

Preface: The Genesis of this Book

What do you do with an idea? Do you walk away from it or do you nourish it? Do you show it to others or do you hide it? In a pre-school story book[1] about an 'idea', these are the questions four-year-olds learn to answer. Pre-schoolers learn that they can 'change the world', with an idea.

The inception of the present book also started with an idea in 2011, when Bahar read and reviewed a tribute volume honoring the work of another scholar.[2] The idea was to develop a similar tribute in honor of Ofelia García – a leading sociolinguist, educational linguist and educator of our time, who tremendously inspired both of us while we both had the privilege of working with her as our doctoral advisor and academic mentor during our memorable years of doctoral studies (2005–2009) at Columbia University's Teachers College. In 2012, when we first discussed the idea of developing a tribute volume in honor of our beloved Ofelia, we were both excited at such a possibility.

We thought of ourselves as a good match, for we had worked with Ofelia on different lines of interest concerning language studies. Bahar's research was on discourse analysis, bilingual education and bilingual community education, whereas Maryam's research concerned the sociological, economic and political aspects of language in schools and societies. At the time, Bahar had just co-edited (with Ofelia García and Zeena Zakharia) a book on the theme of 'Bilingual Community Education and Multilingualism',[3] whereas Maryam's book on the theme of the 'Politics of Educational Borrowing and Lending'[4] was already in press. In spite of our different research focuses, our common transnational perspective made us eager to construct a global lens to guide us in our academic, professional and personal lives. None of these would have been possible had we not had the privilege of working with Ofelia.

A tribute volume for a renowned and accomplished scholar like Ofelia García sounded just right to both of us. 'It would be a meaningful gift, a personal homage and a way of showing our appreciation for her', were the words we said to one another in 2012. Regardless of our immense passion for such collaboration, we could not do it at the time, for we were both busy with new positions, unforeseen health issues and family-related matters. Bahar attempted to restart it a few years later with someone else, but again 'life happened' (a favorite phrase that we borrowed from Ofelia).

When we spoke about this project again in 2020, it was not only the right time but also a historic time for both of us. It was the right time, for throughout the ten years that had passed between conceptualizing the tribute volume idea and actually realizing it, Ofelia's proclivity to produce academic research continued to challenge then current zeitgeist in multilingualism. She had developed further her conceptualization of multilingualism, bilingual education and translanguaging, which led to her research within CUNY-NYSIEB (City University of New York-New York State Initiative on Emergent Bilinguals) and was well-received amongst the sociolinguistic community. It was equally a historic time, for the Covid-19 pandemic had taken hold, threatening the social order – millions were infected, many died, strict social distancing guidelines and lockdowns led to economic uncertainty, job loss and financial anxiety, and still many others yearned for their pre-Covid-19 lifestyle. Within such a circumstance, what did not go away from our minds was the idea of this project; an idea that eventually took flight in August 2020.

Entitled *Remaking Multilingualism: A Translanguaging Approach*, this tribute volume is about the remaking of multilingualism; a collective movement initiated by Ofelia García and her close network of remarkable allies, prolific scholars and leading educators from throughout the world who have devoted their professional and academic lives to the cause of linguistic equality, justice, pluralism, diversity and inclusion in schools and societies worldwide. Using translanguaging as its underlying approach, this book takes the reader beyond named languages and named nation states to place the emphasis on us, human beings, the speakers of different languages and the residents of different parts of the world; it is about us and the ways through which we use all our resources (linguistic, meta-linguistic and socio-cultural) to live, work and communicate with one another in the backdrop of inequality in our highly stratified globalized world of the twenty first century.

This book can be considered a true international collection, which offers its readers a wide array of perspectives, languages, places and writing styles. Like the concept of 'translanguaging', the underlying approach of this book, the contributors of this volume are truly transnational, belonging to various localities of the world. They speak different languages as their first, second first, third or more languages. Regardless of their belonging to various speech communities or nation states, the contributors of this volume care about languages spoken by the people that surround them – their students, families, neighbors, co-workers and communities. Hence, through the pages of this book, we will travel to various localities or geopolitical spaces in the world to learn about the speakers of different languages (Chinese, English, French, Hebrew, Italian, Korean, Persian, Turkish and Spanish, among others), who are languaging or translanguaging here and there throughout the world.

We think that multilingualism should be placed at the heart of our global world because of the extents to which the positive and negative linguistic outcomes of globalization impact the lives of many people worldwide: the rich and the poor, the literate and illiterate, the linguistic majorities and minorities and the monolinguals and bi-/multilinguals of the world. Hence, it is our collective hope, both ours (the editors) and that of the contributors of this volume, that this book with its wide array of perspectives be of interest to people inside academia, including language scholars, professors and students. We equally hope this book will be of interest to those language teachers and practitioners, policy makers and transnational organizations who are involved directly or indirectly in language-related projects, and last but not least, to the citizens of the world, for whom multilingualism is a familiar term but yet vague concept in terms of its immense value for safeguarding the diversity of our planet.

Although this book bears our names as its editors, it is the outcome of a truly collective process, which came to life gradually but gracefully through interactions with many amazing individuals. We are flattered and honored to publish another book with Multilingual Matters. Our special thanks are due to Tommi Grover and Anna Roderick, Managing Director and Editorial Director of Multilingual Matters, respectively, for the excellent job they have been doing in raising awareness about multilingualism, linguistic pluralism and diversity by publishing such books. We would equally like to extend our appreciation to Professor Li Wei and Professor Angel M.Y. Lin, the editors of the Translanguaging in Theory and Practice series, who were very supportive of this project from the very beginning. This book would not have been possible without the chapter authors, to whom we are equally thankful.

In our academic institutions, Maryam would like to thank Rutgers, the State University of New Jersey, in general, and her Department of African, Middle Eastern, and South Asian Languages and Literatures, in particular, for their generous support in making it possible for her to work on this book project during her 2020–2021 Sabbatical Leave. Bahar would equally like to thank Mercy College and her Department of Literacy and Multilingual Studies for all their support. Last but not least, we both like to thank our families for their support, patience and understanding of us during our work on this book.

We would like to close this preface by commemorating our friends, colleagues and professors who were alongside us in our journey with

Professor García, especially Professor María Torres-Guzmán, Dr Ruhma Choudhury and Dr Heesook Cheon, our beautiful friends and gifted individuals from Columbia University's Teachers College, whose untimely passing affected us all deeply.

Maryam Borjian,
Rutgers, The State University of New Jersey

Bahar Otcu-Grillman,
Mercy College, New York

Notes

(1) 'What do you do with an idea?' is the title of a children book by Yamada, K. and Besom, M. (2014). For the read-aloud of this book, please see: https://www.youtube.com/watch?v=0We9zl5J7hQ
(2) Hult, F.M. and King, K.A. (eds) (2011) *Educational Linguistics in Practice: Applying the Local Globally and the Global Locally*. Bristol: Multilingual Matters. This book was a tribute honoring the work of Nancy Hornberger (University of Pennsylvania), another leading scholar of our time, a close colleague and friend of Ofelia García's and a contributor to the present book. We are delighted to have her with us in this project.
(3) García, O., Zakharia, Z. and Otcu, B. (eds) (2013) *Bilingual Community Education and Multilingualism: Beyond Heritage Languages in a Global City*. Bristol: Multilingual Matters.
(4) Borjian, M. (2013) *English Education in Post-Revolutionary Iran: From Indigenization to Internationalization*. Bristol: Multilingual Matters.

Introduction (Part One): The Local Roots and Global Reach of Ofelia García's Multilingualism

Maryam Borjian[1]

> De donde crece la palma.
> [I am] from the land where the palm grows.
> José Martí (1853–1895)

The Cuban royal palm is an elegant and majestically tall tree with roots deeply seated in the Cuban soil, but with an outward-looking gaze that gives passers-by the impression that the tree is in search of all the many things standing before it, in the distant horizon, way beyond the local landscapes and perhaps even overseas. Native to Central America, this tree has inspired generations of poets, singers and artists across territorial borders of Central American nation states. In Cuba, where the splendor of this tree brought it the title of 'royal', it has been a source of inspiration to many, including to José Martí, the 19th century Cuban poet, whose verse adorns the opening of this introduction. This centuries-old tree with its locally grounded roots and globally directed outlook is used here as one of two metaphors (the other will follow shortly) to cast light on the extraordinary life and fruitful academic track record of Ofelia García, a leading intellectual, writer, scholar, sociolinguist, language activist and educator of our time, in whose honor this book is written.

Born in Cuba, García spent a blissful childhood, as she reflected on it many years later (García, 2017), under the cool shade and the wondrous gaze of royal palms. Was it there, as she was developing her roots alongside those of the royal palm, that the tree inspired her to keep her gaze always towards the distant horizon? At the time, the term 'globalization' as we know and talk about it today was not widely known. Yet, the royal palm must have left its imprint on García's mind, for many years later, when she became a professor and scholar, concepts

1

like the locality of roots and the globality of thoughts became central themes of her sociolinguistic investigations. In spite of her close bond with the royal palm, her alliance with her beloved tree came to an abrupt end, when at the age of eleven, she and her family had to leave home to take permanent refuge in the United States due to the radical sociopolitical changes that were taking place in the country.

In America, New York City was their chosen destination. Where could possibly be a better destination than the Big Apple for a girl who was aware of her roots but passionate enough to grow beyond them and learn about the many new things that were awaiting in her new surroundings? This mega metropolis was globalized way before the birth of contemporary globalization. To her, this city must have resembled a magnificent patchwork of hybrid peoples, ethnicities, languages, cultures, customs and traditions that were all like colorful threads that had long before been interwoven into the fabric of a cosmopolitan way of life. Was it then that she felt that she was going to like this city? She was, of course, too young then to make anything out of the city, but gradually its enormous hybridity and diversity must have impressed her greatly for she has stayed ever since and become a New Yorker. Of her many books, *The Multilingual Apple* (García & Fishman, 1997), may best capture García's appreciation of the city's expansive multilingualism.

New York had a lot to offer García, but not the royal palm tree of her yesteryears' childhood. This tree was utterly foreign to the city's cold climate. Instead, New York offered her its finest and most inspirational tree, the linden − known for its tall stature, abundant leaves and beautiful flowers with refreshing fragrances floating into the air every spring. Rooted in Greek mythology as the symbol of love and friendship, the linden has inspired generations of European poets and writers over centuries: from England's William Shakespeare (1564−1616) to the German Wilhelm Müller (1794−1827).

Although the linden tree is cherished for inspiring feelings of protection, love and friendship − all the very good qualities of García's inner self − the tree has also shown her another face of New York City: its towering resilience and strength. Often heaving and cracking through the pavement of the city's wide sidewalks, the spreading roots of linden are there in the walkways to remind the urban passers-by that nature exists and defies our limiting, if not fully selfish, way of life − a way of life through which we have long been marginalizing nature as we push it out of our towns, cities and countries throughout the world. Disregarding such a selfish wish, the linden trees of New York City continue breaking through the pavement as a means of claiming more space for themselves and their roots than the limited space given to them by us or by the city's authorities.

Before New York City could notice the presence of this newcomer young girl on its soil, García was already developing her roots alongside those of the lindens in the city's sidewalks. Are García's enormous strength, resilience and loving and sheltering character the fruits of her alliance with the linden tree? Was it the linden who inspired her to see, question, problematize and challenge another aspect of humans' limiting way of life – the one constructed socially, often by visible or invisible forces (or voices) of authorities as a means of categorizing people to favor some but exclude some others? This I do not know. Yet, as said by Alastair Pennycook (2012), critical resistance requires critical writing. Critical resistance to those forms of authority whose decisions (or unjust policies) limit humans' fluid ways of life (whether social, cultural or linguistic) is another characteristic of García's writings.

Regardless of her enormous passion for learning about all the new things that enclosed her in her adapted home, García's immigrant/refugee status placed her within a vertical chart of sociocultural and linguistic hierarchies, to which she was not accustomed. She first encountered such a categorization in schools, where she was told that her English was not good, because of which she had to be placed in remedial English classes. As for her first language, Spanish, that was regarded as inappropriate or simply irrelevant. All that mattered back then, and perhaps still today, was English – the yardstick used to assess the intellectual abilities of minoritized students in standardized tests in American schools. Thus, at a very early age, she learned, not from books but from her first-hand experiences, what it meant to be an immigrant, a minority or a foreign other, with a foreign language, accent, culture and perhaps, imagination, hopes and dreams, on which she once remarked:

> In making sense of the experiences of others and caring for them, I make sense of myself. I care because I know what it feels like to be told I am stupid because I didn't speak English, to be placed in remedial language arts classes where language use was solely mechanical, to score low in standardized assessments that did not measure what I knew, to be told that my Spanish was not 'good' because it showed the signs of English, to be told to teach in English only when my students only spoke Spanish. My sense of language in the world did not come solely from books, but more from experience. (García, 2017: xiii)

Many years later in the 1980s when she obtained her PhD in Spanish Literature from the Graduate Center of the City University of New York, she knew in her heart that it was language that she wanted to pursue. Although literature never left her and has left its imprints on her poetic style of writing, it was language that drove a heartfelt quest that emerged from within. She wanted to step into the very field that had once categorized her as the foreign other, the inferior other. Determined to make a difference in the lives of minoritized students in schools and their marginalized ethnolinguistically diverse families in the wider society, she began her advocacy for bilingualism, multilingualism and bilingual education; an advocacy for linguistic themes that barely existed at the time, or if they existed they were not the established concepts we know and talk about today. She was determined, nonetheless.

'Where there is a will, there is a way', as the saying goes, and will is what García has had in abundance. Her heartfelt quest soon led her to Joshua Fishman (1926–2015), her life-time mentor, colleague and friend. The two together became a greater whole, using a macro sociolinguistic lens, known as the Sociology of Language, in their sociolinguistic and educational linguistic investigations. Although García always emphasizes (García & Schiffman, 2006) whatever she knows about language, she learned in 'Joshua Fishman 101',[2] she must have awed him too.

Once García began teaching, lecturing and writing, it all poured out so naturally and organically from within. What she had inside her was a vast treasury of lived experiences that were rich, insightful, intellectually of superb quality, but most importantly, honest and truthful. They were the real experiences of real peoples with fluid language practices, patchwork cultures and fragmented identities. They were the lived experiences of real people who lived not in an imaginary world of books but in the real world, the physical and social world that surrounds us all. Who could read about such experiences and still try to deny, toss them out, or label them as irrelevant data?

When García began her academic journey some four decades ago or so, little did she know how she would awe and inspire generations of scholars with her enormous gift of intellectuality. Little did she know of the extensive contributions that she would make to the vast realm of language studies across academic disciplines: from bilingualism and multilingualism to the sociology of language, from language policies and ideologies to language inequalities, injustice and linguistic human rights, from language and globalization to the glocality of knowledge and ideas and from educational linguistics to translanguaging and language teacher training, to name but a few. She has been able to do all this because she has lived the languages about which she writes. She has lived the cultures on which she reflects. And most importantly, she has lived with the people whose lives, languages, cultures and identities alongside their other existential issues and challenges have been voiced in her writings.

Hence, García's story with language is not that of a sociolinguist or of an educator solely but rather that of a soul who has thrown herself into a field, a current or an academic discipline as a means of casting light on the lives of others; not those from the centers or the cores of our towns, cities or countries, but those from the margins, the peripheries, the in-between spaces that exist everywhere and anywhere throughout the world but yet are often forgotten. She uses her gift of intellectuality and knowledge to give voice to the voiceless and power to the powerless people of the margins. Seeing marginality as a source of strength but not a weakness, García stands in the periphery and from there she looks, thinks and writes about the marginalized and minoritized people. This action, in turn, disturbs both the flow and the framework of knowledge, whose boundaries have long been decided by the will of the authorities at the centers, the cores or the metropoles throughout the world. This is, indeed, an act of decolonization on García's part – a decolonization of the field of education and language studies (Thiong'o, 2012).

Like the linden trees of her beloved New York City, through her research García tells us how to challenge various forms of authority, including those of the western intellectuals and their narrow perceptions of language in education and in the wider society. Labeling such a perception a 'monoglossic ideology', rooted in centuries-old monoglossic practices of the western societies, García offers us a fresh lens; a lens constructed by her to remind us of what Jacques Derrida (1974) calls 'différance'. It is a plea to go beyond the Eurocentric and other forms of authority-driven approaches to be able to see the surrounding world and assign meanings to what we see through a 'heteroglossic' or 'transglossic' lens, which will, in turn, allow us to see multilingualism, linguistic diversity, pluralism and inclusion as realities of human lives (whether monolingual, bilingual or multilingual citizens) from throughout the world (García, 2009).

Although native to Cuba and other Central American nation states, the royal palm has transcended the locality of space. Planted as an ornamental tree in many other parts of the world, today the royal palm is no longer territorialized. What makes García's research boundless with enduring legacies is precisely the way her ideas and ideals have gone global, way beyond the geopolitical and territorial borders of nation states. The reason is clear. García's research gives us a vision that goes beyond named languages and beyond nation states to center on the speakers themselves. It is a vison of people, of each and every one of us, languaging here and there throughout the world, while using our entire linguistic repertoire and resources to speak, live, work, dream, love and care for one another (García, 2009).

It would be remiss of us not to mention other individuals who have left their imprints on García's mind and life. One such notable individual is Ricardo Otheguy, an eminent linguist and prolific scholar from the Graduate Center of the City University of New York. About him, she once remarked:

And how can I talk about a husband and colleague? […] Ricardo has been a most patient listener, and he has given me room to disagree, to hold different views. He has never complained about the attention I pay to my students and my work, even though sometimes it takes away from things that we both hold dear. I have learned more from him than from any other, about language, but also about history, politics, and life in general. (García, 2009: xiv)

Along with them happened a happy Cuban-American family. Their three children — Eric, Raquel and Emma — not only made them happy with endless love, but also inspired them with their translanguaging. As proud parents, they watched, talked and listened to their children, and all this languaging germinated the seeds of some of García's scholarship.

Ofelia García's enormous gifts of intellectuality, brilliance of thought coupled with her profound love for humanity are not the only characteristics of her academic endeavors that have awed and inspired many over the past several decades. Her immeasurable humility, warmth of character, abundant love and her sheltering personality have made her a true mentor, colleague and friend to many. Together, we join in this collective volume to honor Ofelia García's enduring commitment to the cause of linguistic pluralism, diversity, justice and inclusion in schools, communities, societies and the nation states of the world — both those of the global North and those of the global South.

Notes

(1) I am grateful to the following individuals who read an earlier draft of this essay and offered me their invaluable suggestions, including Professor Mary Curran (Rutgers University), Professor Nancy Hornberger (University of Pennsylvania), my co-editor of this volume Professor Bahar Otcu-Grillman (Mercy College) and my life-time colleague, spouse and friend Dr Habib Borjian (Columbia University before and Rutgers University now).

(2) 101 stands for an introductory course on any topic for beginners in American universities.

References

Derrida, J. (1974) *Of Grammatology*. Baltimore and London: John Hopkins University.

García, O. (2009) *Bilingual Education in the 21st Century: A Global Perspective*. Malden: Wiley-Blackwell.

García, O. (2017) Why we care: Language in a globalized world. In M. Borjian (ed.) *Language and Globalization: An Autoethnographic Approach* (pp. xiii–xvi). London and New York: Routledge.

García, O. and Fishman, J.A. (eds) (1997) *The Multilingual Apple: Languages in New York* (1st edn). Berlin: Mouton de Gruyter.

García, O. and Schiffman, H. (2006) Fishmanian sociolinguistics. In O. García , R. Peltz and H.F. Schiffman (eds) *Language Loyalty, Continuity and Change* (pp. 3–68). Clevedon: Multilingual Matters.

Pennycook, A. (2012) *Language and Mobility: Unexpected Places*. Bristol: Multilingual Matters.

Thiong'o, N. (2012) The challenge – *ndaraca ya thiomi*: Languages as bridges. In V. Rapatahana and P. Bunce (eds) *English Language as Hydra: Its Impacts on Non-English Language Cultures* (pp. 11–17). Bristol: Multilingual Matters.

Introduction (Part Two): A Tribute to Ofelia García: A Translanguaging Approach

Bahar Otcu-Grillman

> Spanish runs through my heart, but English rules my veins.
> (Study participant, 2016)

Bilingual education in the United States has gone through a lot of turmoil for centuries. It came a long way from the early 18th century, when it was permitted as an essential part of the education system, to the days it became restricted between the mid-19th and mid-20th centuries, then to 1950s, when it gained more opportunities because of national security laws allowing education in foreign languages (García *et al.*, 2013). Today, in the 21st century, still easily manipulated by political tendencies and biased views towards a multilingual and multicultural society, bilingual education and how it is implemented in schools continue to be controversial topics debated by politicians, sociolinguists and educators. For 40 years, Ofelia García has been a leading 'sociolinguist who has specialized in the education of bilinguals',[1] advocating for bilingualism, multilingualism and true bilingual education not only for language minorities but for all, and not only in the United States, but throughout the world.

Ofelia García, who has recently been elected to the National Academy of Education (2018) and been the recipient of countless awards for her scholarship, teaching and mentoring, started her outstanding academic career as a Bilingual and ESL (English as a Second Language) teacher in New York City. Since then, having brought her expertise in teaching bilingual students into her academic career, she has taught, researched and written extensively about bilingual education and multilingualism (see a list for her publications from Multilingual Matters in the Appendix of this book). She visited diverse ethnolinguistic communities in the United States and multiple countries of the world and raised awareness about the teaching of languages other than English, as already depicted in detail by several contributors of this book (see Borjian *et al.*, this volume). She has constantly been in search for the best way to educate children bilingually and wished to go beyond the known norms mostly based on monoglossic beliefs and pedagogies. As such, throughout her career, she challenged the monolingual view that bilinguals are two monolinguals in one and must perform equally well in both of their languages as balanced bilinguals. This view was unfair to bilinguals as it only allowed them the competence of less than half of their full linguistic repertoire (Grosjean, 2016). Through her own, her mentees' and her colleagues' research, García developed her seminal conceptualizations of dynamic bilingualism and translanguaging. This book exemplifies the influence of García's work, especially of the concepts of dynamic bilingualism and translanguaging, in the field of bilingual education via the work of the volume contributors, some of whom were García's doctoral students and some of whom are colleagues.

The Approach

This book takes a translanguaging approach, which Ofelia García introduced, explained and popularized as an essential aspect of her groundbreaking concept of 'dynamic bilingualism' for the first time more than ten years ago (García, 2009). With the term 'dynamic', García (2009) meant that bilingualism was not just about having a first and a second language, or it was not just additive or subtractive; instead, bilinguals have one linguistic system bearing features of named languages. Dynamic bilingualism referred to bilinguals' complex languaging that occurs within this 'one' linguistic system, where 'translanguaging are *multiple discursive practices* in which bilinguals engage in order to *make sense of their bilingual worlds*' (García, 2009: 45, emphasis in original). For instance, she referred to a bilingual 11-year-old's description that opened this chapter, 'Spanish runs through my heart, but English rules my veins'. She mentioned that clearly this student expressed the vitality of his 'one' linguistic system that cannot be put apart, otherwise he would lose his life (Grosjean, 2016). She summarized the connection between dynamic bilingualism and translanguaging stating that 'translanguaging is the enactment of this dynamic bilingualism' (García, 2012). In 2014, García wrote *Translanguaging: Language, Bilingualism and Education* together with Li Wei, published by Palgrave Macmillan. This collaborative work, which offered a complete view of translanguaging, was awarded the British Association of Applied Linguistics Book Prize in 2015.

The term translanguaging originally referred to a pedagogic practice implemented in Wales and involved 'the hearing, signing, or reading of lessons in one language, and the development of the work' in another (García, 2009: 301). Since García's introduction of dynamic bilingualism, through the studies of many other scholars, the term has been extended 'to refer to both the complex language practices of plurilingual individuals and communities, as well as the pedagogical approaches that use those complex practices' (García & Li, 2014: 20). A recent definition of translanguaging made by García is 'the deployment of a speaker's full linguistic repertoire without regard for watchful adherence to the socially and politically defined boundaries of named (and usually national and state) languages' (Otheguy *et al.*, 2015). The present volume makes room for both senses of translanguaging, as a discursive practice and as a pedagogical approach, hence the title of the book, *Remaking Multilingualism: A Translanguaging Approach.*

We acknowledge that there have been criticisms of the translanguaging approach to date. Some scholars criticized the approach as they attributed bilinguals' complex language practices to their two separate linguistic systems instead of one full linguistic system; this was what Otheguy *et al.* (2019) called the *dual correspondence theory.* Some scholars questioned the use of translanguaging as a pedagogical practice in multilingual classrooms, pointing to the challenges of teaching emergent bilinguals in such multilingual classrooms rather than bilingual ones. García and other scholars have provided responses to such criticisms to date. Such criticisms have also been challenged by the chapters in this volume, which we think as an important theoretical contribution to the field.

Organization

The chapters in this book follow a variety of methodological approaches and research designs, offering a representative overview of Ofelia García's work and contributions to various fields and/or subfields studying languaging. There are a total of 20 sections. Twelve full chapters describe research and theoretical considerations, four brief sections and the preface, foreword, introduction and afterword are brief personal narratives. Since this book could also be used as a course textbook in institutes of higher education, each full chapter opens and closes with questions that can be used for class discussions. The breakdown of the contents and abstracts are as follows.

In the Preface, we, as co-editors provide a brief background story to preparing this volume. We also commemorate our professors, colleagues and friends who have inspired us in this journey to celebrate our beloved Professor García.

Bernard Spolsky's note on Ofelia García constitutes the Foreword to the volume. Spolsky accurately writes about Ofelia García's working closely with Joshua Fishman and sharing the following characteristics with him: her exceptionally high productivity, her concern for people more than for languages and her willingness to innovate. Spolsky also points to her major influence on the development of educational linguistics first through her advocacy of bilingualism, and later through her concept of translanguaging, the unashamed use of several parts of one's language repertoire.

The Introduction has two sections. The first part is a personal essay by one of the co-editors, Maryam Borjian, describing the local roots and global reach of Ofelia García's multilingualism. Here, Borjian uses tree metaphors portraying García's roots and connecting them to her exceptional work in multilingualism with a global reach. The second part of the Introduction provides a brief outline of the volume, its approach, and its sections.

The rest of the book is divided into four parts: (1) Remaking Multilingualism, (2) Bilingual Pedagogies and Teacher Education, (3) Bilingual Community Education and (4) Language Policy and Language Ideologies. These sections are thought to constitute the areas of Ofelia García's work from a holistic perspective.

In Chapter 1 under Remaking Multilingualism, Nancy H. Hornberger describes reimagining multilingualism with Ofelia. Here she explores samples of Ofelia's work, weaving in the ways both scholars have crossed since the 1980s, and depicting how they have enriched each other's thinking across their shared conceptual terrain in bilingualism and bilingual education.

In Chapter 2, Suresh Canagarajah discusses how Professor García has mentored him from a distance. Pointing to their shared identity as refugees to the United States from conflict-ridden countries, the author discusses how Ofelia's publications and conversations helped him develop translanguaging perspectives in his own research and teaching.

In Chapter 3, Bahar Otcu-Grillman likens García's academic teachings to a classroom, depicting that her versatility and transcultural activities with her students are promising for a multilingual future of the world. She also shares memories of being Ofelia García's doctoral advisee and colleague.

Chapter 4 is a personal letter of recommendation written for Ofelia García in 2016 for a Lifetime Achievement Award. The author, Lesley Bartlett, opens up about Ofelia García as a mentor and depicts how their collegial relationship supported and excelled her research.

The next part of the volume, Bilingual Pedagogies and Teacher Education, starts with Chapter 5. Jo Anne Kleifgen, who jointly proposed the term 'Emergent Bilinguals' with Ofelia García in a monograph entitled *From English Language Learners to Emergent Bilinguals* (García *et al.*, 2008), examines the confluence of language and digital technology to explore ten adolescents' translanguaging practices as they navigated the bilingual system during classroom instruction on the Civil Rights movement. This study, part of a larger intervention project using a web-based environment to support Latinx emergent bilinguals in NYC schools, was also influenced by Ofelia's thinking. Analysis showed every student engaged in translanguaging, their practices varying in proportion and strategy. Nuances of their translanguaging strategies are illustrated with three students' diverse ways of drawing on sign-systems to accomplish tasks. Findings show that close analysis of emergent bilinguals' trans-semiotic practices can demonstrate their efficacy for learning.

In Chapter 6, Marianne Turner and Angel M.Y. Lin discuss their positioning of translanguaging theory as a majority theory, i.e. it is not a theory applicable to linguistic minoritized students only but is applicable to all students. Such positioning can help reconfigure language education so that it does not privilege the idea of deficit, or the striving towards an unattainable goal. Accordingly, the leveraging and expanding of linguistic repertoires is considered as the primary objective of language education and the learning of any named languages as secondary. The authors draw on the notion of 'transfeaturing' which refers to the use of linguistic features from different named languages (Lin *et al.*, 2020), apply it to García and Li Wei's (2014) translanguaging pedagogical goals and discuss how a transfeaturing focus can give rise to differentiation.

In Chapter 7, Anel V. Suriel and Mary E. Curran document and analyze their approach to urban social justice language teacher education. They focus on a course in their curriculum and the community-engaged pedagogical model, which supports the development of language teacher dispositions grounded in a framework informed by translanguaging (García *et al.*, 2017) and culturally sustaining pedagogy (Paris & Alim, 2017). Within the pedagogical spaces created and the marginalized community members centered, pre-service teachers learn *from, with* and *in* communities. Analyzing teacher candidates' artifacts (reflections, personal stance assignments and course evaluations), the authors document the impact on teacher candidates' dispositions and a need for on-going curriculum and program development.

As its title suggests, Ivana Espinet and Karen Zaino's Chapter 8 refers to Ofelia García's banyan tree metaphor for the interconnectivity and multiplicity of bilingualism and multilingualism. The chapter builds on Ofelia García's work in the context of CUNY-NYSIEB which fostered a collaborative model that engaged educators to a translanguaging pedagogy. It focuses on the work of three New York City teachers who participated in a year-long CUNY NYSIEB study group in which they reflected on what translanguaging pedagogy meant in the context of their classrooms. It describes how these educators took up translanguaging theories and made them their own in the context of their individual teaching practices, along with their reflections on the process.

Chapter 9 by Carmina Makar is on the poetic experience of 25 New York City school teachers as they portray their relationship to their bilingual identity through poems. The chapter honors and draws upon Ofelia García's lifetime work by highlighting key contributions in her scholarship, in particular the role of additive bilingualism and translanguaging in the lived experiences of these bilingual teachers. The qualitative scope of the study pairs translanguaging analysis with photographic discourse analysis. Findings highlight the forces that shape subtractive bilingualism and further support the use of translanguaging as an epistemological paradigm and critical pedagogy. Factors such as shame, deficit paradigms and the silencing of bilingual practices emerge as driving forces as they navigate bilingual identities. Their roles as teachers uncover the powerful potential of becoming bilingual advocates for their students.

Under the Bilingual Community Education section, Chapter 10 by Li Wei and Zhu Hua focuses on parental voices to be heard and taken seriously in the planning and implementation of translanguaging approaches Chinese complementary school education in Britain for children of immigrant and transnational backgrounds. The authors show how translanguaging pedagogies seem to be at odds with the principal objective and traditional pedagogies of these schools. The authors' project engages with the parents in introducing translanguaging into this particular education context. The chapter shows how the process transformed the parents', as well as the schools', understanding and perspectives on growing up bilingual in Britain.

Similar to the previous chapter, Bahar Otcu-Grillman's Chapter 11 discusses translanguaging practices in a bilingual community's educational settings. This time mostly focusing on the students' perspectives, the chapter draws on the findings of a linguistic ethnography of a PreK-5 Turkish community school in New York. It builds on the jointly coined term with Ofelia García, *bilingual community education,* briefly introduces the doctoral study supervised by García and discusses translanguaging data. Findings show that the interviews include more instances of translanguaging than the naturally occurring speech data. They may have felt difficulty expressing themselves in the Turkish interviews and needed to convey meaning via their full linguistic repertoire. In this environment, language proficiency and language choices are inseparable. The children create their own translanguaging space (Li, 2011) while the adults try to accommodate to their language needs despite the school's Turkish-only language policy.

In Chapter 12, Fabrice Jaumont provides an update on a movement called The Bilingual Revolution and how it has encouraged the development of bilingual programming among various ethnolinguistic communities in New York. The chapter celebrates Ofelia García's precept that American society needs a U-turn for bilingual education to its beginnings and proposes starting with the desires of ethnolinguistic communities to bilingually educate their children, rather than starting with government mandates and regulations and focusing only on those who lack (lack English, years of residency or economic means). Such a community-oriented approach is thought to transform and empower children, schools and communities in unprecedented ways.

Under the Language Policy and Language Ideologies section, Chapter 13 by Angela Creese and Adrian Blackledge reports outcomes of a research project which investigates translanguaging for social justice in a welfare advice center in a UK city. The chapter reports an element of the ethnographic study which examined interactions between an advice worker and her Chinese clients in a community center with a remit to support Chinese people in the city. Via translanguaging, the advice worker not only moves between several languages but can also navigate bureaucratic discourse creatively, transforming the social justice outcomes for her clients.

Maryam Borjian's Chapter 14 examines policy actors (who), processes (what and how) and causes (why) of English language policy (LP) in Iran by applying a multi-dimensional framework and drawing on data collected in two stages of fieldwork in Iran. The inclusive and pluralistic approach to LP in this chapter is inspired by the work of Ofelia García. The chapter is grounded in English LP in post-revolutionary Iran, a similar research setting to that of post-revolutionary Cuba that Ofelia García examined in her research. The findings offer new insights into the ways LPs are formed, which may both complement and challenge the previous understanding of the global spread of English.

Chapter 15 by Sarah Hesson foregrounds the perspectives of bilingual Latinx adolescent youth at an after-school program in a K-8 dual language bilingual school. Using her dissertation advisor Ofelia García's theory of dynamic bilingualism and her belief that children's and communities' language practices must be at the center of our pedagogical and policy decisions, Hesson first outlines lessons from youth based on their reported language use and perspectives on bilingualism and translanguaging. She then considers the implications of these lessons for language allocation policy, suggesting an approach to language policy that is grounded in both dynamic bilingualism and youths' lived realities.

Chapter 16 by Sharon Avni applies the concept of translanguaging to a series of activities and performances at American Jewish overnight camps and shows that a distinctive way of camp interactions shapes a new form of American Jewish legitimacy that challenges the hierarchical ordering of homeland/diaspora relations. It identifies the register of camp Hebraized English as a unique form of translanguaging and offers a new way of exploring polycentricity/multiple centers regarding ideas of homeland and diaspora in the contemporary American Jewish experience. The chapter simultaneously shows the creative and ludic nature of translanguaging by extending into non-school-based contexts such as summer camping.

The volume ends with an Afterword written by Jo Anne Kleifgen. In this personal piece, Kleifgen narrates her history of work and play with Ofelia García. Here, we see her emphasis on García's generosity and mentorship, a long time of collegial relationship and friendship which continues to date through the most difficult times such as the Covid-19 pandemic. Dr García being my dissertation sponsor, and Dr Kleifgen being my second advisor at Teachers College Columbia University, this personal account resonated with me, taking me to some point in time I can relate to in this brief history, studying with two great professors. We hope that this volume will elaborate on the discussions on dynamic bilingualism and translanguaging and continue Ofelia's legacy that keeps growing every day. Through the eyes of her colleagues, former students and friends, the volume celebrates Ofelia García and her lifetime commitment to multilingualism and bilingual education within translanguaging perspectives.

Note

(1) Ofelia García's own description of herself in an interview with François Grosjean for *Psychology Today,* March 2016.

References

García, O. (2009) *Bilingual Education in the 21st Century: A Global Perspective.* Malden, MA: Wiley–Blackwell Publishing.

García, O. (2012) Theorizing translanguaging for educators. In C. Celic and K. Seltzer (eds) *Translanguaging: A CUNY-NYSIEB guide for educators* (pp. 1–6). New York: CUNY-NYSIEB.

García, O. and Li, W. (2014) *Translanguaging: Language, Bilingualism, and Education.* New York, NY: Palgrave Macmillan.

Garcia, O., Kleifgen, J. and Falchi, L. (2008) *From English Language Learners to Emergent Bilinguals.* Research Review Series Monograph, Campaign for Educational Equity, Teachers College, Columbia University.

García, O., Zakharia, Z. and Otcu, B. (2013) Bilingual community education: Beyond heritage language education and bilingual education in New York. In O. García, Z. Zakharia and B. Otcu (eds) *Bilingual Community Education and Multilingualism: Beyond Heritage Languages in a Global City* (pp. 3–42). Bristol: Multilingual Matters.

García, O., Johnson, S.I. and Seltzer, K. (2017) *The Translanguaging Classroom: Leveraging Student Bilingualism for Learning.* Philadelphia, PA: Caslon.

Grosjean, F. (2016) What is translanguaging?: An interview with Ofelia Garcia. Psychology Today. Sussex Publishers.

Li, W. (2011) Moment analysis and translanguaging space: Discursive construction of identities by multilingual Chinese youth in Britain. *Journal of Pragmatics* 43 (5), 1222–1235.

Lin, A.M.Y., Wu, Y. and Lemke, J.L. (2020) 'It takes a village to research a village': Conversations of Angel Lin and Jay Lemke on contemporary issues in translanguaging. In S. M. C. Lau and S.Van Viegen Stille (eds) *Critical Plurilingual Pedagogies: Struggling Toward Equity Rather than Equality* (pp. 47–74). Cham: Springer.

Otheguy, R., García, O. and Reid, W. (2015) Clarifying translanguaging and deconstructing named languages: A perspective from linguistics. *Applied Linguistics Review* 6 (3), 281–307.

Otheguy, R., Garcia, O. and Reid, W. (2019) A translanguaging view of the linguistic system of bilinguals. *Applied Linguistics Review* 10 (4), 625–651.

Paris, D. and Alim, H.S. (eds) (2017) *Culturally Sustaining Pedagogies: Teaching and Learning for Justice in a Changing World.* Teachers College Press.

Part 1: Remaking Multilingualism

1 Imagining Multilingualism with Ofelia: Translanguaging and the Continua of Biliteracy

Nancy H. Hornberger

Ofelia García[1] has been shaping bilingual education theory, policy and practice for half a century now and always with imagination. Alongside her determination and deeply rooted commitment to serving the diverse school populations of New York City and the world, her love of literature and the imagination are an ever-present part of her vision for multilingualism and bilingual education. Here, I explore samples of her work in this vein, weaving in also the ways her path and mine have crossed since the early 1980s. Beyond the huge debt we both owe Joshua Fishman and the personal and professional ways our paths have joined, our ideas and commitments have intertwined repeatedly along the trajectories of our careers. From our collaborations in publications to our 'side-by-side' plenary talks[2] and conference presentations, to our mutual mentoring of a new generation of scholars, we have enriched each other's thinking across our shared conceptual terrain in bilingualism and bilingual education, not least our overlapping proposals for the continua of biliteracy (Hornberger, 1989, 2003, 2016) and translanguaging (García, 2007, 2009; García & Li, 2014). The final section of this paper explores these two frameworks for understanding bilingualism and biliteracy – how they overlap, how they differ and how they can contribute to imagining and celebrating multilingualism in our world.

Samples of Ofelia's very earliest work bespeak her advocacy for multilingualism and raciolinguistically minoritized learners,[3] that remain a constant to the present. In her co-edited volume with her lifetime partner and sometime co-author Ricardo Otheguy, *English across*

Cultures, Cultures across English (García & Otheguy, 1989), they suggest that it is precisely the 'common', but also culturally varied, language that causes communication breakdown in inter-ethnic communication in English; that for too long the onus of miscommunication has fallen on the minority interlocutor rather than the dominant one, and that this needs to change; and in her article entitled 'From Goya portraits to Goya beans' (García, 1993), she calls for US Latinx professionals to tend to the overdue task of bringing down the walls (built up over the past five centuries) that separate elite Spanish foreign tradition from popular Spanish US tradition, and to negotiate a valid role for Spanish as a transcendental symbol of Latinx identity.[4]

These are insightful and enduring arguments, but there is also much more here than the wide knowledge and careful analysis that characterize all her work. Like her mentor Joshua Fishman, García commits herself to her work with her heart as well as her head, and in each of these essays, she brings poetry and passion that lend an unusual power to her writing. The reverse imagery of English across cultures and cultures across English, the metaphorical contrast of Goya portraits admired at the museum by elite Spanish scholars and Goya beans eaten at the table by Latinx families living in poverty touch our emotions as well as our intellects as we encounter Ofelia's writings. This quality is, indeed, a trademark of Ofelia's writings, her talks, her teaching and mentoring, her scholarly leadership as a whole. Colin Baker credits Ofelia for sharing her 'powerful and pervading Language Garden analogy' with him in the early stages of writing his bestselling *Foundations of Bilingual Education and Bilingualism* (1993: xii); Ofelia's reading of Cuban poet José Martí's 1883 poem dedicating the Brooklyn Bridge, as she convened her 1999 *International Symposium on Bilingualism and Biliteracy Through Schooling* at Long Island University's School of Education in the shadow of that Bridge, framed the whole conference. This advocacy and poetry remain characteristic of her work to the present (e.g. Flores & García, 2017; García & Otheguy, 2017). Indeed, Ofelia's own poetic use of language illustrates the very point she repeatedly makes about language and its symbolic values.

Thoroughly rooted in New York City after arriving there at age 11 from Cuba with her family, García completed her higher education at the Graduate Center of the City University of New York (CUNY) forty years ago with a PhD in Hispanic and Luso-Brazilian Languages and Literatures, harbinger of and testimony to her lifelong love of Latin American literature. Ofelia's deepest commitment has always been to honoring multilingualism and kids in urban schools, and especially Latinx kids and Latinx communities of New York City. Nationally and internationally recognized for her devoted work and field-shaping scholarship in bilingual education and the education of raciolinguistically minoritized learners – work which has taken her on Fellowships and Visiting Appointments to Uruguay (1996), Cuba (1997), South Africa (2006, 2012), France (2010, 2014), Wales (2012) and Germany (2015–2017), among others – she has been grounded always in a long-term commitment to serving New York City's multicultural and multilingual population and it is there that one must look for the roots of her greatest conceptual contributions.

García's work is rich in empirical detail. Her co-authored studies of Spanish language use and attitudes in two New York City communities (García *et al.*, 1988), the bilingual education of Cuban American children in Dade County's ethnic schools (García & Otheguy, 1987) and the language situation of Cuban Americans (García & Otheguy, 1988) provided useful and detailed new data on topics for which accurate and up-to-date information was hard to come by. Her contributions to *The Multilingual Apple* (García, 1997), a volume she co-edited with Fishman, and to Fishman's own *Can Threatened Languages be Saved?* (García *et al.*, 2001) are more recent examples of the same kind of empirically detailed, informative piece at which García excels.

Beyond clarity and accuracy of detail, however, García's work represents original conceptualizations which move the field forward. Her special contribution to the area of bilingualism and bilingual education in general, and to Spanish-English bilingualism and bilingual education for Latinx in particular, is her ability to continuously evaluate the field and the role of its practitioners from the vantage point of larger historical, linguistic, ethnic and literary perspectives. Her introduction to the 1991 bilingual education volume she edited in Fishman's honor exemplifies how her writings weave layers of themes together in ways that both hold the whole together and elucidate the individual elements as well. The themes here are (using her words): the intertext of Fishman's bilingual education discourse; his 'narrow' loyalty as a Jewish man and 'broad' loyalty as a man with an intellectual contribution to humanity; and his Yiddish activism, Jewish neo-orthodoxy, cultural life and work and the topic of bilingual education. Ofelia's imaginative yet empirically grounded rendering of her mentor's vision and work is repeated in another Fishman festschrift she co-authored 15 years later, honoring the themes of language loyalty, continuity and change in Fishman's contributions to international sociolinguistics, or Fishmanian sociolinguistics, as she and co-author Hal Schiffman call it (García & Schiffman, 2006a).

In the introduction to their *International Journal of the Sociology of Language* issue on US Spanish, García and her co-editor Wherritt wrote that this 1989 collection of papers on Spanish in the United States represented a 'more committed view of Spanish' than the two earlier issues on the topic published in 1974 and 1985. Though cognizant of the pressures on US Spanish at that time arising from its limited and restricted public functions, from the English-only movement and from the historically inexorable pattern of inter-generational shift to English by US immigrants, Wherritt and García nevertheless maintained that '[t]he 1990's still hold the promise of upholding, protecting, and fostering the language and cultural resources of United States Latinos, as Hispanics are incorporated into the social, political, and economic life of the United States' (Wherritt & García, 1989: 8–9). It is to that yet unfulfilled promise that Ofelia García has remained committed, as 'wife, mother, [Latina], ethnic advocate, and bilingual educator' (García, 1991: 19) and it is that commitment which lends a particularly compelling voice to her work.

Our Intertwining Paths and Ideas

Ofelia García's path and mine have crossed and intertwined since the 1980s, initially through our mutual mentor, Joshua Fishman, whom we each met around the same time, I through a summer course with Professor Fishman at the 1980 Linguistic Society of America Summer Institute in Albuquerque (Hornberger, 2017) and Ofelia through a 1981 postdoctoral fellowship in sociology of language and bilingualism with Fishman at Yeshiva University, followed by several years as visiting assistant professor in the program in bilingual developmental psychology at Yeshiva Fishman directed. It is there that I may have first met – or at least heard – Ofelia, who presented at the *Fifth Annual Invitational Conference: Perspectives on Bilingualism: International and Cross-Cultural Perspectives* I attended at Yeshiva in 1986. A few years later, we celebrated Fishman's 65th birthday together at the *SOL on the Horizon: Symposium on the Sociology of Language* in Fishman's honor at the Linguistic Society of America Summer Institute in Santa Cruz (1991), an event commemorated in a three-volume festschrift, one of them on *Bilingual Education* edited by Ofelia (García, 1991) to which I contributed. We again celebrated together on the occasion of Fishman's 80th birthday, this time at Penn and with a pair of edited festschrifts on Fishman's work on language loyalty published by Multilingual Matters (García *et al.*, 2006c; Hornberger & Pütz, 2006).

Ofelia tells us, 'Everything I know, I learned in Fishman 101' (García & Schiffman, 2006a: 3). She was indeed his devoted student, and over the years also his colleague, co-author and co-editor with him of innumerable articles, chapters and volumes, as well as author/editor of articles and books honoring him. She became co-editor with Fishman in 2009 and 2010, respectively, of the landmark journal and book series he founded in the 1970s and edited until his death, the *International Journal of the Sociology of Language* and *Contributions to the Sociology of Language* (Mouton de Gruyter). Most importantly, she was his friend and friend to his family – over many years, Ofelia visited 'Shikl' and his wife Gella regularly, even weekly at times, at their home in the Bronx.

These are just bare outlines of a long, deep and unforgettable scholarly communion of mind, heart, and spirit between the two of them. I have written elsewhere about my own personal encounters with Fishman – many of them in fact also involving Ofelia (Hornberger, 2017).

As our paths continued to cross through the decades, Ofelia's imagination was ever-present and inspirational. She invited me to speak at that 1999 Long Island University conference where she read Martí's poem and sponsored other artists as well; and later at the 2004 *Imagining Multilingual Schools* conference she and colleagues María Torres and Tove Skutnabb-Kangas convened at Teachers College in 2004, where I, like others inspired by the conference theme, ended my talk with these words:

> We need to recognize and celebrate that what may feel to us like stop-gap implementational measures to imagine and create multilingual schools in today's ideologically unfriendly national or global contexts are much more than that. They are in fact imaginative and creative moves that have a strategic role to play in shifting and expanding into more favorable ideological spaces… I am more convinced than ever that we who imagine multilingual schools have the long-term advantage. Threat and fear and restriction can never prevail in the grand scheme of things, but a profuse and rich diversity of ways of speaking, meaning, thinking, valuing and being will. (Hornberger, 2006: 233–234)

That same year, Ofelia and I were 'side-by-side' plenary speakers at the *First International Symposium on Bilingualism and Bilingual Education in Latin America* (2004), held in Buenos Aires, Argentina, where we were treated (together with our husbands and other conference goers) to the beauty of a tango performance and in that context enjoyed time and space to talk about each other's families – a conversation that played a role in her daughter Emma's choice of Swarthmore College (class of '09) where my daughter Ch'uya had graduated class of '97. We have taken a shared interest in the welfare not only of our families but our graduate students as well – Kate Menken went on from her master's in TESOL with me here at Penn to become Ofelia's student and protégé at Teachers College and CUNY Graduate Center, where she is now associate professor; Nelson Flores joined me on the Educational Linguistics faculty in 2012, entrusted to me by his mentor Ofelia upon completion of his PhD with her at CUNY.

Beyond the huge debt Ofelia and I owe Fishman, and these personal and professional ways our paths have crossed, though, our ideas and commitments have intertwined repeatedly along the trajectories of our careers. From her collaborations with and contributions to the *Bilingual Education and Bilingualism* book series I co-edited with Colin Baker and now with Wayne Wright for Multilingual Matters (e.g. García & Baker, 1995, 2007; García *et al.*, 2013), to our plenary talks and conference presentations, to our mutual mentoring of a new generation of scholars, we have enriched each other's thinking across our shared conceptual terrain in bilingualism and bilingual education. Here, too, her imagination is exuberantly evident: for example, when she and Kate Menken edited a volume on educators negotiating language policy in their multilingual classrooms and schools, they imagined educators 'stirring' the metaphorical language policy 'onion' Ricento and I had proposed some two decades earlier and which had hitherto been (un)peeled and sliced but not yet stirred – and was soon to be cooked (García & Menken, 2010; Hornberger & Johnson, 2007; Ricento & Hornberger, 1996; Ruiz, 2011).

Translanguaging and the Continua of Biliteracy

Our intertwining trajectories around bilingualism and bilingual education are perhaps most intriguing to contemplate, however, in our overlapping conceptual proposals around the continua of biliteracy (Hornberger, 1989, 2003) and translanguaging (García, 2007, 2009). At least, they are so to me. In what follows, I explore my perspectives on the emergence and interrelationships of these two concepts – how they overlap, how they differ and how they can contribute to imagining and celebrating multilingualism in our world.

Ofelia's name is practically synonymous with translanguaging, that run-away concept that has captured the imagination of so many in the field of bilingual education. This is as it should be – a reflection of both Ofelia's long and deep scholarship in bilingual education policy and practice and the creativity and imagination she brings to it. *Imagining Multilingual Schools*, the above-mentioned conference she co-organized, brilliantly articulated a theme that brought forth a rich and compelling set of papers at a discouraging time in US education policy when we were reeling from the effects of the relatively new No Child Left Behind Act (García *et al.*, 2006b). Indeed, imagining multilingualism and multilingual education has been a lifelong pursuit of Ofelia's.

In García's highly influential work on translanguaging, the imaginative thread is key to understanding its emergence and political roots. As Ofelia's former student Nelson Flores has eloquently written, García's 2009 *Bilingual Education in the 21st Century*, which he read as chapter proofs in her doctoral seminar in 2008, gave him his 'first glimpse into what it would look like to reimagine conceptualizations of language in ways that start from the perspective of racialized bi/multilingual communities and the implications of this for how we think about language education as part of broader efforts at social transformation' (Flores, forthcoming). This reimagining and its political roots in her commitment to the lives and experiences of Latinx bilingual children and to 'normalizing and extending their linguistic and cultural practices in classroom spaces' are crucial to Ofelia's concept of translanguaging.

Like Flores, I remember very well my first encounter with Ofelia's vision for translanguaging – in my case, as it emerged in the Foreword she wrote for Makoni and Pennycook's now-famous *Disinventing and Reconstituting Languages*, published in 2007 in the Bilingual Education and Bilingualism book series I co-edit. Acknowledging that '[w]hen I was asked to write this Foreword, I had no idea that I would find myself questioning some of my 'venerable' assumptions about language and education or language and minority rights' (García, 2007: xiv), Ofelia began to do just that – to reimagine what language education might look like 'if we no longer posited the existence of separate languages' (2007: xiii). Building from the book's mention of the Welsh *trawysieithu* (Williams, 1994) and from Baker's (2003) translation and clarification of *trawysieithu*/translanguaging as a pedagogical approach that normalizes bilingualism without diglossic functional separation, García suggests that if language is indeed an invention, educators must first and continually observe how people use language and base our pedagogy on that (2007: xiii). She offers Canagarajah's example of language teaching that aims at students' developing negotiation strategies and a repertoire of codes to shuttle between (Canagarajah, 2007); a harbinger of the dozens (hundreds?) of talks, workshops and writings on pedagogical translanguaging suggestions and practices she would offer in the coming years.

In tour de force chapters on Languaging (Chapter 2) and Translanguaging (Chapter 3) in *Bilingual Education for the 21st Century* (2009), García situates the former in a discussion of language categories (e.g. dialect, creole, academic language, standard language) that have real consequences for children in schools; she seeks to shift the focus from 'language' to 'languaging' as multiple discursive practices. Similarly, she situates 'translanguaging' in a discussion of concepts, models and assumptions about bilingualism and bilingual development, seeking to shift the focus to bilingualism NOT as two monolingualisms but rather as bilingual or multilingual discourse practices. For Ofelia, translanguaging is the 'multiple discursive practices in which bilinguals engage to make sense of their bilingual worlds' (García, 2009: 45) – not simply an additive bilingualism (and certainly not a subtractive one), but a recursive and dynamic bilingualism (García, 2009: 51–56).

An important piece of Ofelia's imaginative turn to translanguaging is her engagement with Latin American thought, discussed in Part I of her 2014 book with Li Wei (Ofelia García, personal communication, 1 March 2015; italics and underline are mine). Cuban anthropologist Fernando Ortiz' *transculturación* 'transculturation' described what he called the *contrapunteo* 'counterpoint' of European, African and Indian cultural practices out of which a new reality emerged in Cuba (Ortiz, 1940) – this *trans* inspired Ofelia's vision of translanguaging. Chilean biologists Maturana and Varela's (1973/1998) theory of *autopoiesis* led them to posit that 'all doing is knowing and all knowing is doing' (1973/1998: 26) and that 'it is by *languaging* that the act of knowing ... brings forth a world' (1973/1998: 234–235); and Argentinian semiotician Walter Mignolo's (2000) *bilanguaging* focuses on redressing the power asymmetry of languages and denouncing the coloniality of knowledge. These strands come together in García's vision of translanguaging as complex and fluid discursive practices – and pedagogies – that give voice to bilingual US Latinx speakers, releasing them from monoglossic ideologies whether anglophone or hispanophone.

Similarly, and crucially, the continua of biliteracy framework (Hornberger, 1989, 2003) posits and depends on a dynamic and fluid understanding of communicative repertoire and the multi-dimensional aspects (context-content-media-development) one needs to take into account in creating learning environments that recognize and build on those repertoires. Reciprocally, I posit from the model that the more bi/multilingual students' contexts of language and literacy use allow them to draw from across the whole of each and every continuum, the greater are the chances for their full language and literacy development and expression (Hornberger, 1989).

The continua of biliteracy shares with translanguaging its political roots in pushing to change educational policy and pedagogy in ways that normalize and extend bi/multilingual students' fluid and dynamic communicative practices. The model was formulated in the context of my multi-year, comparative ethnography of language policy in Philadelphia beginning in 1987 – in two public schools and their respective communities. Through participant observation, interviewing, and document collection in and out of school in the long-established Puerto Rican community of North Philadelphia and the immigrant/refugee Cambodian community of West Philadelphia, my students and I sought to understand how national, state, and local policies and programs were situated, interpreted and appropriated in language and literacy attitudes and practices in classroom and community. My 'imagined' continua framework proved useful in analyzing data and drawing conclusions from our collaborative ethnographic research; and by the same token, the ongoing research informed the evolving framework.

The continua of biliteracy also share with translanguaging the re-imagining of bi/multilingualism. A review of research literature on bilingualism and literacy at the time led to thinking about what we were looking at as 'biliteracy' – which I defined as 'any and all instances in which communication occurs in two (or more) languages in or around writing' (Hornberger, 1990: 213). The emphasis on multilingual interaction and interpretation around writing contrasts with definitions that take biliteracy more narrowly to mean (mastery of) reading (and writing) in two languages (or in a second language). Likewise, the emphasis on 'instances' of biliteracy includes communicative events but also actors, interactions, practices, activities, programs, sites, situations, societies and worlds.

Moreover, the communication in these biliteracy instances occurs along complexes of 'continua' – defined as 'interrelated dimensions of highly complex and fluid communicative repertoires' (Hornberger, 2016: 2; see also Hornberger, 1989). In the continua of biliteracy, dimensions of communicative repertoire commonly characterized by scholars, educators and policymakers as polar opposites – such as first versus second languages (L1 vs. L2), monolingual versus bilingual individuals or oral versus literate societies – are understood instead as theoretical endpoints on what are in reality fluid and dynamic continua. Biliteracy use and learning occur in the dynamic, rapidly changing and sometimes contested spaces along and across those continua – something that teachers of bilingual and multilingual learners have of course long been aware of in daily practice, in the face of being repeatedly admonished not to mix the languages.

How then do translanguaging and the continua of biliteracy overlap and how do they differ? Communicative repertoire is clearly key in both translanguaging and the continua of biliteracy, an alternative to 'language' that linguists and sociolinguists have long foreseen as key in contesting inequality. Hymes (1992) put it this way:

> I will talk in terms of 'language'. Most people do, including linguists, and the issue of inequality is historically associated first of all with the notion of 'language.' Ultimately, of course, the true subject is not language in the sense of 'a language,' but repertoire – the mix of means and modalities which we actually practice and experience. Study of communicative repertoire makes issues of inequality all the more salient, if only because it inescapably involves choice among alternatives. (Hymes, 1992: 2)

Exploring translanguaging in relation to the continua of biliteracy, Holly Link and I conceptualized translanguaging as the practices and pedagogy through which biliteracy learners develop their communicative repertoires in bi/multilingual transnational spaces of school and community. Using the metaphor of lenses as a way of bringing different sets of the continua of biliteracy into focus (along the lines of the different lenses the optometrist drops in front of your eyes, changing your focus), we considered in turn the lenses of sociolinguistic *context* as scaled spaces that are simultaneously local and global; *content* as transnational literacies contextualized across national borders; *media* as communicative repertoire including multiple and fluid language varieties, scripts, modes and modalities of communication; and *development* via oral, written, receptive and productive translanguaging across these. Drawing on my ethnographic research in a South African Sepedi-English dual language undergraduate honors degree program in Limpopo and hers in a Latinx diaspora community outside Philadelphia where growing numbers of Spanish-speaking, primarily Mexican origin or Mexican-heritage children have arrived in the last few decades, we suggested that these lenses of the continua of biliteracy serve as pedagogical resources for honing innovative programs, curricula, and practices that recognize, value, and build on the rich and varied communicative repertoires of students, their families and communities. In light of what were then promising openings under the Obama administration reflecting his pro-multilingual stance, we argued for the continua of biliteracy as a pedagogical heuristic to draw on in creating new spaces in our policies and our schools, even in the face of increasingly English-only and high stakes testing policies in the United States under NCLB (Hornberger & Link, 2012).

Both translanguaging and the continua of biliteracy are reimaginings of multilingual communicative repertoires and practices. Both address the urgency of improving education serving urban, raciolinguistically minoritized and in particular US Latinx, students. One was imagined perhaps more specifically – to acknowledge and describe the communicative practices of Latinx students and communities. The other was imagined perhaps more broadly – to account for the contexts, content, and media through which those communicative practices and repertoires develop in and out of school. Ironically, one spread like wildfire across the world, perhaps in part because it offered a ready-to-use term for a rapidly developing paradigm shift away from bounded, unitary 'language' to fluid and dynamic '(trans)languaging'; while the other, broader conceptual framework that preceded it was taken up at first in limited and constrained ways by those who misunderstood it as conveying static or essentialized views of language or literacy, or as being *only* about *literacy* or *only* about *bi*-lingualism, but it has since been widely adopted in Indigenous and immigrant/refugee contexts worldwide (Hornberger, 2016: 134; Hornberger, forthcoming).

Both translanguaging and the continua of biliteracy have in fact been taken up far beyond the contexts in/for which they were imagined. In his chapter introducing Welsh translanguaging pedagogy, Baker argued for using the continua in analysis of success and effectiveness in Welsh language education policy: 'the continua provide a robust tool for critiquing systems (e.g. for biases, absences, unequal power relations)' (Baker, 2003: 88). It has indeed been used as such a tool, not only for evaluating programs but also for designing curriculum, pedagogy and assessment in multilingual settings across the world (Hornberger, 2003, 2016, forthcoming). Most recently, Antia and Dyers apply the continua of biliteracy toward a decolonial pedagogy in South Africa (Antia & Dyers, 2019). Translanguaging has been picked up at such a rate and to such an extent that some worry it has lost its central meaning; here I have stuck close to Ofelia's concept of translanguaging.

Ofelia and I have come to see translanguaging and the continua of biliteracy as different starting points that ultimately arrive at the same destination.[5] In the end, what is important is not so much how they overlap or how they differ, but how they can contribute to imagining and celebrating multilingualism in our world. To the extent that our twin concepts of translanguaging and the continua of biliteracy contribute to furthering socially just and equitable cultural and linguistic diversity in our schools and in our world through educational research, policy and practice, they will be fulfilling our purpose for 'imagining' them in the first place.

Notes

(1) I at times use Ofelia's first name and at times her last, honoring both our personal friendship and her stature as world renowned scholar. At times I also represent Ofelia's thoughts here without benefit of checking with her given that the volume is intended to be a surprise for her. Any misinterpretations or misunderstandings are of course my own.
(2) By this I mean that we were both invited plenary speakers at the same conference, a rather special experience for colleagues.
(3) I have opted to retroactively use the term *raciolinguistically minoritized* rather than the earlier terms *language minority* or *language minoritized* in reference to linguistically and culturally diverse children/learners/families/communities that have been historically marginalized in the US and around the world. I do this in recognition of groundbreaking work by García's student Nelson Flores and others that makes explicit the raciolinguistic ideologies underlying that marginalization (Flores, 2019; García & Otheguy, 2017: 56).
(4) I have opted to retroactively use the inclusive term *Latinx* (rather than *Latino/a*) throughout this article, even for articles or writings which pre-date widespread adoption of that term.
(5) We were most recently reminded of this hearing our side-by-side plenaries at the 1st International Conference on Literacy, Culture and Language Education, held at the School of Education, University of Indiana, Bloomington, Indiana, in October 2018.

References

Antia, B.E. and Dyers, C. (2019) De-alienating the academy: Multilingual teaching as decolonial pedagogy. *Linguistics and Education* 51, 91–100.

Baker, C. (1993) *Foundations of Bilingual Education and Bilingualism* (1st edn). Clevedon: Multilingual Matters.

Baker, C. (2003) Biliteracy and transliteracy in Wales: Language planning and the Welsh National Curriculum. In N.H. Hornberger (ed.) *Continua of Biliteracy: An Ecological Framework for Educational Policy, Research, and Practice in Multilingual Settings* (pp. 71–90). Clevedon: Multilingual Matters.

Canagarajah, S. (2007) After disinvention: Possibilities for communication, community and competence. In S. Makoni and A. Pennycook (eds) *Disinventing and Reconstituting Languages* (pp. 233–239). Clevedon: Multilingual Matters.

Flores, N. (2019) Translanguaging into raciolinguistic ideologies: A personal reflection on the legacy of Ofelia García. *Journal of Multilingual Education Research* 9, 45–60.

Flores, N. (2022) Foreword: The transformative possibilities of translanguaging. In M.T. Sánchez and O. García (eds) *Transformative Translanguaging Espacios: Latinx Students and their Teachers Rompiendo Fronteras sin Miedo* (pp. xix–xxi). Bristol: Multilingual Matters.

Flores, N. and García, O. (2017) A critical review of bilingual education in the United States: from basements and pride to boutiques and profit. *Annual Review of Applied Linguistics* 37, 14–29.

García, O. (ed) (1991) *Bilingual Education: Focusschrift in Honor of Joshua A. Fishman on the Occasion of his 65th Birthday*. Philadelphia, PA: John Benjamins Publishers.

García, O. (1993) From Goya portraits to Goya beans: Elite traditions and popular streams in U.S. Spanish language policy. *Southwest Journal of Linguistics* 12 (1–2), 69–86.

García, O. (1997) New York's multilingualism: World languages and their role in a U.S. city. In O. García and J.A. Fishman (eds) *The Multilingual Apple: Languages in New York City* (pp. 5–50). Berlin: Mouton de Gruyter.

García, O. (2007) Foreword. In S. Makoni and A. Pennycook (eds) *Disinventing and Reconstituting Languages* (pp. xi–xv). Clevedon: Multilingual Matters.

García, O. (2009) *Bilingual Education in the 21st Century: A Global Perspective*. Malden, MA: Wiley-Blackwell.

García, O. and Baker, C. (eds) (1995) *Policy and Practice in Bilingual Education*. Clevedon: Multilingual Matters.

García, O. and Baker, C. (eds) (2007) *Bilingual Education: An Introductory Reader*. Clevedon: Multilingual Matters.

García, O. and Menken, K. (2010) Stirring the onion: Educators and the dynamics of language education policies (looking ahead). In K. Menken and O. García (eds) *Negotiating Language Policies in Schools: Educators as Policymakers* (pp. 249–261). New York, NY: Routledge.

García, O. and Otheguy, R. (1987) The bilingual education of Cuban American children in Dade County's ethnic schools. *Language and Education* 1, 83–95.

García, O. and Otheguy, R. (1988) The language situation of Cuban Americans. In S. McKay and S. Wong (eds) *Language Diversity: Problem or Resource?* (pp. 166–192). New York, NY: Harper and Row.

García, O. and Otheguy, R. (eds) (1989) *English Across Cultures - Cultures Across English: A Reader in Cross-cultural Communication*. Berlin: Mouton de Gruyter.

García, O. and Otheguy, R. (2017) Interrogating the language gap of young bilingual and bidialectal students. *International Multilingual Research Journal* 11 (1), 52–65.

García, O. and Schiffman, H.F. (with the assistance of Z. Zakharia) (2006a) Fishmanian sociolinguistics (1949 to the present). In O. García, R. Peltz and H.F. Schiffman, with G.S. Fishman (eds) *Language Loyalty, Continuity and Change: Joshua A. Fishman's Contributions to International Sociolinguistics* (pp. 3–68). Clevedon: Multilingual Matters.

García, O. and Li, W. (2014) *Translanguaging: Language, Bilingualism and Education*. New York, NY: Palgrave Macmillan.

García, O., Evangelista, I., Martinez, M., Disla, C. and Paulino, B. (1988) Spanish language use and attitudes: A study of two New York City communities. *Language in Society* 17, 475–511.

García, O., Morín, J. and Rivera, K.M. (2001) How threatened is the Spanish of New York Puerto Ricans? In J.A. Fishman (ed.) *Can Threatened Languages be Saved?* (pp. 44–73). Clevedon: Multilingual Matters.

García, O., Skutnabb-Kangas, T. and Torres-Guzmán, M.E. (eds) (2006b) *Imagining Multilingual Schools: Languages in Education and Glocalization*. Clevedon: Multilingual Matters.

García, O., Peltz, R., Schiffman, H.F. and Fishman, G.S. (2006c) *Language Loyalty, Continuity and Change: Joshua A. Fishman's Contributions to International Sociolinguistics*. Clevedon: Multilingual Matters.

García, O., Zakaria, Z. and Otcu, B. (eds) (2013) *Bilingual Community Education and Multilingualism: Beyond Heritage Languages in a Global City.* Bristol: Multilingual Matters.

Hornberger, N.H. (1989) Continua of biliteracy. *Review of Educational Research* 59 (3), 271–296.

Hornberger, N.H. (1990) Creating successful learning contexts for bilingual literacy. *Teachers College Record* 92 (2), 212–229.

Hornberger, N.H. (ed) (2003) *Continua of Biliteracy: An Ecological Framework for Educational Policy, Research, and Practice in Multilingual Settings.* Clevedon: Multilingual Matters.

Hornberger, N.H. (2006) Nichols to NCLB: Local and global perspectives on U.S. language education policy. In O. García, T. Skutnabb-Kangas and M. Torres-Guzmán (eds) *Imagining Multilingual Schools: Languages in Education and Glocalization* (pp. 223–237). Clevedon: Multilingual Matters.

Hornberger, N.H. (2016) Researching the continua of biliteracy. In K. King, Y.J. Lai and S.A. May (eds) *Research Methods in Language and Education,* (3rd edn, Vol. 10, Encyclopedia of Language and Education, pp. 1–18). Cham: Springer.

Hornberger, N.H. (2017) Joshua A. Fishman: a scholar of unfathomable influence. *International Journal of the Sociology of Language* 243, 17–28.

Hornberger, N.H. (forthcoming) Researching and teaching (with) the continua of biliteracy. Unpublished manuscript.

Hornberger, N.H. and Johnson, D.C. (2007) Slicing the onion ethnographically: Layers and spaces in multilingual language education policy and practice. *TESOL Quarterly* 41 (3), 509–532.

Hornberger, N.H. and Link, H. (2012) Translanguaging and transnational literacies in multilingual classrooms: A biliteracy lens. *International Journal of Bilingual Education and Bilingualism* 15 (3), 261–278.

Hornberger, N.H. and Pütz, M. (eds) (2006) *Language Loyalty, Language Planning, and Language Revitalization: Recent Writings and Reflections from Joshua A. Fishman.* Clevedon: Multilingual Matters.

Hymes, D.H. (1992) Inequality in language: Taking for granted. *Working Papers in Educational Linguistics* 8 (1), 1–30.

Maturana, H. and Varela, F. (1973/1998) *The Tree of Knowledge: The Biological Roots of Understanding.* Boston and London: Shambhala.

Mignolo, W. (2000) *Local Histories/Global Designs: Coloniality, Subaltern Knowledges, and Border Thinking.* Princeton, NJ: Princeton University Press.

Ortiz, F. (1940) *Contrapunteo cubano del tabaco y el azúcar.* Caracas: Biblioteca Ayacucho.

Ricento, T.K. and Hornberger, N.H. (1996) Unpeeling the onion: Language planning and policy and the ELT professional. *TESOL Quarterly* 30 (3), 401–428.

Ruiz, R. (2011) Afterword: Cooking with Nancy. In F.M. Hult and K.A. King (eds) *Educational Linguistics in Practice: Applying the Local Globally and the Global Locally* (pp. 173–178). Bristol: Multilingual Matters.

Wherritt, I. and García, O. (eds) (1989) U.S. Spanish: The language of Latinos. *International Journal of the Sociology of Language* 79, entire.

Williams, C. (1994) Arfarniad o ddulliau dysgu ac addysgu yng nghyd-destun addysg uwchradd ddwyieithog (PhD). University of Wales, Bangor, Wales.

2 A Mentor from Afar

Suresh Canagarajah

There are some mentors who serve as guides and motivators even when you don't have direct interactions with them frequently. Professor Ofelia García has served in that capacity for me for a long time. She enlightened me on the possibility of translingualism and motivated the research and teaching I am doing now. The resonance of her work might be related to the fact that we are both immigrants and exiles, and have a multilingual background from the Global South. I remember from a conversation with Ofelia her experiences of arriving in the United States from Cuba as a small girl. This social background probably explains Ofelia's openness to the complex communicative practices of multilingual people. It also explains her critical orientation to dominant linguistic and pedagogical paradigms in the centers of scholarship in the Global North. Since I am myself from the Sri Lankan Tamil community, and had to flee the ethnic discrimination in my postcolonial South Asian country, her research insights and pedagogical practices made perfect sense to me.

My biggest regret in my professional life is not getting to interact more with Ofelia when I taught at the City University of New York from 1994 to 2007. It was Ofelia who took the initiative to make connections with me. She invited me to give a lecture at Teachers College, where she was working at that time, in November 2005. I wasn't doing research related to translingualism[1] at that time. I spoke about diversifying our approaches to English language. She listened supportively and we had a useful conversation over lunch after the talk. I got to know more about Ofelia's work and family. Among other things, she told me that teaching in a four-year college was not the best fit for me, as I was capable of handling the challenges in a research-intensive university and mentoring graduate students. She helped me raise my sights to more rewarding professional contributions.

Perhaps inspired by her confidence in me, I moved to Penn State in July 2007. It was while here that I read her book *Bilingual Education in the 21st Century: A Global Perspective* that was published in 2009. That book changed my perspectives on language practices and pedagogies. I was impressed with Ofelia's ability to convey complex theoretical issues with great clarity, apply them insightfully to classroom interactions and offer constructive pedagogical recommendations. As another colleague who read the book told me, 'There is something in it for everybody'. What he meant was that whether the reader was a researcher or practitioner, or whether the reader was interested in theoretical, historical, scholarly or teaching concerns, the book addressed areas of such diverse interests. This has been Ofelia's hallmark even in the lectures I have heard her deliver. She is a rounded scholar who can shuttle across diverse professional concerns with ease. The book was so insightful that I started using some of the informative charts and figures Ofelia included there to illustrate translingualism in my own lectures. When I wrote to Ofelia for permission to use a figure in my article, she was so generous that she told me not to bother about crediting her for it. This attitude reminded me of my own Tamil community where we have great humility towards knowledge. We hold that knowledge is so vast and changing that no one can claim to own it.

As I continue to do my own research on translingualism and translate it to my teaching and professional practices, I still find Ofelia a good role model for the path ahead for me. I am impressed with the way Ofelia can merge research, theory and pedagogy. I am particularly inspired by her investment in teachers and students. She can leave the ivory towers of the university to step into public school classrooms in under-resourced neighborhoods, observe the challenges and concerns of students and teachers and develop practices that can be useful to them. She is also a great collaborator and advisor, working together with teachers and graduate students to develop useful pedagogical recommendations for classrooms. On many occasions, I have directed my own students to her website for pedagogical applications. Her work on the CUNY New York State Initiative on Emergent Bilinguals is detailed and thorough in offering guidelines for teachers at various levels of teaching. I remember one graduate seminar when students overwhelmingly rejected the translingual approach, saying that it was only of theoretical significance and had no pedagogical relevance for teachers. Stung by their criticism, I searched the internet to see what I could offer them. I was relieved to discover the CUNY NYSIEB website where Ofelia and her collaborators made available detailed pedagogical recommendations and guidelines. I was happy that there were efforts of this nature available for my students.

I am also impressed with Ofelia's efforts to make inroads into policy circles and state educational agencies. Rather than staying outside state structures as a critic of dominant pedagogical policies, she has worked with education officials and policy makers to transform education from within the system. She has served the New York City Department of Education (NYCDOE) in many capacities: i.e. as Co-Chair, Best Practices for English Language Learners; Distinguished Advisory Board member of the ELL Teacher Academy; and New York City Board of Education Chancellor's Board on Promotion and Standards. She has also served the New York State Education Department (NYSED): in NYSED Steering Committee, Bilingual Common Core Initiative; NYSED LEP/ELL Committee of Practitioners; NYSED Rubrics Workshop for Regents Accreditation; New York State's Learning Standards for Native Language Arts; New York State Regents' Professional Standards and Practices Board for the Teaching Profession; and NYSED Higher Education State Assessment Advisory Board.

She continues to challenge me on how to go beyond dichotomies such as research/practice, descriptive/political or pedagogies/policies, and make more holistic contributions to our field. In recent years, there have been useful criticisms of the translingual approach. Some critics argue that translingualism has lost its political edge when it focuses too much on textual or identity concerns (Block, 2018). Others claim that it is of mere theoretical interest and has no practical usefulness in a society and education dominated increasingly by restrictive language ideologies and structures (Kubota, 2014). But Ofelia's lifetime of professional contributions show how someone can address these domains in an integrated manner. One domain feeds into the other, and the diverse areas energize each other. Her teaching complexifies her theorization. Classrooms complicate her politics. Her research informs her policy reformulations. I will continue to explore how to go beyond the separation of these domains and treat them in an integrated manner in my professional practice. But one thing that goes against me in following her footsteps is Ofelia's superhuman energy!

Note

(1) I use translingualism as an umbrella term to describe the many terms Ofelia has used in her publications, such as plurilinguailsm, dynamic bilingualism and translanguaging. It also includes the term I often use, translingual practice.

References

Block, D. (2018) The political economy of language education research (or the lack thereof): Nancy Fraser and the case of Translanguaging. *Critical Inquiry in Language Studies*, Adance Publication, 1–21. https://doi.org/10.1080/15427587.2018.1466300.

Kubota, R. (2014) The multi/plural turn, postcolonial theory, and neoliberal multiculturalism. *Applied Linguistics* 37, 474–494.

3 Ofelia García's Global Classroom

Bahar Otcu-Grillman

Professor Emeritus Ofelia García has been a unique mentor and a colleague to me. With her productiveness and mentorship, which is second only to her warmth and modesty, Ofelia[1] inspired me as she did many of her doctoral students, mentees and new scholars to follow in her footsteps. Her nurturing nature and resourcefulness made her remarkable. While at Teachers College (TC, hereafter), I took several of Ofelia's inspirational courses such as Languages, Societies and Schools, and doctoral seminars. She taught contemporary topics in sociolinguistics and bilingual education, covered topics of social justice, medium of instruction, language policy and planning and evoked in us an awareness of diversity and minority education in the United States and around the world. She introduced us to great scholars in the field either in her classes or in her guest-lecture series, through which she brought many leading scholars to TC. I had the pleasure to meet notable figures such as Adrian Blackledge, Angela Creese, Suresh Canagarajah, Thomas Ricento, Elana Shohamy, Tove Skutnabb-Kangas, Robert Phillipson, Bernard Spolsky, Ricardo Otheguy – her beloved husband and colleague – and Joshua Fishman, Ofelia García's life-long mentor and colleague. Some of these impressive scholars, alongside others from around the world, have joined us here in this collective volume, for which I am honored.

Ofelia not only taught us bilingual education and multilingualism, but also made sure we experienced it together by sustaining our diversity in various ways. She kept us, her students, close and always stayed in touch via emails, phone calls, brief gatherings and collaborations. As Ofelia's students from the United States, the Americas, Europe, Middle East or Asia, we attended several fiestas in her home and even in those of her colleagues, where learning never stopped. I remember many lovely intellectually stimulating conversations at Christmas parties in her home, driven by delicious albondigas a la Habanera, mezes and vino. I also recall Joshua Fishman's cozy apartment in Riverdale, New York, where we not only had great academic conversations but also experienced his family's unique Jewish hospitality. One time, when Professor Fishman was getting out of a car that he had arrived in, Ofelia, having assisted him, turned to me and said, 'you will also be like this, helping me walk when I grow old'. As a doctoral student away from home, I had emotional moments with this thought. It allowed me to imagine growing older near Ofelia, like a relative or even a daughter. I also recall attending Joshua Fishman's 80th birthday celebration symposium at the University of Pennsylvania in 2006 – an unforgettable event. There, Ofelia introduced me to Nancy Hornberger briefly as well. It was heartwarming to see Ofelia with her friends, celebrating her own mentor, with the members of Professor Fishman's family. Ofelia's extended network is magical like this; she connects you to people in the field, even though they may be at the other end of the world. My friendships from Ofelia's classes and networks transcend the borders of the United States to Bangladesh, Iran, Japan, Korea, Mexico, Pakistan, Uzbekistan and Turkey, to name a few of these locations. Ofelia is thoughtful of her relationships, be it with her students, colleagues or friends, no matter where they are. When she sees you, she not only asks about you and your family and remembers all the names of your family members, but also asks if you have recently heard from a specific colleague, how they are doing and so on. She opened the doors of multilingualism and multiculturalism to us so brilliantly, supported us morally and academically and happily became present in our lives.

Ofelia is not only a hardworking and accomplished scholar with a broad scholarly network, but she is also a supportive colleague and leader. In the last year of my doctoral studies, I approached her to ask if it would be interesting to write a book together about community-based language schools. She became very interested, encouraged me to get started sooner than later, but I did not have that kind of courage or readiness. Soon, when I found us working on *Bilingual Community Education and Multilingualism* (with Zeena Zakharia), I got to know her motivating, disciplined work style and saw what a talented and courageous writer she was. Throughout our work on the book and our doctoral seminars, she always advised, 'don't be afraid to say things'. Ofelia helps you develop your ideas, articulate them and put them into proper words. When you are stuck and suffering from writer's block while working on your book chapter or dissertation, she gives a simple advice: 'sit down and write'. You take her advice and see that you can really write once you sit down! Ofelia supports her students and colleagues morally and academically, publishes with them and gives them the self-confidence they need to achieve anything and everything. She visited me at my home when I had just had my second baby and was afraid to take my children to places by myself. Ofelia encouraged me to drive then, and now I can drive our own minivan thanks to her confidence in me.

Ofelia's teaching is never without humor and fun. She is an impressive storyteller with always an interesting story to tell; it is uplifting to hear and listen to her. I attended many of her speeches at conferences, and always learned something new about bilingual education and multilingualism (also, all-terrain vehicles and Latinx pop culture!). Many years after graduation, when I went to present my paper in this volume in Ottawa in 2018, I had a chance to listen to her speak again and see how much Canadians loved, laughed with and respected her. Canada is not too far from the United States, but it indicated that, everywhere in the world, people love her and have an interest in her work.

Ofelia's advocacy is above everything else. Her lifetime work on bilingual education and multilingualism, initially with Professor Fishman, and her translanguaging approach later, have provided the advocacy for those who speak minority languages and the guidance for educators and policymakers who regulate the minorities' education. I am thankful to her for everything she did for me and others, for every idea she nurtured and pursued and for everyone she inspired to change the world.

Note

(1) As a timid doctoral student, I first called Ofelia García, Professor García. But with her friendliness and asking us to call her by her first name, we called her Ofelia. I refer to her as Ofelia also in this essay.

4 A Letter for Ofelia García[1]

Lesley Bartlett

1 December 2016

Selection Committee
[...]
[...]

Dear Members of the Selection Committee,

I write to express my strongest recommendation for the nomination of Professor Ofelia García for the [...] award. Other letters have outlined her prodigious, continuous and strong scholarship in the field of bilingual education and the significant contributions she has made theoretically and empirically to the field. Instead of repeating that information, in this letter I would like to describe her impact, as a mentor, on my career. In truth, I am herein writing a heartfelt love letter to Ofelia.

I was already working at Teachers College, Columbia University, when Ofelia, a senior scholar, moved to the institution. I remember distinctly the widely shared buzz of feeling very lucky that we had been able to hire her. She joined a department that, it is fair to say, was suffering from years of low-grade in-fighting. Ofelia had an immediate humanizing effect on discourse in the department. She politely called out inappropriate behavior, and she encouraged all of us to reframe, focus on strengths and plan for the future. It was astounding to me how her presence reoriented conversations.

At this time, I was early in my career. I had exhausted the writing I could do from my dissertation on youth and adult literacy programs in Brazil and I was casting about for a local project on language and literacy with which I could engage. Ofelia graciously shared resources on bilingual education in New York, and she tutored me through my reading. Together, and with a group of sharp graduate students, we planned a research project in a remarkable bilingual high school for newcomer Latinx youth. Access was made possible thanks to Ofelia's wide network. We pulled together shoestring budgets to conduct the research. It was an amazing learning experience for me. I was particularly impressed by Ofelia's manner of engaging with teachers as organic intellectuals with informed analyses of language policies and practices. I learned as much writing a book with Ofelia, based on the data, as I had in the preparation for the work. It was a truly educational experience, in which she always generously highlighted and heralded my contributions, making me feel like an equal partner.

On a more personal note, throughout this period of research, I also gave birth to two children. The general sense in the department was that you could have children, as long as it didn't interfere with your work. Ofelia was the only senior scholar to encourage me. She talked with me about her own struggles as a young mother and scholar. She helped me think through how to balance competing demands. When my son faced a health scare, she comforted me and gave advice. Her emotional support was essential to my persistence during this period.

I sometimes wonder where I would be now, had it not been for Ofelia's many kindnesses. Her generosity of spirit has been a blessing to all who have had the privilege to work with and learn from her. I can think of no one more deserving of this award. Thank you for considering this letter.

Sincerely,

[Signed]

Lesley Bartlett, Ph.D. Professor
The University of Wisconsin-Madison

Note

(1) This is a letter of recommendation written for Ofelia García for an award. The award name and address have been redacted so that the letter could be presented to a broader audience in this volume.

Part 2: Bilingual Pedagogies and Teacher Education

5 Emergent Bilinguals and Trans-Semiotic Practices in the New Media Age

Jo Anne Kleifgen

Pre-Reading Discussion Questions

(1) How would you explain to a colleague or family member how the designation 'emergent bilingual' best describes students who come to school speaking a language different from the school language? What does 'emergent bilingual' offer over other labels ascribed to language-minoritized students?

(2) Besides spoken and written language modes, what other semiotic (meaning-making) resources are available for learning?

Introduction

Imagine a classroom where students enter without having to leave their ways of speaking at the door. What happens when these students, who are emergent bilinguals, are free to draw on their full meaning-making repertoires to learn? And what happens to learning when these students have equal access to digitized semiotic resources for learning? In this study, I examine the classroom practices of eighth grade Latinx students working with a web-based platform designed to support academic writing development. The study documents how students collaborate with one another and with teachers as they learn about a topic in social studies, using bilingual along with other semiotic resources available to them in the online research and writing space.

The chapter begins with a discussion of the term 'emergent bilingual', tracing the different labels assigned to language-minoritized learners of English in the United States by official institutions and the attendant dissonance between what research says about educating these students and educational policies and practices that have tended to thwart their access to an equitable education. Next, I offer a theoretical and empirical rationale, focusing on social-semiotic approaches to research on resources for learning. Then, to provide a context, I discuss the larger intervention project from which the data for this study are drawn. The chapter continues with a case study of a class of Latinx middle school students using the online system to learn and write about the US Civil Rights Movement, which includes a close analysis of three students' practices during a task activity in class. A summary discussion of the findings and recommendations concludes this chapter.

Why Emergent Bilinguals?

The term 'emergent bilingual' was first proposed in a monograph (García et al., 2008) prepared for the Campaign for Educational Equity while Ofelia García was on the faculty at Teachers College, Columbia University. The term arose out of a dissatisfaction with the labels appropriated and applied to students learning the language of the classroom. For over half a century, language-minoritized students in the United States have been identified by several different labels, based often on prejudicial beliefs. These designations changed over time, depending on shifting federal and educational policies. In the late 1970s, the term 'limited English proficient' (LEP) was established, thereby placing emphasis on students' learning deficits rather than their learning potential; the label is used to this day by many federal agencies, including the Department of Education (DOE), where the term appears extensively throughout its website. Other such restrictive school-based labels include 'English as a second language' students, 'English language learners' or simply 'English learners', all terms that focus on a monoglossic ideal that ignores bilingual communities' fluid language practices (García, 2009a).

Another frequently used label, 'bilingual students', might appear at first blush to be an improvement, since it no longer overtly places the English language in the sole position of primacy. However, it has become a short form for students studying in bilingual education programs where they are learning English, the majority language used in school. Thus, 'bilingual' has become a euphemism for 'non-English'. Joshua Fishman bemoaned the US language-educational policy, the Bilingual Education Act of 1968, as: 'primarily an act for the Anglification of non-English speakers and not an act for Bilingualism [...]. "Bilinguals" are thus non-English mother-tongue speakers; "bilingual teachers" are those who teach them; "bilingual programs" are those that Anglify them' (Fishman, 1981: 517). Over time, even 'bilingual' fell out of favor, and the pendulum of labels began to swing back to English-only: 'bilingual programs' became 'dual-language programs,' and official acknowledgment of a student's home language was effectively silenced when, in 2002, the DOE renamed the Office of Bilingual Education as the Office of English Language Acquisition.

Names of other offices have followed suit since then (Crawford, 2004; García, 2009b). Yet, despite the official silencing at the national level, support for bilingual education remains evident at the state and district levels (Goldenberg & Wagner, 2015).

The 'emergent bilingual' designation materialized during a research initiative at Teachers College. In reviewing the research on linguistic minorities' access to education in the United States, our research team, including Ofelia García, Lorraine Falchi and myself, recognized the limiting ways these students were named and began to imagine a better way to characterize who they are. After considering several variations, we adopted the new term 'emergent bilinguals'. Our final report, which eventually became a monograph in January, 2008, opened with a simple declaration: 'English language learners are in fact *emergent bilinguals* ...' (García *et al.*, 2008: 6, emphasis in the original). We argued that inequities in the students' education evolve from an incomplete understanding of who the students are: speakers of a home language who become learners of an additional language through schooling until they become bilingual, and who continue to function in their home language along with the language of the school. The report illustrated the dissonance between what research says about educating emergent bilinguals and policies enacted, such as No Child Left Behind in 2002, which emphasized English-only and high stakes testing. The monograph was expanded into a book, *Educating Emergent Bilinguals* (García & Kleifgen, 2010, 2018) designed for educators and policy makers, providing theoretical foundations, research findings, alternative teaching and assessment practices and innovative approaches to engagement with parents and community. The second edition offers updates on research, policy and pedagogy and includes a new chapter on the affordances of technology for an equitable education of emergent bilinguals, an area which receives special attention in the research intervention project described in this chapter.

It is important to bear in mind the context surrounding the choice of this term: while it is true that any person learning an additional language can be called an emergent bilingual, including a 'majority' language speaker studying another language, the concept of emergent bilingual was brought forward primarily to address the plight of language minoritized students, schooled in inequitable circumstances, to propose ways of repairing disparities and opening paths to full access to learning.

Theoretical Framework

The research described in this chapter is grounded in social semiotic thinking, in which language is understood as part of a broader, complex repertoire of semiotic resources that people draw on to make meaning in their communicative practices. An early discussion of this theoretical grounding can be found in Valentin Vološinov's outline of the philosophy of language ([1929]1973), a volume that has been called 'the first extensive Russian prolegomenon to semiotics' (Matejka, 1973: 163). The work focuses on human social interaction at the level of the utterance. Vološinov called different semiotic means 'signs' − words, gestures, images, music; these signs each have meaning potential that can be realized conjointly in social interaction.

Michael Halliday elaborated on these ideas in his work on language as a mode of social action (e.g. Halliday, 1978; Halliday & Hasan, 1985). Halliday's theory of social semiotics views language as a system of signs that is socially constructed and that interacts with other semiotic systems in the culture. Where Vološinov wrote of signs, Halliday introduced the concept of 'semiotic resources' − actions and objects that people draw on in social interaction. Language and these other systems are also called 'modes'. Social semiotics primarily addressed the spoken and written modes, neglecting other sign systems that work together with linguistic ones to accomplish meaning. Yet, in Goodwin's words, 'neither talk, nor language itself, are self-contained systems, but instead function within a larger ecology of sign systems' (Goodwin, 2007: 27−28).

Toward the turn of the century, researchers began to examine the affordances of other modes of communication. Gunther Kress and his colleagues introduced the term 'multimodality' to investigate ways in which people communicate through images, color, film and sound (Kress & van Leeuwen, 1996; van Leeuwen, 1999, 2011), and later to demonstrate how different modes are combined into 'ensembles' (Kress, 2003: 70) of meaning making that vary with each given communicative situation (e.g. Kleifgen, 2006). These modes are fluid and changeable when taken up and applied in different social contexts, including educational contexts. Kress was a member of the New London Group (1996) − academics concerned about pedagogy − who called for recognizing 'multiliteracies', a concept that accounts for both the increasing linguistic diversity of learners and the growing availability of digitized modes of communication (see Cope & Kalantzis, 2000; Cope et al., 2022); their work signaled the added complexity of new media technologies where learner access to multimodal resources extends beyond the boundaries of the classroom.

This 'multimodal turn', however, largely neglected to attend to the integral relationship among *all* communicative modes, including the linguistic modes. In an age of increased bi/multilingualism, complex language and literacy practices of multilinguals were not being included in the multimodal whole. The case study that follows begins to fill this gap by examining the confluence of language use and technology and exploring what I call the 'trans-semiotic' (Kleifgen, 2019) practices of emergent bilingual adolescents as they navigated a multimodal online system during classroom instruction.

Case Study of Emergent Bilinguals' Trans-Semiotic Practices

Background

The data for this study are drawn from a larger four-year intervention project called STEPS to Literacy (Kleifgen & Kinzer, 2014), funded by the Institute of Education Science.[1] The overarching goal of this project was to support Latinx adolescents' academic writing in the science and social studies content areas by combining (1) a web-based space for student research and writing with (2) a pedagogical approach that acknowledges these students as emergent bilinguals, recognizing and supporting their full semiotic repertoires as resources for learning. Project team members designed and tested a multimodal web-based software, which contained curricular units and a library of digital resources for students' investigations. The interface permitted student choice to read teacher-made prompts in Spanish or English and to write notes and essays in either language (see Kleifgen *et al.*, 2014, for a more detailed description).

The multiyear intervention was carried out in public middle schools located in Harlem and the Bronx in New York City, where classroom cohorts of eighth grade Latinx students participated in units of six to eight instructional sessions taught by teacher-researchers, who were members of the project team. The units were designed in collaboration with the schools' classroom teachers for inclusion in the online system and were based on topics from the eighth-grade curriculum. This case study examines one of the participating classrooms in the third year of the intervention project.

Setting and participants

This study of emergent bilinguals' trans-semiotic practices took place in a Bronx public middle school, one of several schools that formed part of the larger research intervention. In an eighth-grade English learner classroom, ten Latinx students, four girls and six boys, participated in six instructional sessions covering a unit on the US Civil Rights Movement. The students had been pre-tested for English knowledge, showing that they represented various ranges of experience with spoken and written English. The teacher-researcher engaged in translanguaging, and students could rely on others for help and clarification in English and Spanish. They carried out collaborative research and analysis and the production of notes for future essay drafts. They were told not to be concerned with mechanics (spelling, grammar, etc.) during note taking but instead to focus on interpreting information and expressing ideas as they created notes, or new 'knowledge artifacts' (Kleifgen, 2013; Ronan, 2014).

During the sessions, these students examined resources available in the web-based learning space, which included over 30 artifacts related to the topic: photographs of historical figures; of segregated schools, parks, lunch counters, water fountains; and of protests and police actions, along with maps and graphs. Students also had access to bilingual recordings and transcripts of Martin Luther King's speeches and other texts covering civil rights activities across various regions of the country. With guided instruction, students explored the historical materials and collaborated, using their home language resources along with English to grasp concepts, form ideas and take notes to synthesize the resources examined before developing drafts in response to a teacher-created prompt.

The adults in the classroom included members of the project team – the teacher-researcher, the technology (tech) specialist, and myself – and the regular classroom teacher.

Data collection and analysis

Focusing specifically on the students' collaborative on-line research and note-taking practices, the case study addressed two questions: The first examined how, over the course of six instructional sessions, the students deployed their home language (Spanish) and developing language (English), that is, how their translanguaging practices unfolded as they worked across web-based spaces to complete research and note-taking tasks. For the second question, the study focused on three students, Kenny, Jessica and Mauricio (pseudonyms), each representing differing levels of emergent bilingualism, and explored how these students combined their linguistic and embodied modes with other semiotic modes – e.g. historical texts, videos, images, maps – to learn about Martin Luther King Jr's 'I Have a Dream' speech. The findings for this portion of the research are presented below in the form of vignettes.

Primary data sources included video-camera and screen-capture recordings of the classroom interaction. Screen-capture software on each computer permitted direct observation of every student's actions on the web-based interface. Figure 5.1 is a diagram of the classroom configuration, student-seating chart (indicating locations of the three focal students) and placement of recording equipment.

Sixty-six hours of recorded data were transcribed and coded for language choice in spoken and written modes during on-line and off-line activities. These, along with selection choices students made of other semiotic resources on-line and in the classroom, were coded and analyzed using ELAN (Wittenburg et al., 2006), a tool for creating annotations of digital recordings. Observers' field notes supplemented the analysis and interpretation of the recorded data.

Findings: Classroom trends in translanguaging

I begin with an overview of the translanguaging practices of all ten emergent bilinguals during the instructional sessions. In terms of the

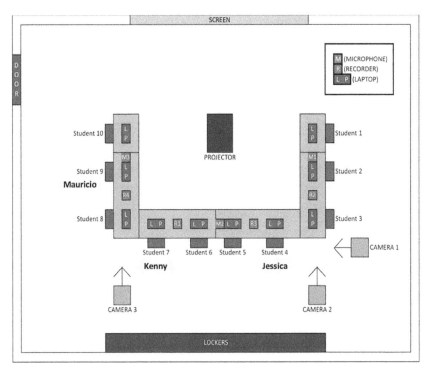

Figure 5.1 Classroom configuration, seating chart and recording devices

Spanish-English flow in the classroom, the overarching finding shows that students and instructors engaged in translanguaging practices throughout all the sessions. Both languages were present in class discussions as well as on- and off-line reading and writing activities.

While all students engaged in Spanish-English translanguaging, their language choices – spoken and written – varied in terms of proportion and strategy. The spoken discourse in the classroom showed pervasive translanguaging, which could be attributed to the teacher's instructional interactions with the students, thus setting the tone for fluid language practices as a normal way of communicating. As the students began to use the interface to work in collaboration with their peers on the assigned tasks, they typically used spoken Spanish in assignment-related interactions among their peers or when interacting individually with the teacher or other bilingual adults in the room.

However, whenever the students turned from interpersonal interaction to interaction with the web-based system, their language choices varied: the findings show differences in which language they chose to commit the spoken, shared information to their written notes. Regarding language choice for reading and writing in the web-based system, students could choose to read text resources and take written notes in either language, and within these choices, some patterns emerged. A summary of all ten students' language choices for reading and writing (indicating the three focal students' patterns) is presented in Table 5.1:

Table 5.1 Emergent bilinguals' written language choices in the web-based system

Students	On-line text resources	On-line note taking
Student 1	English	English
Student 7 **Kenny**	English	English
Student 10	English	English
Student 5	English (one exception)	English (one exception)
Student 2	English (one exception)	Spanish and English
Student 8	Moved from Spanish to English	Spanish and English
Student 4 **Jessica**	Moved from Spanish to English	English (one exception)
Student 3	Spanish	Spanish
Student 6	Spanish (one exception)	Spanish
Student 9 **Mauricio**	Spanish	Spanish

These findings show variations in the reading and writing choices that were made in the web-based system. Four students: 1, 7 (Kenny), 10 and 5 worked predominantly in English; three students: 3, 6 and 9 (Mauricio) worked predominantly in Spanish and three students: 2, 8 and 4 (Jessica) made substantial use of both languages.

Findings: Vignettes of three emergent bilinguals: Kenny, Jessica and Mauricio

Translanguaging practices

Nuances of the emergent bilinguals' sequential translanguaging strategies with differing patterns of language choice are illustrated with three students' varied translanguaging practices to accomplish tasks. The first focal student, Kenny, was the only one of the three born and educated in the United States. His parents were immigrants from the Dominican Republic; he reported speaking at home to his mother in Spanish and to his 27-year-old sister in English. He was comfortable with everyday interpersonal communication in the Spanish and English varieties reflective of his neighborhood's Black and Latinx cultural and linguistic practices. He reported spending time collecting and sharing Latinx and rap music on his home computer, which was another indication of his personal identification with his community. In school, he habitually read and wrote in English while completing classroom tasks, though his academic discourse was still developing in both languages. This practice was borne out during the instructional sessions: he read the English version of text documents to take notes and write in English. In teacher led discussions where translanguaging took place, he contributed in both languages. During group or paired activities, he requested help in English from adults about the content of resources and what to write, but he engaged with other students about assigned tasks primarily in Spanish. Because of his online experience and skills, he also used Spanish to assist peers in navigating the instructional interface.

Jessica, who immigrated with her parents to the United States from Honduras, was a year older than her classmates. She reported speaking Spanish at home and was observed by teachers to have 'advanced writing proficiency in Spanish' while beginning to develop her English literacy. Her teachers reported that she was studious, had a quiet disposition and spoke 'a little English' in class. During the instructional sessions, Jessica offered translanguaged responses during teacher-led discussions. She requested assistance in Spanish from peers or adults in the room about what to write or how to navigate the web-based system. As for reading and writing, her commitment to building competence in written English was evident as shown in how her literacy practices shifted over time from Spanish to English: in session one, she read and took notes in Spanish. In sessions two through five, she read the Spanish version of text resources, then used the English versions of online materials or handouts as a basis to write her notes in English. In the final session, she worked primarily in English.

Mauricio, a newcomer from the Dominican Republic, reported speaking Spanish and 'some English' at home. At school, he wrote almost exclusively in Spanish. In contrast to Kenny, who had the background experience of living and studying in the United States, Mauricio's funds of knowledge and identity were rooted in his home country. As such, he came to school with a higher content-area learning curve to gain understanding of American historical events like the Civil Rights Movement and so studied content through the home language while developing his spoken and written English. Mauricio was highly verbal during classroom discussions, participating in Spanish and displaying English receptive competence by responding in Spanish to questions that the teacher posed in English. His engagement with peers was in Spanish. While working with texts associated with the assigned tasks, Mauricio requested assistance in Spanish to interpret events. He read Spanish versions of online texts to take notes and write in Spanish.

To obtain a snapshot of the three students' relative emergent bilingualism, their utterances in the two named languages were isolated (recognizing that in practice, languages are not bounded) and coded for analysis. Table 5.2 presents a comparative summary of the three students' spoken language use for all sessions based on coding of individual utterances, which included student-to-teacher talk and peer-to-peer talk:

Table 5.2 Spoken utterances of the three focal students – all sessions

	Spanish	English	Mixed	Total
Kenny	175 (33%)	335 (64%)	13 (0.25%)	523
Jessica	121 (83%)	19 (13%)	6 (4%)	146
Mauricio	416 (97%)	10 (2%)	2 (0.05%)	428

The analysis shows that Kenny spoke the most in class (523 utterances), and his utterances were primarily in English (64%), while Mauricio produced 428 utterances, which were almost entirely in Spanish (97%). Jessica was shown to be less verbal in class, confirming teacher-reported impressions, with only 146 utterances, 83% of them in Spanish. These findings provide evidence for how, as emergent bilinguals, they were each drawing on their developing bilingual repertoires in this specific classroom situation where there was freedom and support to do so.

Trans-semiotic practices

Translanguaging never happens in a vacuum; it occurs as an integral part of a complex of meaning-making resources. The second part of the analysis consists of a close examination of the three focal students' translanguaging in concert with their use of other semiotic resources that were available online and in their surrounds, i.e. their trans-semiotic practices, to accomplish assigned tasks. This analysis explores how students' use of the linguistic modes combines with other modes to construct meaning in a learning situation. The fifth instructional session was propitious for this examination because, by then, students had become familiar with the web-based technology and with the freedom to translanguage in class. In addition, their online trans-semiotic investigations (historic texts, photographs, maps) during the prior four sessions engendered new knowledge, laying the groundwork for study and writing about the new civil rights event they were about to examine.

In this session, they participated in a detailed exploration of another semiotic resource: a videorecording of the 'I Have a Dream' speech by Martin Luther King Jr. The session began with the teacher's introduction to King, activist and leader of the Civil Rights Movement. She reviewed some key events studied in prior sessions – the history of segregationist laws and protests by individuals fighting for change – and projected on the overhead screen a few familiar artifacts from the library of resources in the interface: a US map of the segregated south and Washington, DC (the setting for King's speech), and a time line of events in the Movement – all to create a context for the day's activity. The video was then projected playing a two-minute portion of King's speech, followed by a teacher-led analysis of his words in a whole-class discussion, taking different social, political and geographic perspectives.[2]

The students also received two handouts: a Spanish-English excerpt of the speech and a set of guiding questions based on different perspectives (social, political, geographic) to use for note taking. After the video was played, the teacher, translanguaging throughout, invited the students to talk about the main message King was conveying to his audience, suggesting that they refer to the printed version of the speech. She reminded them of the images of segregation they had examined before and of the supreme court decision that segregation was illegal. In the ensuing discussion, there were student contributions in both languages. Next, students were invited to collaborate with a peer to take notes describing King's 'dream' and the social and political changes he imagined.

Vignettes of the three focal students' sequential actions during the discussion and note-taking phases follow.

Kenny

Kenny participates actively during the class discussion of the video, giving evidence of prior knowledge about King: He speaks up in English, confirming that King was a leader and a preacher, noting that activist meetings occurred in African-American churches, and stating that King eventually was assassinated. Yet Kenny and his classmates are having trouble interpreting some of King's words describing how black people felt, such as 'sweltering with the heat of injustice'. Their regular classroom teacher intervenes, offering an explanation to scaffold the students' understanding. She reframes the words, using an expression familiar to New York City urban youth: 'Kenny, you know when you all get very stressed, you're angry and upset, you say you're 'tight'?' Kenny responds with 'Oh, yeah' nodding along with his peers.

As students turn to their computers for the note-taking task, Kenny and his classmate Nanci are instructed to take their notes based on a political perspective. Kenny opens the interface, reads the prompt in English, looks through the library of resources and selects the English version of the text of King's speech. Nanci, using Spanish, asks him for assistance, and he turns to help her find the on-line text of King's speech on her computer.

He then proceeds to read the excerpt on his screen and refers to a handout placed next to his keyboard to examine the guiding questions based on a political perspective: 'Who had power?' and 'What laws and decisions did the government make about segregation?' After a pause, he consults with the tech specialist (TS) standing behind him about what to write in answer to the first guiding question. He turns with his hand raised to ask her:

K: 'Martin Luther King had the power, right?'   (pointing to handout)
TS: 'Power?'
K: 'Or wasn't it, like, the government?'
TS: 'Yeah, who was in charge'/...
K: /'the gover'/
TS: /'Who was the boss?'
K: 'The government?'
TS: (nods)

Kenny requests confirmation regarding who held power, first suggesting King, then the government. The tech specialist rephrases the question from the more abstract 'holding power' to a more colloquial response ('who was in charge'; 'who was the boss') as a language accommodation technique typically used by teachers to scaffold learning (Kleifgen, 1985).

After this exchange, Kenny begins to produce a first note: 'the government had the power of the states'. Meanwhile, Nanci asks him in Spanish for help about what to write; he struggles to explain, and after a few attempts, he simply tells her to write a response to the first question, pointing to his own on-screen notepad: 'Contesta la pregunta, haz lo alli. 'Quien tiene el poder' y tú lo escribes alli' (Answer the question, do it there. 'Who has power' and you write it there). While they both speak to each other in Spanish about how to interpret the guiding questions and respond in writing, both are still in the process of developing an academic register in either language, so they labor to articulate their ideas in talk as well as in writing.

Kenny continues to muse over the handout of guiding questions, then raises his hand to ask the tech specialist for assistance in interpreting the second question about the laws and decisions made by the segregationist government. Figure 5.2 is a screen-capture recording, showing Kenny's opened notepad and his request for help from the tech assistant.

He poses the question, and she encourages him to recall some of the online images of segregated spaces he has examined in prior instructional sessions:

K: What was the laws?   (pointing to second guiding
                                                question)
TS: What have you learned about, right?
        Remember you learned that, like, the
        schools were segregated, you learned
        about the water fountains, all of that?
K: (nods)
TS: Those are all of the laws that the   (nods)
        governor makes.

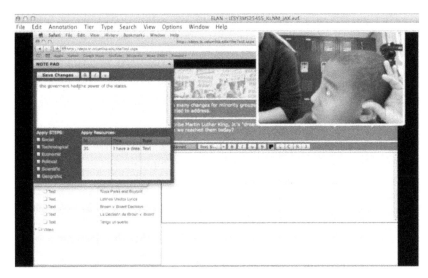

Figure 5.2 Screen capture of Kenny's notepad and his request for help in interpreting text

The reminder about prior examinations of images, which represent segregationist laws imposed by powerful people like the governor of Alabama, helps Kenny to address the second guiding question. He returns to his notetaking: 'the governor decision was that it should be segragated. the laws was that colored was to use water fountains and different restaurant different school'. He is able to contrast what King dreamed for all Americans with what the government enforced on people of color.

As Kenny continues with his notes in English, Nanci again appeals for help; he tries in Spanish to explain the discriminatory laws imposed by the governor of Alabama. After several false starts he finally says, 'Alabama necesita estar segregado' (Alabama must be segregated). Nanci complains that his words are confusing her: '¡Es que tú hablas demasiado enredado!' (It's that you speak too tangled up!). Kenny completes his notes just as the class is ending:[3]

> The goverment had the power of the states. the governor decision was that it should be segragated. the laws was that colored was to use water fountains and diffrent restaurant diffrent school.what affect the civil rights was that they could of done nothing or change nothing

His notes can be summarized as: The governor held state power and made laws enforcing segregation of water fountains, restaurants, schools; these laws could not have been changed without the civil rights movement.

He saves his notes and, using the message function, sends a copy to classmates, logs out and quickly adds a new tab to open a space for free online storage and searches for 'con lo Pie', by Chimbala, a Dominican rapper; just at this moment, the teacher researcher looks over his shoulder, smiles, and says the bell is about to ring. He grins, closes the link and leaves the classroom.

In this vignette, Kenny was seen to come to an understanding of the King speech by several means. First, born, raised, and schooled in the United States, he brought prior cultural knowledge to the lesson, along with his spoken language repertoire – Dominican Spanish and Black English vernacular. His teacher and the tech specialist adapted their English to Kenny's ways of speaking: The teacher introduced a term familiar to his neighborhood dialect to scaffold understanding of King's more complex metaphorical phrases. The tech specialist used simplified English register to explain the more abstract register of political ideas; both transactions facilitated the making of meaning across linguistic registers (informal to formal speech) and modes (spoken to written).

Further, Kenny's interactions with others and with the texts were enveloped by other semiotic means: images. He was able to act on the tech specialist's reminders about photographs of segregation, which he had analyzed during earlier sessions. These additional semiotic resources facilitated Kenny's understanding of the meaning of power, laws, and segregation. In this case, the recalled images were resemiotized into the creation of a textual interpretation in his note (Iedema, 2003; Ronan, 2015).

Jessica

At the beginning of the class session, while the King speech is projected on the overhead, Jessica has her eyes fixed on the screen, paying close attention to the first half of the video; then, she begins to follow the written text on the handout, tracing her fingers along the words until the video ends. During the teacher-led translanguaged discussion, she participates by volunteering answers in Spanish to questions posed by the teacher in English.

For the online note-taking task, she and her peer collaborator, Ricki, are asked to focus on guiding questions from a social perspective. With help from the tech specialist who points to icons on her computer screen, Jessica logs into the interface, locates the prompt for notetaking and begins reading. She and Ricki confer briefly in Spanish about what constitutes a social perspective. She opens the digital notepad, moving it to a convenient place on the screen, then looks down at the handout of the speech next to her keyboard to begin her interpretation of the King speech. After some pause, she turns to Ricki for help in how to get started but gets no response: '¿Qué es lo que hay que hacer?' (What do we have to do?), '¿Qué es lo que hay que escribir?' (What do we have to write?). She asks a third time: '¿Yo…. Qué puedo poner?' (I…. What can I put?). This time Ricki looks at her handout but still does not respond; he is distracted, sending off-task messages to other classmates.

The tech specialist comes to her aid, showing her two text files in the library of resources by pointing to 'I have a dream' and 'Tengo un sueño' links. Jessica opens the text in Spanish, and begins to read it on the screen. She has placed the digitized text on the left of the screen and has moved the notepad next to it. She scrolls up and down, examining the speech, then she types slowly with one finger: 'Dr.Martin'. But instead of comparing the Spanish and English digital files, she refers to the Spanish digitized version, then puts her finger on the handout to read the printed English version to use as a basis for taking notes in English. She looks up at the screen continuing to type 'Luther King'. Next, she turns the handout over several times to read the Spanish and corresponding English texts and types 'he say a the people' into the on-screen notepad. At this point her notepad reads 'Dr. Martin Luther King he say a the people'. Her bilingual reading pattern continues for several minutes, when, turning to Ricki again and tapping him on the elbow, she says:

J: 'Mira eso'
      ((Look at that))
J: 'Ricki, esta palabra significa 'sueño', ¿verdad?'   (pointing to 'dream'
      ((Ricki, this word means 'dream', right?))   on the handout)
R: 'No'   (takes a fleeting glance at her handout)
J: 'Esto'   (pointing again)
      ((This))
R: (looks again)
R: 'Sí, significa 'sueño' '
      ((Yes, it means 'dream'))

With the translation confirmed, Jessica continues typing her note: 'he have an dream'. Jessica is now intensely focused on both sides of the handout. From this point until the session ends, over a period of 15 minutes, her note-taking pattern includes using the paper handout to read the Spanish translation of the speech – turning it over to study the English, sometimes placing her pencil on the text to mark the place, and using the English version as a basis to type her interpretation in the notepad with her left hand (Figures 5.3 and 5.4).

The tech specialist periodically checks Jessica's screen, pointing and using English to assist her in navigating the system; Jessica smiles and nods in response. She continues working after the bell has rung. At the end of the session, she has written these notes on her notepad, which take a social perspective by focusing on Martin Luther King's

Figures 5.3 and 5.4 Jessica reading the handout and typing a note into the on-screen notepad

interactions with the audience and his dream that people of all races in the south will come together in unity:

> Dr. Martin Luther King he say a the people he have an dream, Dr. Martin King talk about the have an dream to an day on the red hill of George. He say the slaves owners will be able to sit down together

Jessica saves her changes and quickly gathers her belongings. She is the last student to leave the room.

This vignette shows that, after closely watching King's speech and participating in the introductory discussion around visuals projected on the overhead screen, Jessica's strategy for note taking was to give steady attention to the Spanish and English texts of King's speech, while also consulting in Spanish with Ricki and receiving assistance in navigating the system from the tech specialist.

Jessica's interactions with others and with bilingual texts exemplify a pervasive use of an embodied semiotic mode: the pointing gesture. Pointing gestures represent an interstitial action connecting various other semiotic means, and all the classroom participants made use of this semiotic mode. In Jessica's case, pointing linked talk with on-screen icons, and printed texts with evolving on-screen notes: the tech specialist pointed to places on the computer screen for mutual orientation and direction, which Jessica acknowledged. Jessica also used pointing, but not to align another person to a semiotic field; she used pointing to keep herself oriented between bilingual words on the handout and the new words she would inscribe on the screen. She juxtaposed reading, pointing and writing to structure her cognition.

Jessica's focus on the linguistic modes for building meaning shows a determination to use her well-developed literacy in the home language as a resource to gain understanding through a comparative reading of the King speech and then to produce a novel written interpretation of its social significance in another language, English.

Mauricio

Mauricio is highly engaged with Martin Luther King's delivery on the overhead video. He has been watching intently at the beginning and is now following closely the Spanish translation on the handout for the remainder of the speech. Just as King's repeated refrain ends with an oratory flourish: 'I have a <u>dream</u> today', Mauricio looks up and nods his head extending an emblematic 'thumbs up' gesture, saying something inaudible that seems to endorse King's words (Figure 5.5). He continues nodding affirmatively as King's supporters applaud.

When the video concludes, the teacher begins a debriefing with the class asking: 'What do you think his main idea was? ¿Cuál es su

Figure 5.5 Mauricio affirming King's speech with gestures

idea principal?' Mauricio immediately raises his hand to answer, but the teacher calls on another student, who offers an answer in Spanish regarding unity among the races. Meanwhile, Mauricio keeps his hand raised trying to gain the teacher's attention. By the time she recognizes him, he says: 'Lo que iba a decir ya dijeron, Miss' (What I was going to say they already said, Miss). But, undeterred, he continues participating, offering in Spanish accurate interpretations of King's words.

To begin taking notes, Mauricio opens the digitized Spanish version of the speech and the notepad, placing them side by side on the screen. The teacher tells Mauricio and a peer, Elena, to take notes using a geographic perspective. The teacher observes Mauricio scrolling the text of the speech and leans in to ask questions to help him get started:

T:	'¿Qué está diciendo que quiere que pase?'
	((What is he saying he wants to happen?))
M:	'Que él ya no como que no aguanta más
	el que hay horita la injusticia'.
	((That he is, like, fed up with what is
	now injustice))
T:	'Um-hum'.
M:	'La opresión'.
	((The oppression))
T:	(reads his note in Spanish to herself)
T:	'What does he imagine for Alabama? ¿Qué es
	su sueño para Alabama?'
M:	'Unirlos'.
	((to unite them.))
T:	'Right. You can write that.
	'Martin Luther King…''
M:	(begins copying King's full name into his notepad)
M:	'Voy a escribir que…'/
	((I'm going to write that…))
T:	/'Qué sueño tiene
	para el sur'.)
	((What dream he has for the south.))
M:	OK. (begins typing into notepad)

In this exchange, the teacher is attempting to guide Mauricio to geographic references in the speech. In his replies, however, Mauricio describes injustice, oppression and King's dreams of uniting both races, demonstrating not only his understanding but also his emotional response to the speech. This emotional interest is realized semiotically in his writing in a way that is unexpected (Leander & Boldt, 2012); it does not conform to the assigned task. Mauricio types rapidly on the notepad stating that King's dream is to unite whites with blacks, who should be able to study together in the same school, and that people – whites and blacks – should unite with no more injustice:

> Martin luther king el sueno del es unur a to dos los blancos con nos negros que puedan ir a una misma escuela estudiar juntos que las personas se una todos los blanos y los negros y que las cosas no sean injustas para ellos ...

> [Martin luther king the dream is to unite all the whites with the blacks that they can go to the same school study together that people unite all the whites and blacks and that things are not unjust for them ...]

Studying the Spanish translation of the speech on the handout, Mauricio, to satisfy the task assignment, writes further that King wants this to happen in the south and in the entire continent, but then he adds that black people are sweltering (sofocados) 'with the heat of injustice', and they are tired of what has been done to them:

> ... y quiere que pase eso en el sur en todo en continente pero el pide que lo agan en el sur porque ya estan sofocados por el calor de la injusticia para ellos que ya estan cansados de lo que le estaban asiendo

> [... and he wants this to happen in the south in the whole continent but asks that they do this in the south because they are already sweltering with the heat of injustice for those who are finally tired of what they were doing to them].

Mauricio saves his notes as the bell rings, concluding the class session.

Mauricio's vignette represents the actions of a student in the earlier stages of emergent bilingualism. He demonstrated a growing receptive competence in spoken English as seen in his gestural responses to the King video, his subsequent oral contributions, in Spanish, to the whole-group discussion, and his responses to the teacher's translanguaging as he began note taking. His actions during the video phase of the session illustrate the moment when, for the first time, Mauricio learned about King and his role in the Civil Rights Movement. Mauricio, a newcomer to US history and culture, was becoming a 'legitimate peripheral participant' in a community of practice (Lave & Wenger, 1991: 29). The video constituted a crucial semiotic resource for new knowledge, which, through the classroom discourse, became a scaffold for his note taking to follow.

For Mauricio, this video-recorded semiotic resource was a motivating force for building meaning in his interaction with the teacher about what to write and in the text he produced. His notes in Spanish evidence not only the acquisition of knowledge about a historical event that occurred in what for him is a new country, but also an intense emotional identification with the event. While his notes made a brief reference to the geographical perspective that was assigned to him, most of his writing demonstrated empathy with people's pain and struggles for freedom and justice.

Like Jessica, Mauricio relied on bilingual texts to study and design his notes in response to a prompt. In his case, the home language was an essential scaffold to learning subject matter content while in the process of developing spoken and written English.

Summary and Conclusion

In terms of language practices, the ten emergent bilinguals in this case study engaged in Spanish-English translanguaging, drawing on both languages collaboratively and flexibly for learning. Spoken Spanish outweighed spoken English between peers as they were discussing and analyzing online and offline texts. Regardless of language choice, however, spoken communication was used as a resource for writing. Students' paths to writing varied in language choice across prompts and written resources within and outside the web-based space. The research showed that the home language was a scaffold to learning subject matter content, and that students' participation in translanguaging enabled them to approach with more confidence their academic writing tasks.

Looking across the vignettes portraying three students' interactions with multiple resources around note-taking practices, findings also show how translanguaging was enveloped by additional semiotic forms. The students engaged in *trans-semiotic practices*, a term that accounts for all potential resources in any given field of action to assemble meaning, and, in the case of schooling, to create new knowledge artifacts. In this study, there was mutual elaboration of talk, gesture, moving and still images, and text. We saw how embodied actions – postural orientation, a gaze, a hand raised, a tap on the elbow, a thumbs-up or pointing for mutual orientation – served as semiotic links between talk, text and other semiotic materials in the setting, such as icons, graphics, photographs and video recordings. These additional modes amplified talk and text-based information about important historical events. Historical images and a video played a role through overhead projections from the web-based space and through discursive recall of digital resources explored in prior lessons. For emergent bilinguals, the availability of all these semiotic forms became important scaffolds for understanding subject-matter content as well as learning a new language.

The three vignettes provide fine-grained accounts of how students can take up translanguaging differently, leveraged according to their diverse ways of speaking and varied stages along the path to bilingualism. They also show how emergent bilinguals, while drawing on their multilingual/multidialectal repertoires, select and respond to other semiotic means differently – with aspiration, curiosity, emotion – based on prior knowledge, experiences and diverse ways of knowing, as they strive to interpret new understandings through writing. An essential ingredient in this process is the classroom teacher who adopts a trans-semiotic pedagogy. In this case study, teachers affirmed the students' experiences, emotions and identities; accommodated to their evolving bi/multilingual repertoires; facilitated the integration of other semiotic modes using new media; and treated emergent bilinguals, not as inferior, but as learners with potential.

The findings also confirm what has been demonstrated many times over but which bears repetition here: access to and thoughtful use of appropriate digital media is essential in today's diverse classrooms (e.g. Darling-Hammond *et al.*, 2014). High quality internet technologies must be afforded to emergent bilinguals for equal access to all available meaning-making modes for study and deeper understanding (Kleifgen *et al.*, 2014; Smith *et al.*, 2000).

In sum, schooling should not take place in a linguistic and digital straitjacket; when barriers to linguistic and technological resources are removed, emergent bilingual students can draw on their developing bi/multilingual repertoires and, with access to other semiotic forms, attain their maximum learning potential.

Post-Reading Discussion Questions

(1) What are trans-semiotic practices? How is translanguaging included within this broader ecology of semiotic systems?
(2) Provide examples of how learners draw on multiple modes to express meaning. Include examples showing how translanguaging is enveloped by other meaning-making modes in the classroom.

Acknowledgments

This work would have been impossible without the expertise and collaboration of my invaluable colleague and project Co-PI, Charles Kinzer, along with our team of dedicated graduate students at Teachers College, Columbia University. I especially wish to express gratitude to two of our former students, Andrea Lira, now on the faculty of the Pontificia Universidad Católica de Chile, for her many hours of meticulous coding and analysis of the language data for this case study, and to Briana Ronan, now associate professor at California Polytechnic State University, for her significant contributions to data analysis over the duration of the project and her subsequent published work. Andrea and Briana, both gifted bilingual teachers, also conducted the instructional sessions for the intervention.

Notes

(1) Project Number R305A09047. The Institute of Education Science (IES) is the research arm of the US Department of Education.
(2) Students used a heuristic called STEPS+G developed by Charles Kinzer (Kinzer, 2000), a guide to exploring events/topics through the lenses of Science, Technology and the social studies (Economic, Political, Social and Geographic).
(3) All student talk and note taking reported in this chapter is reproduced exactly as spoken/written. Students in this study were encouraged to draft notes with a focus on ideas rather than on mechanics.

References

Cope, B. and Kalantzis, M. (2000) *Multiliteracies. Literacy Learning and Design of Social Futures*. London: Routledge.

Cope, B., Kalantzis, M. and Tzirides, A.O. (2022) Meaning without borders: From translanguaging to transposition in the era of digitally-mediated meaning. In K.K. Grohmann (ed.) *Multifaceted Multilingualism*. Amsterdam: John Benjamins.

Crawford, J. (2004) *Educating English Learners: Educational Diversity in the Classroom* (5th edn). Los Angeles, CA: Bilingual Educational Services.

Darling-Hammond, L., Zielezinski, M.B. and Goldman, S. (2014) *Using Technology to Support At-Risk Students' Learning*. Stanford, CA: Stanford Center for Opportunity Policy in Education (SCOPE) and Alliance for Excellent Education.

Fishman, J.A. (1981) Language policy: Past, present, and future. In C.A. Ferguson and S.B. Heath (eds) *Language in the USA* (pp. 516–526). New York: Cambridge University Press.

García, O. (2009a) Emergent bilinguals and TESOL: What's in a name? *TESOL Quarterly* 43 (2), 322–326.

García, O. (2009b) *Bilingual Education in the 21st Century*. Boston, MA: Basil Blackwell.

García, O. and Kleifgen, J. (2010) *Educating Emergent Bilinguals: Policies, Programs, and Practices for English Language Learners*. New York: Teachers College Press.

García, O. and Kleifgen, J. (2018) *Educating Emergent Bilinguals: Policies, Programs, and Practices for English Learners* (2nd edn). New York: Teachers College Press.

García, O., Kleifgen, J. and Falchi, L. (2008) *From English Language Learners to Emergent Bilinguals*. Research Review Series Monograph, Campaign for Educational Equity, Teachers College, Columbia University.

Goldenberg, C. and Wagner, K. (2015) Bilingual education: Reviving an American tradition. *American Educator* 39 (3), 28–32.

Goodwin, C. (2007) Participation, stance, and affect in the organization of activities. *Discourse and Society* 18 (1), 53–73.

Halliday, M.A.K. (1978) *Language as Social Semiotic. The Social Interpretation of Language and Meaning*. Baltimore, MD: University Park Press.

Halliday, M.A.K. and Hasan, R. (1985) *Language, Context and Text: Aspects of Language in a Social-Semiotic Perspective*. Geelong: Deakin University Press.

Iedema, R. (2003) Multimodality, resemiotization: Extending the analysis of discourse as multi-semiotic practice. *Visual Communication* 2 (1), 29–57.

Kinzer, C.K. (2000, December) Exploring new technology applications in literacy education; Exploring new Internet applications for literacy growth (Double Symposium). Papers presented at the National Reading Conference Annual Meeting, Scottsdale, AZ

Kleifgen, J. (1985) Skilled variation in a kindergarten teacher's use of foreigner talk. In S. Gass and C. Madsen (eds) *Input and Second Language Acquisition* (pp. 89–114). Rowley, MA: Newbury House.

Kleifgen, J. (2006) Variation in multimodal literacies: How new technologies can expand or constrain modes of communication. *WORD* 57 (3), 303–324.

Kleifgen, J. (2013) *Communicative Practices at Work: Multimodality and Learning in a High-Tech Firm*. Bristol: Multilingual Matters.

Kleifgen, J. (2019) The 'translanguaging and multimodality' conundrum: How to avoid reification pitfalls. Paper presented at the Multilingual and Multicultural Learning: Policies and Practices Conference, Charles University, Faculty of Arts (Prague, Czech Republic, 14–15 December).

Kleifgen, J. and Kinzer, C.K. (2014) *STEPS to Literacy: An Integrated Digital Writing Space for English Language Learners. Final Report: Executive Summary*. Washington, DC: Institute of Education Sciences. Project 305 A09047, US Department of Education.

Kleifgen, J., Kinzer, C.K., Hoffman, D., Gorski, K., Kim, J., Lira, A. and Ronan, B. (2014) An argument for a multimodal, online system to support English learners' writing development. In R.S. Anderson and C. Mims (eds) *Digital Tools for Writing Instruction in K-12 Settings: Student Perception and Experience* (pp. 171–192). Hershey, PA: IGI Global.

Kress, G. (2003) *Literacy in the New Media Age*. London: Routledge.

Kress, G. and van Leeuwen, T. (1996) *Reading Images: The Grammar of Visual Design*. London: Routledge.

Lave, J. and Wenger, E. (1991) *Situated Learning. Legitimate Peripheral Participation*. New York: Cambridge University Press.

Leander, K. and Boldt, G. (2012) Re-reading 'A pedagogy of multiliteracies': Bodies, texts, and emergence. *Journal of Literacy Research* 45 (1), 22–46.

Matejka, L. (1973) On the first Russian prolegomena to semiotics. In V.N. Vološinov *Marxism and the Philosophy of Language*, Appendix I, (pp. 161–174). Cambridge: Harvard University Press.

New London Group (1996) A pedagogy of multiliteracies: Designing social futures. *Harvard Educational Review* 66 (1), 60–93.

Ronan, B. (2014) Moving across languages and other modes: Emergent bilinguals and their meaning-making in and around an online space. Unpublished doctoral dissertation, Teachers College, Columbia University.

Ronan, B. (2015) Intertextuality and dialogic interaction in students' online text construction. *Literacy Research: Theory, Method, and Practice* 64, 379–397.

Smith, B., Pacheco, M.B. and Khorosheva, M. (2000) Emergent bilingual students and digital multimodal composition: a systematic review of research in secondary classrooms. *Reading Research Quarterly* https://doi.org/10.1002/rrq.298

van Leeuwen, T. (1999) *Speech, Music, Sound*. London: Macmillan.

van Leeuwen, T. (2011) *The Language of Colour: An Introduction*. New York: Routledge.

Vološinov, V.N. ([1929]1973) *Marxism and the Philosophy of Language* (L. Matejka and I.R. Titunik, trans.). Cambridge: Harvard University Press.

Wittenburg, P., Brugman, H., Russel, A., Klassmann, A. and Sloetjes, H. (2006) ELAN: A professional framework for multimodality research. In N. Calzolari, K. Choukri, A. Gangemi, B. Maegaard, J. Mariani, J. Odijk and D. Tapias (eds) *Proceedings of the Fifth International Conference on Language Resources and Evaluation*. Genoa: European Language Resources Association.

6 Using 'Transfeaturing' to Explore Differentiation in the Pursuit of Translanguaging Pedagogical Goals

Marianne Turner and Angel M.Y. Lin

Pre-Reading Discussion Questions

(1) How does a translanguaging stance position the way we think about language in general?
(2) Can monolingual students engage in translanguaging practices?

Introduction

Translanguaging theory has developed in contexts where minoritized speakers' language use is compared to that of monolingual speakers of a dominant language (mostly English) (e.g. García & Li, 2014; García & Lin, 2016; Li & Zhu, 2013). Monolingual standards position minoritized speakers as deficient, and do not do justice to speakers' linguistic resources as a whole: translanguaging as both a theoretical and pedagogical construct as well as a stance has sought to rectify this. Translanguaging theory foregrounds a speaker's 'idiolect' (Otheguy *et al.*, 2015), meaning that the focus shifts from a bounded view of a named language (from the perspective of that language), to the extended, holistic repertoire of a speaker from the speaker's perspective. This perspective on language is a deliberately disruptive one, and has implications for linguistic hierarchies, or the privileging of particular named languages, such as English, and ways of using them to communicate. Languages education in schools is considered to be problematic when viewed through this translanguaging lens, since there is a strong focus on learning a standardized, named language based on prefigured monolingual norms.

In this chapter, we develop our view that it is possible to reconfigure languages education through the lens of translanguaging theory and, by so doing, develop translanguaging into a majority theory that is applicable to all speakers (Turner & Lin, 2020). From this perspective, the leveraging and expanding of linguistic and semiotic repertoires is the primary objective in education and the learning of any named languages is secondary. We consider it to be important to include all speakers if translanguaging is to maintain its disruptive sense because a majority language theory has the potential to disrupt monolingual speakers' sense of 'rightness' as well as the emergent bi/multilingual speakers' sense of deficit. In order to further this line of thought, we draw on the notion of *transfeaturing* which refers to the use of different kinds of linguistic features (Lin *et al.*, 2020) and apply it to García and Li's (2014) translanguaging pedagogical goals. We argue that taking up these goals with a transfeaturing focus can give rise to differentiation, which is expanded in Turner (2019a) beyond instructional differentiation in the classroom to include working with differences in students' linguistic repertoires as a resource for everyone's learning, working with different levels of student engagement with languages and with idiosyncratic characteristics of languages.

Cummins considered theory and practice to be 'infused within each other', and we join him in understanding that theoretical claims 'should be judged by criteria of adequacy and usefulness', adequacy meaning that empirical data is taken into account and usefulness that it 'can be used effectively by its intended audience to implement the educational policies and practices it implies or prescribes' (2009: 4). Although we are driven by these two criteria, and also view usefulness in terms of social equity – usefulness for marginalized groups needs to be central – we would also like to add that heteroglossia on which translanguaging is based (see Bakhtin, 1981) refers to *intra*-language differentiation and stratification, and translanguaging commonly focuses on language practices associated with more than one named language. Bakhtin took the position that monoglossia is a myth, and we share this position and stance, seeking to highlight the everyday-ness of hybridity for monolinguals, as well as bi/multilinguals. Kubota (2016, 2020) reminds us that translanguaging theory is premised on the privileging of linguistic plurality and hybridity, but it may be monolingual/monocultural individuals and groups that are victims of inequality and asymmetrical power relations. Kubota was concerned that 'our scholarly promotion of the multi/plural turn may primarily function as a way to legitimate and reaffirm our own hybrid and plural subjectivities rather than as an aid to transforming the lives of the people we refer to' (2016: 484). As we extend the idea of hybridity to language practices as a whole, we take into account Kubota's exhortation to be cognizant of who is included and who is excluded in the privileged positioning of hybridity (2016).

We will begin by discussing translanguaging pedagogical goals (García & Li, 2014), and then we will explain transfeaturing and the way it relates to a focus on the navigation of linguistic difference in the classroom. The rest of the chapter will be devoted to discussing pedagogical goals in relation to differentiation, and the role of transfeaturing. We will draw on empirical studies to demonstrate how practice is informing our position towards differentiation and the development of translanguaging theory into a majority theory. We are indebted to Ofelia García for pushing the boundaries of language in a way that aligns theory very clearly with classroom practice and takes social equity as a defining principle. We seek to stay true to these values in our own work as we apply and extend translanguaging theory and pedagogy in our own contexts.

Translanguaging as Pedagogy

It is long established that home languages can be leveraged as an active resource for minority speakers learning in dominant language (English) classrooms (e.g. Cummins & Swain, 1986; Lucas & Katz, 1994; Moll *et al.*, 1992). Recent studies also attest to this, and findings show that teachers can play a relatively passive or more active role in the encouragement of home language practices. Encouragement can be contained to students with limited English language proficiency or it can be extended to everyone. For example, in her study conducted in a linguistically diverse Australian secondary school, French (2016) found that students demonstrated hybrid language practices, metalinguistic awareness, and knowledge of *linguae francae* other than English, and that some teachers accepted this, but did not actively leverage students' linguistic repertoire in teaching and learning. In another study in two different primary schools in the United States, Pacheco (2018) found that teachers were using different teaching strategies to draw on immigrant students' home languages in the classroom. In a third study, Blair *et al.* (2018), also investigating two primary school settings in the United States, showed how extended language practices were positioned as an asset for everyone (see also Prasad & Lory, 2019; Turner, 2019a). These examples show a continuum of lesser to greater commitment to the privileging of extended language practices in the classroom (see de Jong, 2018). The need for the teacher to consider how to differentiate as a result of students' understanding and/or what kinds of language resources they are able to bring into the classroom appears only when there is a more active commitment to classroom translanguaging.

Conceptualizing the leveraging of students' extended language practices in class as translanguaging, rather than code switching, is useful because the focus can be firmly on the speaker rather than on this or that (named) language. There are different pedagogical goals related to translanguaging (see García & Li, 2014) and these include the development of students' linguistic resources and their crosslinguistic and metalinguistic awareness, learning and the display of knowledge, the affirmation of bi/multilingual identities and the critique of inequities and language hierarchies. García and Li (2014) also considered two more dimensions to be important. The first is meaning making: a word-for-word translation of a text (with no extra activity that has a focus on meaning) does not count as translanguaging. The second is that instruction needs to be differentiated for monolinguals, emerging bilinguals and bilinguals. Aligning instruction to these categories is one way of thinking about differentiation, but not the only way. We seek to show how differentiation can be considered more broadly, without necessarily conforming to these categories, and we will do this via a focus on transfeaturing.

Transfeaturing and Differentiation

The idea of transfeaturing draws on translanguaging theory and also seeks to extend it into a more overarching theory of language. As a more general theory, the heteroglossia within each named language (alongside language as a whole) is additionally brought into focus, and this is consistent with translanguaging, which challenges the idea that languages are unified and compartmentalized systems. There is space to consider all kinds of languaging in translanguaging theory because monolingual speakers have different kinds of styles, registers and dialects (Li, 2018; Lin *et al.*, 2020). In interview with Angel Lin, Lemke (Lin *et al.*, 2020: 51) referred to these three aspects of languaging as 'loosely structured clusterings' and 'overlappings'. Language features might be shared among dialects or they might not, leading Lemke to speculate that 'there really is not such a thing as a dialect, there is only dialectal variation' (Lin *et al.*, 2020: 51). The notion of dialectal variation reinforces a central point in translanguaging that it is very difficult − if not impossible − to draw firm boundaries around dialects and languages. It also draws attention to similarities between different kinds of language resources. Transfeaturing is thus useful for thinking about language practices because it can be used to refer to the use of language features that may overlap or be very different for speakers in various classroom settings.

Speakers are as central to the concept of transfeaturing as they are to translanguaging. The speakers are the primary focus, not any particular language. The communicative purpose governs the way they use language resources, and these purposes can be highly controlled in institutionalized contexts, such as high stakes assessments and job interviews. When contexts are less controlled, transfeaturing is common, and this is the lived reality of speakers (Lin *et al.*, 2020). Transfeaturing might occur through the use of different styles and registers as much as through use of different named dialects and languages. Lin *et al.* (2020) discussed the use of transfeaturing in less controlled settings as a form of indexing, and Lemke, drawing on Li's (2018) discussion of people speaking to each other in Hokkien Chinese, other Chinese 'dialects', Malay and English, explained it this way: 'The whole process of combining these different forms, deploying these different resources, indexes the relationship between the speakers. And I would say that … what is being said would not have exactly the same meaning if it were all being produced in the same language variety' (Lin *et al.*, 2020: 53).

In the remaining part of the chapter, we use the concept of transfeaturing to explore differentiation, and we use the term differentiation in its everyday sense of distinguishing between people, things or ideas. We then relate the term to the classroom in that we consider the overarching objective of differentiation to be student learning or, more specifically in the case of our discussion, to lead to translanguaging pedagogical goals. Transfeaturing is a useful way of thinking about differentiation because it can draw nuanced attention to what speakers share and what they do not share within and across language practices commonly associated with particular named languages. It can also incorporate the idea of engagement with certain practices because there is a twin focus on the *overlappings* of these practices and the indexing of relationships between speakers. If we understand speakers to use an idiolect, or their linguistic repertoire (cf. Otheguy *et al.*, 2015), to communicate, the way this idiolect overlaps with the idiolect of others (or does not) is a significant aspect of effective communication.

Differentiated instruction for monolinguals, emerging bilinguals and bilinguals is a discrete goal of translanguaging pedagogy (García & Li, 2014), but other ways of thinking about differentiation can address the remaining goals. These forms of differentiation include noticing the extent to which the linguistic repertoire of speakers in the classroom is shared or not shared (*overlappings*), students' engagement with their language practices (indexing) and the potential value of *not* differentiating. Paying attention to the features of students' linguistic repertoire, as well as to student engagement, can result in different kinds of – and degrees of – differentiation, and can apply across monolingual, emerging bilingual and bilingual categories. We will now discuss this through reference to empirical studies.

Features of Language Practices

In classrooms where the profile of the students is linguistically diverse, various kinds of language practices may be shared across what are considered to be named languages, and differentiation can be understood in relation to the kinds of features intrinsic to these practices. For example, different named languages can share a script (German and French) or share elements of a script (Chinese and Japanese). Other features of languages can also be shared, such as cognates (Italian and English), or features might help deepen students' understanding of concepts because they are *not* overlapping and may provide more access to complex meanings. Noticing and leveraging language features that may overlap in students' linguistic repertoires (or may not) can help meet three translanguaging pedagogical goals: the learning and display of knowledge, the affirmation of bi/multilingual identities, and crosslinguistic and metalinguistic awareness.

First, whether or not the named language associated with the students' home/community language practices shares a script with the dominant language may have implications for the translanguaging pedagogical goal of learning and display of knowledge and also the affirmation of bi/multilingual identities. For example, in a study on three Australian primary schools with a large number of second-generation students from a diverse range of linguistic backgrounds (see Turner, 2019a, 2020), the teachers devised activities whereby students needed to bring their home/community language practices into class in written form. Students mostly came from backgrounds where the script was different from the Roman alphabet (for example, Telugu, Vietnamese, Arabic, Russian, Chinese), and some of the teachers noted that many students were not able to write. In this case, teachers differentiating between spoken and written language features might have been able to help the students' learning and display of knowledge. Much of the literature on translanguaging in schools has focused on European languages and English, and students have been able to use overlapping literacy features of different named languages. For some languages (such as Chinese and Japanese), where second generation immigrant children are learning how to write in community language schools, it can take a lot of time and effort to learn the script. Thus, in order to affirm multilingual identities, it is important to focus on the actual, rather than presumed, linguistic repertoire of the student.

The degree to which language features overlap can also influence crosslinguistic and metalinguistic awareness. Cognates are a good example of this. For example, students with an Italian or Spanish background can gain a better understanding of language in general by noticing cognates, something that Beeman and Urow (2013) drew attention to in their book *Teaching for Biliteracy* aimed at guiding teachers in Spanish-English dual immersion programs in the United States. A *lack* of overlap in the features of language practices can also be useful as a way to enrich students' understanding of a concept. In a study on content and language integrated learning (CLIL) in which one Grade 8 class in Australia was learning science in Japanese, the Japanese support teacher realized the potential of directly translating concepts such as 'organism' [生物] and 'zygote' [受精卵] from *kanji* (Chinese characters): these direct translations helped the students understand the concept because they came back from the Japanese as 'living/thing' and 'accept/semen/egg' (see Turner, 2019b). The degree to which language features overlap can be important because the features can be leveraged in class in different ways.

Student Engagement

Strategic leveraging of language features by teachers in class can embed practices incorporating these features more firmly in everyday classrooms, and this can be important to the sustainability of translanguaging pedagogical goals and strategies in general. Students' extended linguistic repertoire can continue to be marginalized if teachers understand it to be fun but not central to teaching and learning (Turner, 2019a). It is also important to note that the language choices of speakers index their various relationships in situated domains of use. For example, second-generation migrant students who are very comfortable speaking the dominant language might be unsure about using their home/community language practices in class, but can be encouraged if a popular student leads the way (Turner, 2020). There can also be a great range of engagement with extended language practices among students. A primary school student growing up in Australia may choose to speak English to his Japanese mother when she speaks Japanese to him and read books in English rather than in Japanese, whereas another student speaks and reads in Japanese at home. There can also be a range of engagement with languages being taught at school.

A focus on transfeaturing can help think about differences in this engagement. The privileging of bi/multilingual identities, the learning and display of knowledge, and metalinguistic and crosslinguistic awareness are all goals that can benefit from differentiation on the basis of students' desire to index their belonging to a particular community of practice. Both examples discussed here are drawn from studies on learning a language formally at school (Turner, 2019a). In one study, Year 8 students in an advanced Japanese language class in Australia brought the *shogun*-related *kanji* they were learning in their language class into various history classes on the *shogun* (it was a big school and the students were spread across different classes). Of 28 students, two had a Japanese heritage and 23 were Chinese-heritage students. Chinese-heritage students *not* in the advanced Japanese language class were observed to begin writing more than the stipulated words using Chinese characters. Also, students with no logographic language practices in their linguistic repertoire reported in a survey that they had enjoyed using kanji/Chinese characters when asked what they liked about the unit of work. The advanced language students were invited to do the assessment in Japanese, and four students took up this opportunity. These differences in engagement can be understood through the lens of transfeaturing, in this case *overlappings* between *kanji* and Chinese characters, and the difference, or exotic nature of the characters, for students with no exposure to a logographic script. In particular, the Chinese and Japanese heritage students' linguistic repertoire was affirmed outside the language classroom, and the learning and display of knowledge was facilitated in different ways depending upon the degree to which students chose to engage.

In another study in Australia, differentiation occurred in a Year 7 humanities classroom where Italian was being used to instruct students. An Italian content and language integrated learning (CLIL) program was running in the school but only seven Year 7 students had opted in to the program. Since it was only a small group of students, they shared a class with a larger group and then had one lesson on their own in Italian each week. Three of the Year 7 students who had opted in to the CLIL program had an Italian heritage, reporting that the biggest driver for them was to be able to talk to grandparents in Italian. The teachers of the larger group of students decided to incorporate Italian into the humanities class. Even though a majority of students had not opted in to the CLIL program, they were studying Italian as a subject area. The teachers chose to use *overlappings* in language features: Italian was positioned as a series of sleuthing activities, whereby the students were detectives looking for 'cognate clues' in both speech and writing. Students were reported to engage enthusiastically with this. Here again, it was the *overlappings* between language features in the distributed linguistic repertoire of the classroom that allowed for the kind of differentiation that promoted student engagement. Learning was promoted by the positioning of content-and-language-integrated activities as stimulating and fun, and the transfeaturing was also part of the broader translanguaging pedagogical goal of metalinguistic and crosslinguistic awareness.

Disrupting the Status Quo

Encouraging an understanding of transfeaturing, which recognizes how practices associated with one named language such as English can differ so greatly, also allows for the constructive possibility of *not* differentiating. This understanding can help to disrupt the monolingual language norms of classrooms because it privileges the extended linguistic repertoires of bi/multilingual students, while also being inclusive of monolingual students. In situations where the dominance of a particular language is unquestioned, the translanguaging pedagogical goal of critical discussions around linguistic hierarchies and social structures might need to be triggered by this kind of linguistic disruption. If transfeaturing is explored holistically as a phenomenon that pertains to everyone in the classroom and not only (emerging) bi/ multilingual students, this can then create spaces of discomfort for monolingual students that can provide rich learning opportunities for everyone, if carefully navigated by teachers.

An example of disrupting the status quo in this way is taken from a study on the leveraging of students' home language practices in three Australian primary schools (Turner, 2019a, 2020). In the study, which engaged in-service teachers in professional learning on translanguaging pedagogy, seven mostly monolingual teachers were invited to complete language maps – a form of identity text that depicts the variety of a speaker's language practices over time in different domains of use (see D'Warte, 2013, 2015). The way that features of English language vary depending on style, register and dialect was explained to the teachers as a way to facilitate the creation of these maps, and also to show them how monolingual students could be included. The teachers then worked towards student production of language maps in their classrooms (see Figures 6.1 and 6.2), and later used these maps as a springboard for leveraging students' home/community language practices for teaching and learning. They unanimously reported that the students with different language backgrounds loved doing the language maps and also the later activities, although one teacher also reported that one monolingual student complained that it was boring.

Transfeaturing was thus found to allow an entry point into the incorporation of students' home/community language practices in class in a way that privileged an extended repertoire, and also in a way that did not necessarily exclude monolingual teachers or students. Teachers were mainly monolingual and it offered a lens on language they could use their own experiences to explore. They initially spoke of being bilingual as something that the students were but, in the course of the study, began to understand it as a process of engaging in language practices as indexed by particular (situated) communities of practice (see Turner, 2019a). The way that the teachers did not choose to vary instruction was significant to the possible achievement of the translanguaging pedagogical goal of critical reflection. Allowing monolingual students to experience discomfort because they do not feel they know enough in a language-rich environment has the potential to be a very real way to help them think critically about how students who are new to language practices associated with English so often feel in the context of formal learning in an English-speaking country (cf. Palmer et al., 2019). Making connections with the languages classroom is an additional way to show monolingual students that they can use the learning of a language at school to work towards the goal of an expanded linguistic repertoire themselves.

Figure 6.1 Example of a language map

Figure 6.2 Example of a language map

Discussion and Conclusion

In this chapter, we have sought to show how translanguaging pedagogical goals can be furthered through attention to transfeaturing. These goals presuppose teachers' commitment, not only to accepting/ affirming students' language practices but also to working with them actively and strategically. Once teachers begin to use translanguaging in a pedagogical sense, the way they understand language is arguably even more important, given that the theory underlying this pedagogy positions language differently from the common 'out there' bounded notions of different languages. The concept of transfeaturing draws on scholarship conducted under the umbrella of translanguaging theory and may help to develop understanding of translanguaging because it emphasizes the fundamental hybridity of language and semiotic repertoires, even when associated with monolingualism (see Lin *et al.*, 2020). If monolingual teachers – and bilingual teachers who see their languages as pertaining to very different domains of use – have a way to understand translanguaging in relation to themselves, they may find it easier to embrace translanguaging pedagogical goals.

A focus on hybridity, or variation, in transfeaturing also allows for an equal curiosity about what might be the same: the overlappings among language features or what speaker' idiolects might have in common. By explicitly focusing on the variations and overlappings of *all* language practices, transfeaturing has the potential to help translanguaging theory to become a majority theory. Linguistic hierarchies can be such that the sophistication of bi/multilingual speakers' language practices can be affirmed and celebrated, but only in situated domains of use. If instruction is only differentiated according to whether students are monolingual, emerging bilingual and bilingual (see García & Li, 2014), then monolingual students can continue with the 'core business' of learning in that language with no sense of disruption and little access to understanding the nature of their peers' knowledge. A desire to fit in with dominant practices can then leave many second-generation immigrant students choosing this language, and by the third generation, the dominant language has overwhelmed language practices associated with other languages (see Eisenchlas *et al.*, 2013). Translanguaging pedagogy takes speakers as the focus, and the range (and depth) of language practices of students might need to be taken into account, as well as any languages being taught at school, when aiming for pedagogical goals. Transfeaturing can act as the link between the heteroglossia of an idiolect that is considered (by the speaker and/ or others) to be monolingual and the heteroglossia of an idiolect that is considered to be emerging bilingual or bilingual.

The bridging potential of transfeaturing is directly connected to the classroom: teaching and learning practices have informed the theory (cf. Cummins, 2009). Across different studies, teachers' innovations resulted from noticing similarities and differences in the kinds of language practices to which their students had access, and the way they could work with student engagement. This led to creative approaches to differentiation. Adapting (differentiating) instruction according to the three categories (monolingual, emerging bilingual or bilingual) appeared to be more challenging for the teachers. In institutionally monolingual teaching and learning environments, differentiating instruction for emerging bilingual students who are having trouble understanding can be intuitive for teachers, but why should you differentiate for bilinguals when they can understand perfectly well? This mindset perpetuates an understanding of deficit because language practices are considered a scaffolding tool to be used until no longer needed and maintains baseline instruction as monolingual. A privileged positioning of heteroglossic hybridity may be present in schools for emerging bilinguals, but this may not result in what scholarship promotes (cf. Kubota, 2016) if power differentials are such that the students are attempting to move out of this category as fast as they can.

In sum, we understand García and Li's (2014) translanguaging pedagogical goals to be central to teaching and learning. García's body of work, especially that linking translanguaging to the classroom, has also been of enormous benefit in taking inequity and the sociopolitical dimension of languages at school as a point of departure. We have discussed transfeaturing and various approaches to differentiation as a way to help teachers in sustainable and effective ways because we attribute so much importance to these goals and this project in general. We further consider that the positioning of translanguaging theory as a majority, social semiotic theory can assist teachers in conceptualizing communication as a range of language and semiotic practices that may be associated with one or more named languages in settings where linguistic diversity amongst students – and school-based languages education – is the norm.

Given the majority focus, developing translanguaging theory in this way has implications for teacher education programs. In these programs, at least in countries such as the United States, Canada and Australia, there are a growing number of practical resources to help teacher educators guide pre-service and in-service teachers' thinking on ways to leverage students' home/community language practices in class. This is heartening, but translanguaging tends still to be the domain of the language teacher or the teacher who teaches students who are considered to be English language learners (or learners of the dominant language). Language is fundamental to learning, but it is so often explored in teacher education in relation to the dominant named language as it is taught at school, not in relation to students' actual language practices. Making translanguaging more than a response to an English language (dominant language) learning problem in the minds of teachers is a worthwhile endeavor, and teacher education programs can play a significant role. Further research on translanguaging as a majority theory has the potential to generate different kinds of options for language-in-education policy planning.

Post-Reading Discussion Questions

(1) How might positioning translanguaging theory as a majority theory benefit minoritized students? What might be some points of caution?
(2) How can transfeaturing guide thinking on ways to differentiate (or not) between the various kinds of language resources students are bringing to class? Can you think of different kinds of examples to those given in the text?

References

Bakhtin, M.M. (1981) *The Dialogic Imagination: Four Essays by M.M. Bakhtin*. Translated by C. Emerson and M. Holquist and edited by M. Holquist. Austin, TX: University of Texas Press.

Beeman, K. and Urow, C. (2013) *Teaching for Biliteracy: Strengthening Bridges Between Languages*. Philadelphia, PA: Caslon Publishing.

Blair, A., Haneda, M. and Nebus Bose, F. (2018) Reimagining English-medium instructional settings as sites of multilingual and multimodal meaning making. *TESOL Quarterly* 52 (3), 516–538.

Cummins, J. (2009) Transformative multiliteracies pedagogy: School-based strategies for closing the achievement gap. *Multiple Voices for Ethnically Diverse Exceptional Learners* 11 (2), 38–56.

Cummins, J. and Swain, M. (1986) *Bilingualism in Education: Aspects of Theory, Research and Practice*. Harlow: Longman.

De Jong, E.J. (2018, Keynote) *Taking a Multilingual Stance: Quality Education for ELLs*. Minnesota-TESOL, Minneapolis, Minnesota.

D'Warte, J. (2013) Pilot project: Reconceptualising English learners' language and literacy skills, practices and experiences. University of Western Sydney. See http://researchdirect.westernsydney.edu.au/islandora/object/uws:23461 (accessed September 2020).

D'Warte, J. (2015) Building knowledge about and with students: Linguistic ethnography in two secondary school classrooms, *English in Australia* 50 (1), 39–48.

Eisenchlas, S., Schalley, A. and Guillemin, D. (2013) The importance of literacy in the home language: The view from Australia. *SAGE Open* 3 (4), 1–14.

French, M. (2016) Students' multilingual resources and policy-in-action: An Australian case study. *Language and Education* 30, 298–316.

García, O. and Li, W. (2014) *Translanguaging: Language, Bilingualism and Education*. New York, NY: Palgrave Macmillan.

García, O. and Lin, A.M.Y. (2016) Translanguaging in bilingual education. In O. García, A.M.Y. Lin and S. May (eds) *Bilingual and Multilingual Education (Encyclopedia of Language and Education)* (pp. 117–130). Cham: Springer.

Kubota, R. (2016) The multi/plural turn, postcolonial theory, and neoliberal multiculturalism: Complicities and implications for applied linguistics. *Applied Linguistics* 37 (4), 474–494.

Kubota, R. (2020) Promoting and problematizing multi/plural approaches in language pedagogy. In S.M.C. Lau and S. Van Viegen Stille (eds) *Critical Plurilingual Pedagogies: Struggling Toward Equity Rather than Equality* (pp. 47–74). Cham: Springer.

Li, W. (2018) Translanguaging as a practical theory of language. *Applied Linguistics* 39 (1), 9–30.

Li, W. and Zhu, H. (2013) Translanguaging identities and ideologies: Creating transnational space through flexible multilingual practices amongst Chinese university students in the UK. *Applied Linguistics* 34 (5), 516–535.

Lin, A.M.Y., Wu, Y. and Lemke, J.L. (2020) 'It takes a village to research a village': Conversations of Angel Lin and Jay Lemke on contemporary issues in translanguaging. In S.M.C. Lau and S. Van Viegen Stille (eds) *Critical Plurilingual Pedagogies: Struggling Toward Equity Rather than Equality* (pp. 47–74). Cham: Springer.

Lucas, T. and Katz, A. (1994) Reframing the debate: The roles of native languages in English-only programs for language minority students. *TESOL Quarterly* 28, 537–561.

Moll, L., Amanti, C., Neff, D. and Gonzáles, N. (1992) Funds of knowledge for teaching: Toward a qualitative approach to connect homes and classrooms. *Theory into Practice: Qualitative Issues in Educational Research* 3 (2), 132–41.

Otheguy, R., García, O. and Reid, W. (2015) Clarifying translanguaging and deconstructing named languages: A perspective from linguistics. *Applied Linguistics Review* 6 (3), 281–307.

Pacheco, M. (2018) Spanish, Arabic, and 'English-Only': Making meaning across languages in two classroom communities. *TESOL Quarterly* 1–27. DOI: https://doi.org/10.1002/tesq.446.

Palmer, D.K., Cervantes-Soon, C., Dorner, L. and Heiman, D. (2019) Bilingualism, biliteracy, biculturalism and critical consciousness for all: Proposing a fourth fundamental goal for two-way dual language education. *Theory into Practice* 58 (2), 121–133.

Prasad, G. and Lory, M.P. (2019) Linguistic and Cultural Collaboration in Schools: Reconciling Majority and Minoritized Language Users. *TESOL Quarterly* 1–26. DOI: https://doi.org/10.1002/tesq.560.

Turner, M. (2019a) *Multilingualism as a Resource and a Goal: Using and Learning Languages in Mainstream Schools*. Cham: Palgrave Macmillan.

Turner, M. (2019b) The positioning of Japanese in a secondary CLIL science classroom in Australia: Language use and the learning of content. *Journal of Immersion and Content-Based Language Education* 7 (2), 192–211.

Turner, M. (2020) Incorporating Australian primary students' linguistic repertoire into teaching and learning. In Z. Tian, L. Aghai, P. Sayer and J. Schissel (eds) *Envisioning TESOL Through a Translanguaging Lens: Global Perspectives* (pp. 185–202). Cham: Springer.

Turner, M and Lin, A.M.Y. (2020) Translanguaging and named languages: productive tension and desire. *International Journal of Bilingual Education and Bilingualism* 23 (4), 423–424.

7 Translanguaging in an Urban Social Justice Teacher Education Program

Anel V. Suriel and Mary E. Curran

We were '... provided with a wonderful environment to push ourselves to think beyond the parameters we began the class with [and] ... encouraged ... to think critically about the course content and understand the material as it applies to teaching and the world around us'
Language teacher candidate feedback, Fall 2019

Pre-Reading Discussion Questions

(1) How is a translanguaging perspective infused in your teacher education program?
(2) What teacher education activities support the development of a translanguaging stance?

Introduction

When preparing future teachers, our goal is to support the development of teachers who create liberating, humanizing and stimulating learning spaces that engage and celebrate students' linguistic and cultural practices. To do this, we support them, as the teacher candidate indicated in the introductory quotation, to deeply reflect upon and transform their beliefs about language and learning while they are in our program in order to 'think critically about the course content and understand the material as it applies to teaching and the world around us'. In our own reflection as we prepared to write this chapter, as language teacher educators we observed how the legacy of Ofelia García's scholarship contributes to a paradigm shift in language education, and provides us with a cutting-edge framework for preparing new language (ESL, world language and bilingual) educators and *all* future and in-service educators. Recently, at Rutgers Graduate School of Education, we created an Urban Social Justice Teacher Education Program with the goal of preparing teachers with the knowledge, skills and dispositions to teach and advocate for all students, while learning from and with the communities they serve. In this newly designed program, we have been able to infuse García's translanguaging framework for teaching emergent bilinguals into all licensure areas. The redesigned program now requires teacher candidates to take courses in urban education and teaching emerging bilinguals; conduct clinical placements in partnership districts; and participate in community-engaged programming. In this chapter, we focus on the way that García's work has had a Graduate School of Education-wide impact on both our initial licensure programs and our language teacher education programs. Specifically, we focus on two courses: Teaching Emerging Bilinguals (required for all licensure areas) and Principles of Language Learning (required for ESL, world language and bilingual licensure). We describe these courses and García's influence upon their development, discuss our next steps as we evaluate our efforts, and how we will move forward with this work.

Ofelia García's work has had a big impact on the two of us as well. Anel V. Suriel first encountered García's work as a New York City Teaching Fellow and dual language educator in New York City. Her advisor, Dr Yvonne deGaetano, Associate Professor at CUNY Hunter College and the program coordinator for the bilingual Teaching Fellows, introduced Anel to García's *Bilingual Education in the 21st Century: A Global Perspective* (2009), which transformed her classroom pedagogy. As a result of following García's work, Anel engaged translanguaging pedagogies and practices in both her dual language and transitional bilingual classrooms in New York and New Jersey. Additionally, Anel has and continues to use García's research and books, such as *Educating Emergent Bilinguals: Policies, Programs, and Practices for English Language Learners* (García & Kleifgen, 2010, 2017) to advocate for equitable and social justice practices for emergent bilingual students. This includes Anel's adoption of the terms *emergent bilingual* and *home/target language* over English language learner (ELL) or ESL student and L1 or L2, and advocacy for equitable practices that include heteroglossic assessment practices, translanguaging pedagogies and the meaningful inclusion of bi/multilingual families in school-based programs. This advocacy has continued in her scholarship, which aims to document the decision-making processes teachers make when grounded in a translanguaging framework, and what a translanguaging practice looks like in the classroom and when conducting professional development workshops. García's work forms the theoretical foundation for all of Anel's graduate student course syllabi, including the use of *The Translanguaging Classroom: Leveraging Student Bilingualism* (2017) as the textbook for her section of the course, Methods of Teaching and Assessing English as a Second Language. García's body of work is the inspiration and cornerstone of Anel's current research on bilingual education policy, practice and assessment.

Mary Curran's colleague at Rutgers, Dr Wallis (Wally) Reid, is a good friend of Ofelia García and her husband, Ricardo Otheguy. Wally frequently spoke about García's work, and he introduced Mary to Ofelia when she visited Rutgers after the publication of *Bilingual Education in the 21st Century* (2009). For the next few years, before he retired, Wally shared stories from *las sobremesas* (after-dinner conversations) he had with García and Otheguy, some of which led to multiple publications, including the 2015 article, 'Clarifying Translanguaging and Deconstructing Named Languages: A Perspective from Linguistics', in which they used a culinary simile to explain and define translanguaging as 'the deployment of a speaker's full linguistic repertoire without regard for watchful adherence to the socially and politically defined boundaries of named (and usually national and state) languages' (Otheguy *et al.*, 2015: 283). This simile of menus, recipes and food allowed the authors to demonstrate the need 'to debunk the myth of the lexically and structurally-defined named national language' (Otheguy *et al.*, 2015) and demonstrate the way defined national languages are social constructs. They then applied this critique to educational practices and assessments. This work, along with García's large body of scholarship, influenced Mary and her colleagues in many ways, especially as they collaborated on planning, implementing and evaluating community-engaged language learning initiatives, and in their program-wide revision.

García's translanguaging framework served as a foundation and lens for professional development, curriculum and materials design and implementation of several community-engaged programs Mary Curran is involved in which put Rutgers 'Jersey Roots, Global Reach' trademark into action as relationships are built between university students and members of local and global communities. Some of the projects include:

- The Conversation Tree: Community-Based Language Partnerships (which links Rutgers New Brunswick students and adults in the community for opportunities to practice English);
- the Community-Engaged Education in Yucatán Program (an annual study abroad program in Mexico for GSE teacher candidates); and
- the Rutgers GSE Community-Schools Partnership Network Tutoring Program (in which Rutgers students tutor local K-12 students at libraries, schools and community organizations).

As we prepare university and community leaders and facilitators to participate in our community-engaged programming, we focus on the need to center the linguistic and cultural resources of the students, adult participants and communities at the core of our collective efforts. This requires an affirmation of the idiolect, heteroglossic practices, and cultural repertoires of each participant. It also requires acknowledging and avoiding the tendencies so common in traditional classes, where the focus is on one national, standard variety of a language and grammatical accuracy, and where a deficit-approach disposition is often the lens applied to participants' existing linguistic and cultural repertoires (which has the material and psychological effect that language choices may be discriminated against or corrected as inaccurate) (Otheguy *et al.*, 2015). Our professional development for all of these programs includes an introduction to guiding principles aligned with a translanguaging framework, including celebrating multilingualism and encouraging participants to draw upon their entire linguistic and cultural repertoires; designing activities building on participant interests and strengths; providing language practice in the natural authentic ways that make up our lived experiences; and developing belongingness and communities of practice.

At the same time, Mary and her colleagues' exposure to García's scholarship and a translanguaging framework impacted the redesign of the Rutgers GSE Urban Social Justice Teacher Education Program, most specifically in two courses: Teaching Emerging Bilinguals I and II (required courses for all teacher candidates). Details about the application of the framework in these courses follow.

Our Context: Rutgers GSE Urban Social Justice Teacher Education Program

At Rutgers Graduate School of Education, we prepare Bilingual, Biology, Dance, English Language Arts, English as a Second Language, Math, Physics, Social Studies, Special Education and World Language Teachers. We recently redesigned our five-year and post-baccalaureate two-year graduate programs to put social justice at the core of the teacher candidates' curricular and clinical experiences. According to the GSE website, our new Urban Social Justice Teacher Education Program is designed to develop teachers to be engaged in and committed to excellence, equity and social justice in their teaching practice. Our new program design requires that all teacher candidates develop meaningful understandings of linguistically, culturally and economically diverse students and their experiences and communities; critically analyze the social, economic, historical and political dimensions of urban settings and schools; effectively teach diverse students, including those from historically marginalized backgrounds; identify and disrupt instances and patterns of discrimination and marginalization; and teach and advocate for all students, while learning from their communities. Details about the program can be found on the GSE website (see http://catalogs. rutgers.edu/generated/gse_current/pg66.html).

Our teacher candidates complete four semesters of coursework and clinical practice, which lead to both a master's degree in education and a New Jersey teaching license. The four semesters include clinical experiences, and all teacher candidates are required to take the following four courses: Teaching Emerging Bilinguals I and II, and Urban Education I and II. These courses and Classroom Organization in Inclusive and Special Classrooms, and the community-engaged course, Students, Communities and Social Justice, are core course requirements, in addition to discipline-specific courses. A video describing the program reform can be found here: https://www.youtube.com/ watch?v=3HMySIDMcEg.

The program is based upon a critical, funds of knowledge framework (Moll *et al.*, 1992), which positions learning *from, with* and *in* communities and centers the linguistic and cultural repertoires of students and their families (España & Herrera, 2020; Flores & Aneja, 2017; Paris & Alim, 2017). Our Students, Communities and Social Justice course is an important new addition to our program, as it aims to bridge the university and community so teacher educators and candidates collaborate with district leaders, community organizations and parents to provide community services – for example, as part of the Conversation Tree Program, facilitating 'Conversation Cafés' in the local community for adults looking for opportunities to practice English, or organizing a book drive and creating reading spaces at local clinics. We share these experiences at an annual GSE conference, in which teacher candidates, teachers, administrators and community members present innovative pedagogical activities informed by a social justice perspective. As candidates move through the program, we support them as they acknowledge, affirm and build on community strengths, while confronting their own deficit orientations, reflecting upon their and others' educational experiences and considering their roles, responsibilities and possible actions when teaching for social justice. We see this sustained focus on social justice as a radical revision to traditional teacher education programs. It is only natural that Ofelia García's work informs our practice.

Teaching Emerging Bilinguals I and II

In our program, each teacher candidate has the opportunity to develop a translanguaging lens to apply to their disciplinary pedagogical efforts through the two required courses: Teaching Emerging Bilinguals I and II. Employing this lens requires a shift in traditional language ideologies and commonly held dispositions toward language use. Not only does it require that we stop using deficit, monolingual frameworks to interpret our students' linguistic and cultural practices, it requires that we move from taking an *outsider* perspective as we try to understand our students' linguistic practices to an *insider*, translanguaging perspective which teachers can employ when promoting and encouraging students' access to their full, unique linguistic repertoire in their academic activities (García *et al.*, 2017). This shift requires the construction of a counter narrative to challenge the existing traditional narrative in which there is a monolingual target of one dominant, standard, named language that operates from a position of power in educational practices and assessments. Creating counter narratives requires a deep understanding of history, politics and the way power operates in favor of dominant interests (Flores & Aneja, 2017). We help our teacher candidates understand that how we orient to language is not objective so they can make informed, judicious pedagogical decisions in order to provide space and support for their future students where they can draw on and develop their full linguistic repertoires, and as such, their entire selves (España & Herrera, 2020).

Teaching emerging bilinguals I (TEB I)

This two-part course, created and continually updated by a team of language education faculty, doctoral students and part-time lecturers, supports students as they develop an understanding of the strengths and needs of emerging bilinguals, their families, communities and a foundation upon which they can build a set of general and content-specific pedagogical practices. In TEB I, the focus is on dispositions and fostering perspectives toward emerging bilinguals that includes a developing critical multilingual awareness (García, 2008) of the traditional narrative regarding English as the standard dominant language, the relationship between language and power, and the social-political context of learning English and other languages in a US public school setting. We consider the impact of deficit labeling and thinking (García, 2008; Moll *et al.*, 1992), and we begin the course by reflecting on the class title and our use of the term, *emerging bilinguals*, referencing García's (2009) use of the term, 'emergent bilinguals' to put our asset-based approach in action. We use 'emerg*ing*' bilinguals to not only highlight our students' bilingualism as a positive characteristic, but also how it is a dynamic, growing entity, one which is full of potential and an advantage, which builds on the strengths of students' first language as a resource. We also explain that this label, while we use 'bilingual', also refers to our students' and their families' *multi*lingual practices as well. Moreover, this label can be applied to all of us, in a positive way, as we develop our potential as multilinguals. Course content includes the history and battle for educational equity in the United States, language rights as protected in education policy, key court cases defending language rights and the local New Jersey state code regarding languages and education. In TEB I, key assignments include, for example, an immersion simulation experience (Curran, 2003), watching and debriefing the video 'Immersion' (Media That Matters, 2009); writing and discussing reflections on weekly reflection questions; and conducting a linguistic landscape ethnographic inquiry (Curran, 2018) in a partnership district.

The linguistic landscape assignment (see Appendix 7.1) is one we return to over the course of the program. For this assignment, candidates observe the language in signage in the community where they are conducting their clinical placement. Candidates research community demographics and analyze their findings (for example, in terms of 'bottom up' (handwritten) versus 'top down' (official) signs, order and font size of the languages, etc.) to reveal the symbolic messages about power, language, and community membership in the linguistic landscapes where they are teaching (Cenoz & Gorter, 2006). This assignment gives them the opportunity to observe and critically analyze how language(s) are used in the community. Which are visible? Which are marginalized? And how does the landscape reflect the multilingualism of the community demographics. For details of this assignment, see Appendix 7.1.

Some of the key guiding questions for reflections from the Teaching Emerging Bilingual I course syllabus are:

- Why is this course called Teaching Emerging Bilinguals?
- Who are emerging bilinguals?
- What do emerging bilinguals need from and bring to schools and educators?
- What is academic English?
- How can educators design culturally responsive instruction?
- How is our public space symbolically constructed? What role does language play?

Teaching emerging bilinguals II (TEB II)

In TEB II, we focus on building a toolkit of strategies and practices that support language development and heritage language preservation while practicing critical multilingual awareness and culturally sustaining pedagogies (García, 2008; Paris & Alim, 2017). In this second half of the course, key assignments include describing disciplinary/language relationships, developing and adapting lesson plans, creating language-rich classroom environments and making theory-practice connections via reflections on clinical experiences. Students revise lesson plans in their disciplines, highlighting the ways they plan to support language development and sustain their students' linguistic and cultural practices. Some of the key questions from the course syllabus are:

- What is the academic language of the disciplines: for example, of science, math, language arts and social studies?
- What strategies best support the development of language for content learning?
- How do we support the development of students' complete linguistic and cultural repertoires?

Teaching Emerging Bilinguals I and II are still works in progress. We are pleased that these courses reach all students at the Graduate School of Education now; however, we know that there is always room for improvement, which requires our own life-long learning, constant reflection, listening to student feedback, and making changes to the course. For example, a recent addition to the first course has been scholarship by April Becker-Bell (2020), who writes about linguistic justice, in which the focus is Black language – which had been an area of silence in course design.

Principles of Language Learning

While students of all disciplines take the two Teaching Emerging Bilinguals courses, the Principles of Language Learning course is taken by bilingual, ESL and world language teacher candidates in their first semester with the goal of familiarizing teacher candidates with the history and range of theories of language learning. We promote a sociocultural framework to language learning (Johnson, 2006; Lantolf, 2000) which draws on the metaphor of language 'participation' versus language 'acquisition', and centers language use in our lived experiences and our socialization into language communities – becoming members who use languages for real purposes, or becoming marginalized from access to those communities. In 2019, the course was revised and updated to include an understanding of dynamic bilingualism theory and equitable inclusion of community (García & Kleifgen, 2010, 2017). Teacher candidates are exposed to scholarship to guide their decision-making processes for planning, implementing and assessing instruction in language classrooms. Through the course readings and analysis of classroom work samples, teacher candidates are encouraged to view home language as an asset and leverage the entire linguistic repertoire for new learning and language use with participants (Vogel & García, 2017).

The class offers both an introduction to language learning scholarship and opportunities to view the theory through practice in our community. In addition to being a traditional seminar style course, the course requires that teacher candidates participate in an after-school Conversation Café at a local elementary school, where our students facilitate conversation practice. While offering parents, guardians, and community members the opportunity to practice English in a safe, informal space, this community-engaged component provides a rich experience in which teacher candidates can observe and reflect upon the theories of language learning in action, through authentic language use. Our goal is that through their participation in this activity, and by engaging in reflection upon it through the lens of scholarship, teacher candidates are building an emerging pedagogical stance on language learning that is strength based and rooted in equity.

After each community engaged session, teacher candidates are asked to reflect on a thematic question based on the weekly readings and their experience at the Conversation Café. Some of these questions include:

- How do new language learners *acquire* vocabulary and negotiate meaning?
- What is the best age for learning a new language?
- What is the role of grammar in acquiring a new language?
- What is the role of interaction and feedback on language learning?
- Why learn a new language? How can we problematize the concept of 'motivation'?

Teacher candidates' reflections on these questions, based on their personal experiences in the Conversation Café and as language learners, as well as the readings, prepare teacher candidates to think deeply about and create a critical, social justice stance on language learning that can guide them in their future decision-making process as teachers.

The Principles course ends with a resounding call to advocacy and social justice. In the second to last session, teacher candidates are introduced to raciolinguistics (Rosa & Flores, 2015) and advocacy for equitable practice (García, 2017). In the following session, the last session of the course, teacher candidates reflect on their growth by comparing their current perspectives on language learning to beliefs they expressed on the first day of class in a survey on language learning beliefs (Lightbown & Spada, 2013), using the lenses of the scholarship and their experiences in the Conversation Cafés. Teacher candidates use these reflections to finalize a personal stance on language learning, the final writing assignment for the course (see Appendix 7.2).

For the final assignment, teacher candidates are asked to reflect on the theories and readings of the course and create a philosophical statement of practice around language teaching and learning. This statement allows teacher candidates to begin crafting their own translanguaging stance (García *et al.*, 2017) that will ground their future classroom practice in social justice. Teacher candidates directly experience the impact of engaging the entire linguistic repertoire (García & Kleifgen, 2010, 2017) for new language learning in their interaction with Conversation Café participants. This provides practical experience with the strength-based perspectives they encounter in much of their theoretical research and readings, and transforms the teacher-as-master, student-as-language-recipient paradigm (Palpacuer-Lee *et al.*, 2017). Grounding this work in García's translanguaging framework not only helps challenge and deconstruct hierarchical power structures (Freire, 2000), but it also establishes students' and families' bi/multilingual language practices and experiences as the center for teaching and learning. As a result, as future teachers, our goal is that our teacher candidates are more readily able to interpret students' bi/multilingual language uses from a heteroglossic lens. In turn, they are more able to engage instructional practices that leverage all language for learning, equitably assess the content learning and linguistic proficiency of emerging bilinguals, and become edu-activists (España & Herrera, 2020) on behalf of bi/multilingual learners.

Moving Forward

As we reflect on the legacy and importance of Dr García's work on our teacher preparation program, we can report that her scholarship has had both language program-specific and program-wide impact. Engaging in this reflection itself (Zeichner, 2007) has given us the opportunity to more deeply consider the power of her work, and to consider next steps we need to take with regard to teacher education program development, our community-engaged activities and our future research.

In terms of our program, we are proud that all of our graduates leave with an exposure to the tools to create counter narratives about language and our lived experiences that will allow them to construct transformative pedagogical approaches which center and affirm their students' linguistic and cultural repertoires. However, we are well aware that an exposure is not enough, and that our graduates enter the educational field which has already been shaped by institutional racism, linguicism, and other forms of discrimination. They face a challenging, uphill battle to create change. We must continually work to find ways to support our teacher candidates and teach them to remain steadfast in the face of opposition – to create powerful pedagogical tools while they are in our programs, networks among our graduates so we can continue to support their efforts, and alliances with like-minded colleagues in their schools and places of employment.

We also have learned from informal feedback from graduates, that the perspectives we promote in the Teaching Emerging Bilinguals courses are not sustained or promoted in other courses they are required to take while in their degree program. This requires more work on behalf of our faculty to clarify our vision, more explicitly define what we mean by an 'urban social justice teacher education program', support faculty professional development, and engage in curriculum revision. This is much easier said than done, as not all faculty share the same beliefs. However, we are committed to paving a new path with this work.

Additionally, as we continue to review our language education courses, we are working to further incorporate translanguaging pedagogies even more deeply into the content of more courses. Currently, we are revising both our Language and Culture and Bilingual/Bicultural Education courses. Both of these courses will now aim to dismantle monoglossic and raciolinguistic ideologies (Flores & Rosa, 2015) in educational discourse and practice and engage heteroglossic stances for teaching and learning. Both courses will also include a local and/ or global community-engaged language learning component that will continue to offer an experiential context designed to support the transformation of teacher and student dispositions toward language learners in US classrooms. We also are now layering in a focus on Black Language, acknowledging the work of Baker-Bell (2020) and the Baker-Bell *et al*.'s (2020) demands for Black linguistic justice. We stand in solidarity with these demands and commit ourselves to their inclusion in our revisions to our language education courses.

We have and continue to incorporate the scholarship of Drs Nelson Flores, Kate Seltzer, Carla España and Luz Herrera (all former students of Ofelia García) into our course revisions and in our commitment to equity and social justice in education. Flores' work on raciolinguistics continues to inform our review and selection of course materials, and his scholarly articles have been incorporated into both the Principles of Language Learning and Bilingual/Bicultural Education courses as required readings. Additionally, España and Herrera's (2020) book *En comunidad: Lessons for Centering the Voices and Experiences of Bilingual Latinx Students* is a key text for the Language and Culture course, as well as a project in Bilingual/Bicultural Education, and *The Translanguaging Classroom,* co-authored by García and Seltzer alongside Suzanna Ibarra Johnson is a required textbook for our ESL methods class. As we look to the future of language education, we are indebted not only to Ofelia García's work, but we also continue to be influenced by her legacy in the work of her former students, formidable scholars in their own right.

However, we know there is much work to be done. As such, we are creating a research agenda. It includes research on teacher candidate dispositions and assessing the way they understand and apply translanguaging frameworks in their clinical teaching experiences and after graduation. Additional research is still required to document concrete instructional and assessment frameworks that dismantle monoglossic ideologies in ESL, world language and bilingual/ multilingual education programs. We need research that continues to document how to differentiate translanguaging from code switching, and ways teachers can undo symbolic language borders (Valdés, 2017) that create discursive practices that continue to categorize bi/multilingual language students as deviant from nativist subject norms (see Flores, 2013, 2020; Flores *et al.*, 2020). Moreover, we need to evaluate and document which teacher education pedagogical techniques are most effective with teacher candidates as well.

As we continue in our efforts, we are learning from and with our school district and community partners. We have created listening and brainstorming sessions in which we gather to share resources and strengths, and work to design programming that values heteroglossic practices and are mutually beneficial for both the community members and our teacher candidates. We work to align our professional development training modules and session plans for these community-engaged activities with a translanguaging framework. We are discovering wonderful symbiotic relationships, as we are sharing ways of thinking and speaking about languages with the community, while we are sharing the ways languages live in the community. As such, we have the transformative effect of influencing both the university and the organizations' practices and guiding principles.

We recognize that a focus on teacher dispositions and arming students with theory and instructional tools are only a first step on the difficult journey ahead to expanding heteroglossic ideologies in language education and normalizing bi/multilingual language practices for teaching and learning. We remain committed to this work, guided by our mission for social justice in education practice, and we are grateful for Dr Ofelia García's guidance through her extensive research and scholarship. Her efforts have helped us embrace dynamic multilingualism and translanguaging in the support all of our students. At the same time, we are cautious of the need to develop a critical translingual approach (see Hamman, 2018; Seltzer, 2019) that remains vigilant of power dynamics and language hierarchies in order to be critical of silences and one-way uses of translanguaging which can be damaging and engaged in ways that protect the status quo, instead of sustaining minoritized languages in bilingual education programs (Palmer, 2009; Zheng, 2019). We look toward the future, following in Ofelia García's footsteps, as we work to prepare the next generation of educators, 'eduactivists', who are ready to dismantle deep-seated and minoritizing practices while creating new norms that empower students in their bi/multilingual identities and language practices for equity and social justice (España & Herrera, 2020).

Post-Reading Discussion Questions

As other teacher education programs seek to incorporate translanguaging frameworks within their coursework, we offer these reflective questions:

(1) How does a translanguaging lens impact our teacher candidates' dispositions and beliefs about students and families? About language? About instruction? About the concept of academic language?
(2) What opportunities are provided to teacher candidates to engage with translanguaging frameworks across their pedagogical content coursework, and how do we encourage them to reflect on emerging heteroglossic ideologies around teaching and learning and the way this will influence their decision-making processes in the classroom?

Acknowledgements

Designing the Teaching Emerging Bilinguals I and II and the Principles of Language Learning courses is an ongoing team effort. Appreciation for their input, insights, hard work and care for these courses' development goes to Rutgers faculty, doctoral students and part-time instructors Tasha Austin, Juliane Bilotta, Julie Ochoa and Christelle Palpacuer Lee.

References

Baker-Bell, A. (2020) *Linguistic Justice: Black Language, Literacy, Identity and Pedagogy.* Routledge.

Baker-Bell, A., Williams-Farrier, B., Jackson, D., Johnson, L., Kynard, C. and McMurtry, T. (2020, July) *This Ain't Another* Statement! This is a DEMAND for Black Linguistic Justice! Conference on College Composition & Communication. See https://cccc.ncte. org/cccc/demand-for-black-linguistic-justice (accessed November 2020).

Cenoz, J. and Gorter, D. (2006) Linguistic landscape and minority languages. In D. Gorter (ed.) *Linguistic Landscape: A New Approach to Multilingualism.* Clevedon: Multilingual Matters.

Curran, M.E. (2003) Linguistic diversity and classroom management. *Theory into Practice* 42 (4), 334–341.

Curran, M. (2018) The Linguistic Landscape: Preparing teachers to see, hear and affirm the community. Paper presented at the American Education Research Association Annual Meeting (New York City, April 13–17).

España, C. and Herrera, L. Y. (2020). *En Comunidad: Lessons for Centering the Voices and Experiences of Bilingual Latinx Students.* Oxford: Heinemann.

Freire, P. (2000) *Pedagogy of the Oppressed (30th anniversary edn).* New York: Continuum.

Flores, N. (2013) Silencing the subaltern: Nation-state/colonial governmentality and bilingual education in the United States. *Critical Inquiry in Language Studies* 10, 263–287.

Flores, N. (2020) From academic language to language architecture: Challenging raciolinguistic ideologies in research and practice. *Theory into Practice* 59 (1), 22–31. https://doi.org/10.1080/00405841.2019.1665411.

Flores, N. and Rosa, J. (2015) Undoing appropriateness: Raciolinguistic ideologies and language diversity in education. *Harvard Educational Review* 85 (2), 149–171.

Flores, N. and Aneja, G. (2017) 'Why needs hiding?' Translingual (re)orientations in TESOL teacher education. *Research in the Teaching of English* 51 (4), 441–463.

Flores, N., Phuong, J. and Venegas, K. (2020) 'Technically an EL': The production of raciolinguistic categories in a dual language school. *TESOL Quarterly* 54 (3), 629–651. https://doi.org/10.1002/tesq.577.

García, O. (2008) Multilingual language awareness and teacher education. In J. Cenoz and N. Hornberger (eds) *Encyclopedia of Language and Education* (2nd edition Vol 6. Knowledge about Language, pp. 385–400). Berlin: Springer.

García, O. (2009) *Bilingual Education in the 21st Century: A Global Perspective.* Wiley-Blackwell.

García, O. (2017, October) Translanguaging. *Multilingualism & Diversity Lectures (MuDiLe).*

García, O., Johnson, S.I. and Seltzer, K. (2017) *The Translanguaging Classroom: Leveraging Student Bilingualism for Learning.* Philadelphia, PA: Caslon.

Hamman, L. (2018) Translanguaging and positioning in two-way dual language classrooms: A case for criticality. *Language and Education* 32 (1), 21–42. https://doi.org/10.1080/09500782.2017.1384006.

Johnson, K.E. (2006) The sociocultural turn and its challenges for second language teacher education. *TESOL Quarterly* 40 (1), 235–257. https://doi.org/10.2307/40264518.

Kleifgen, J. and García, O. (2017, 2010) *Educating Emergent Bilinguals: Policies, Programs, and Practices for English Language Learners.* New York, NY: Teachers College Press.

Lantolf, J. (2000) *Sociocultural Theory and Second Language Learning.* Oxford: Oxford University Press.

Lightbown, P. and Spada, N. (2013) *How Languages are Learned* (4th edn). Oxford: Oxford University Press.

Media That Matters (2009) See Immersion at https://www.youtube.com/watch?v=I6Y0HAjLKYI (accessed November 2020).

Moll, L., Amanti, C., Neff, D. and González, N. (1992) Funds of knowledge for teaching: Using a qualitative approach to connect homes and classrooms. *Theory Into Practice* (2), 132–141.

Otheguy, R., García, O. and Reid, W. (2015) Clarifying translanguaging and deconstructing named languages: A perspective from linguistics. *Applied Linguistics Review* 6 (3), 281–307.

Palmer, D. (2009) Middle-class English speakers in a two-way immersion bilingual classroom: 'Everybody should be listening to Jonathan now…' *TESOL Quarterly* 43, 177–202.

Palpacuer-Lee, C. and Curtis, J. (2017) Into the realm of the politically incorrect: Intercultural encounters in a service-learning program. *International Journal of Multicultural Education* 19 (2), 163–181. https://doi.org/10.18251./ijme.v19i2.1239.

Paris, D. and Alim, H.S. (eds) (2017) *Culturally Sustaining Pedagogies: Teaching and Learning for Justice in a Changing World.* New York, NY: Teachers College Press.

Rosa, J. and Flores, N. (2017) Unsettling race and language: Toward a raciolinguistic perspective. *Language in Society* 46 (5), 621–647. https://doi.org/10.1017/S0047404517000562.

Rutgers Graduate School of Education (2020) Urban Social Justice Focus https://gse.rutgers.edu/academic-programs/five-year-teacher-education-programs. (Accessed November, 2020).

Schönwetter, D., Sokal, L., Friesen, M. and Taylor, K. (2002) Teaching philosophies reconsidered: A conceptual model for the development and evaluation of teaching philosophy statements. *International Journal for Academic Development* 7 (1), 83–97. https://doi.org/10.1080/13601440210156501.

Seltzer, K. (2019) Reconceptualizing 'home' and 'school' language: Taking a critical translingual approach in the English classroom. *TESOL Quarterly* 53, 986–1007.

Valdés, G. (2017) Entry visa denied: The Construction of symbolic language borders in educational settings. In O. García, N. Flores and M. Spotti (eds) *Oxford Handbook of Language and Society* (pp. 321–348). New York, NY: Oxford University Press.

Zeichner, K. (2007) Accumulating knowledge across self-studies in Teacher Education. *Journal of Teacher Education* 58 (1), 36–46.

Zheng, B. (2021) Translanguaging in a Chinese immersion classroom: An ecological examination of instructional discourses. *International Journal of Bilingual Education and Bilingualism* 24 (9), 1324–1339, DOI: 10.1080/13670050.2018.1561642.

Appendices

Appendix 7.1: Linguistic Landscape Assignment (Abbreviated)

Teaching Emerging Bilinguals I

Linguistic Landscape assignment

The purpose of this Linguistic Landscape assignment is to become familiar with the diverse communities of New Jersey, through an ethnographic observation of the public display of language, in one of our partner school districts. This assignment offers an opportunity for you to tell an empirical and reflective story about the multilingual context in which you will be working as a teacher. This is also an opportunity for you to understand how language is an actor and a resource in our multilingual urban world. In conducting this ethnographic small-scale research project, you will enter the familiar, sensory world of your future students and their families, and critically position yourself as a language user, a community member and an educator, within a local and global context. As a future teacher, it is important you gain an understanding of your school community, and an understanding of the role of language as a resource. The observation and teamwork skills you will activate for this assignment will be useful in your professional development at the Graduate School of Education, on the job and beyond.

Your Linguistic Landscape project will take the form of a five-minute multimodal presentation. You will perform this group presentation on Week 6 of the Teaching Emerging Bilingual I class. You will be assessed on your performance and on the group inquiry processes. To complete this Linguistic Landscape assignment, you will complete three parts with your group: (1) Observation and data collection; (2) Analysis and critical reflection and (3) Presentation. Each part is described below:

Part 1. Observation and data collection

Select a bounded location in the school district you are investigating, for instance at least two blocks of an avenue or a commercial street. Note and/or sketch which areas of the street you are investigating, marking street numbers and street sides, and who seems to be ' in charge' of each section of the street. You can also include a map and add the required information. Remember that signs can be a piece of written text, and/or a visual text that includes writing. Document each sign by taking photographs. Pay specific attention to signs that include more than one language. Collect information from census data as well, looking historically for changes.

Part 2. Analysis

Begin the analysis of the data you have collected in Part 1, focusing on the meanings associated with the signs you have collected, for themselves and in context. Use concepts from the Cenoz and Gorter (2006) text in your analysis (which languages are represented; font type and size; order of language use; matching/mismatches between community demographics and languages observed; etc...). Consider how the linguistic landscape is used by the community and what it represents about its identity. How would newcomers to this community perceive the linguistic landscape? What does the linguistic landscape mean for you as a teacher?

Part 3. Presentation

Present the results of your investigation in a five-minute multimodal group presentation., consider the following questions: (1) What linguistic resources are available in the community you investigated and for what purposes? (2) How do language communities use the linguistic landscape? (3) In what ways does the linguistic landscape reflect global flows and mobility? (4)What does the completion of this assignment mean to you as a teacher and how can this impact your approach to practice?

Appendix 7.2: Personal Stance on Language Learning Assignment (Abbreviated)

Principles of Language Learning

Personal stance on Language Learning final paper

The personal stance on language learning is an original professional statement of your teaching philosophy(ies) related to language learning and education (adapted from Schonwetter *et al.*, 2002). The claims and definitions within it should be firmly grounded in both your learning and experience. This should be done through personal reflection of your learning and experiences as informed by language acquisition theory and research. It also includes declarative statements of your language learning philosophies as related to and reflected in your practices. With each question, be sure to cite and reference relevant and influential theories and research, and be sure to reflect on our class readings, discussions, community-engaged language learning sessions and experiences. It will be helpful to reflect on your responses to the activity on Day 1 Survey on Language Learning (Lightbown & Spada, 2006), and your reflections to our community engaged language learning sessions. Your personal stance should not exceed five pages.

You may find it helpful to revise this statement after completing a larger portion of your graduate course work and throughout your career as a classroom language teacher. You may also choose to include this statement in a teaching portfolio.

Please guide your writing based on the following questions:

- *What is language learning?*
- *How are new languages learned and acquired?*
- *Who is an emergent bilingual?*
- *What is the relationship between the language student and teacher?*
- *How are new language learning and new language learners to be evaluated?*

8 Where the Banyan Tree Grows: Nurturing Teachers' Translanguaging Pedagogy through a Study Group

Ivana Espinet and Karen Zaino

Pre-Reading Discussion Questions

(1) What linguistic resources do your students bring to your classroom?
(2) How do you incorporate your students' and families' linguistic resources into the design of your classroom instruction?

When I shared with one of my colleagues about my students' work, she said 'Oh, you can have regular Junot Díazes[1] in your classroom'. I'm like, 'Exactly!' (Michelle, second grade teacher)

I see a lot of really fun [languaging] that is happening in the classroom and in their work and how [my students] are bringing not only their linguistic understanding but also different cultural understandings of some of the themes that we've been talking about, like love and liberation and what it looks like to them. (Nisa, 12th grade ELA teacher)

Introduction

This chapter shares the work of two New York City teachers, Nisa and Michelle. Through their participation in a translanguaging study group organized by the CUNY New York State Initiative on Emergent Bilinguals (CUNY-NYSIEB), they began to implement a translanguaging pedagogy in their classrooms. We begin the chapter by providing a brief history and a summary of the vision of the CUNY-NYSIEB project. Next, we present an overview of translanguaging pedagogy and describe the translanguaging study group which both authors facilitated. Lastly, we present a case study of the work of each teacher and analyze the implications.

Both authors are former students of Ofelia García and were also part of the CUNY-NYSIEB team. Our approach to working with teachers of emergent bilinguals was rooted in the translanguaging pedagogy that evolved from Ofelia García's work. Over the years, Ofelia fostered spaces for collaboration that engaged educators in reimagining their schools and classrooms. Our work and the work of the teachers that we feature in this chapter are examples of how she inspired educators to open a space in which they could carefully analyze how learning was attuned to emergent bilinguals' identities and socioemotional development.

The CUNY-NYSIEB Project

In 2011, as New York State was confronting what was seen as the failure of many schools with a large number of students they classified as English Language Learners,[2] officials from the New York State Education Department (NYSED) reached out to the Research Institute for the Study of Language in Urban Society (RISLUS) and the PhD Program in Urban Education at The Graduate Center of the City University of New York. Ofelía Garcia, Ricardo Otheguy and Kate Menken[3] met with NYSED and agreed to work with New York State to support these schools. As a result, New York State provided funding to start the CUNY New York State Initiative for Emergent Bilinguals (CUNY-NYSIEB). The team knew that they could not continue to work from the same theoretical constructs and pedagogical practices that had failed so many children (García & Otheguy, 2020). They developed the vision for CUNY-NYSIEB which included two non-negotiable principles for participating schools:

(1) Embrace bilingualism as a resource in education so the entire linguistic repertoire of emergent bilingual children is used flexibly and strategically in instruction in order to engage the children cognitively, academically, emotionally and creatively.
(2) Support for a school-wide multilingual school ecology so the entire range of language practices of all children and families are evident in the school's textual landscape, as well as in the interactions of all members of the school community. (CUNY-NYSIEB, 2011)

Over the years, the CUNY-NYSIEB team, comprised of CUNY faculty and doctoral students, worked with teachers, school administrators, parents, students and community members to implement translanguaging theory/practice in schools heavily populated with emergent bilingual students. In her book *Bilingual Education in the 21st Century*, Ofelia García had used the banyan tree, common in Southeast Asia, which is grounded vertically and horizontally, with aerial roots that expand to the sides, as a metaphor for the interconnectivity and multiplicity of bilingualism and multilingualism. The ideological foundations of the project – the roots – emerged from Ofelia's work in that book. The CUNY-NYSIEB team worked together to develop and extend a theory of translanguaging that engaged with the practices; those practices, in turn, informed the evolution of the theory. Throughout the years, the core CUNY-NYSIEB principles guided the work. Little by little, as translanguaging pedagogy in CUNY-NYSIEB schools was developed, theory and practice have evolved and like the banyan tree, the work has extended and grown.

Translanguaging Pedagogy

When teachers enact translanguaging pedagogy, they purposefully and strategically leverage their students' entire linguistic repertoire for learning. García *et al.* (2017) use the metaphor of the translanguaging *corriente* to refer to the 'flow of students' dynamic bilingualism that runs through our classrooms and schools' (García *et al.*, 2017: 21). In the United States, this flow has been traditionally suppressed, as the dynamic non-dominant language practices of bilingual students and families are often devalued in educational settings. A critical translanguaging approach advocates for educators to recognize and challenge deficit perspectives of bilingual students that are informed by raciolinguistic ideologies of language deficiencies (Martin *et al.*, 2019). In order to do so, educators need to bring the *corriente* to the surface and strategically leverage the creative potential of its streams, torrents and cascades. Thus, the purposes of translanguaging in the classroom are to:

(1) Support students as they engage with and comprehend complex content and texts.
(2) Provide opportunities for students to develop linguistic practices for academic contexts.
(3) Make space for students' bilingualism and ways of knowing.
(4) Support students' bilingual identities and socioemotional development (García *et al.*, 2017).

In the context of this chapter, we examine how two educators who participated in a translanguaging study group began to enact pedagogical practices that further those goals.

The Translanguaging Study Group: Co-Creating Spaces for Reflection

Early on, the CUNY-NYSIEB team understood that changing the teachers' and administrators' stances toward their bilingual students was essential. In order to develop such a stance, teachers need to experience translanguaging and how it works in their classroom and have spaces for reflection on their practices. One of the ways by which the project supported this was by facilitating groups and providing materials that schools could use to conduct collaborative descriptive inquiry sessions in the context of professional learning communities or study groups (Aponte & Ascenzi-Moreno, 2019; García & Ascenzi-Moreno, 2012).

The teachers whose work we share in this chapter participated in a year-long study group modeled after the work of the Prospect Center Descriptive Review (Himley & Carini, 2000), as well as the teacher inquiry groups developed by Fitcham Dana and Yendol-Silva (2003). The purpose of the study group was to provide structures for educators to collaborate in designing translanguaging transformational spaces. Both authors co-facilitated the study group. When we began our meetings, everyone had different levels of familiarity with translanguaging. During the year, each teacher created small projects that focused on creating spaces that challenged linguistic boundaries and hierarchies in their classroom so as to challenge the hegemony of English. We met once a month to reflect and think about questions, challenges and insights that emerged from their work. The general structure of the study group included discussions about readings, practical applications, connections to conceptual issues and observations and examinations of student work. During each session, we devoted some time for each teacher to share ideas that they wanted to implement in their classrooms and get feedback and suggestions from their peers. In addition, each of the facilitators met with the individual teachers and visited their classroom to provide support.

In the following sections, we describe the work of two of the teachers in the study group, Nisa and Michelle, as they began to explore how to design instruction that was centered on language practices of their students.

Michelle's Second Grade Multilingual Classroom

Michelle teaches at a public school in Brooklyn that serves students from kindergarten through fifth grade. She also speaks Spanish. Her general education second grade class had twenty-five children. While only half of the class had been identified as Multilingual Language Learners/English Language Learners (MLL/ELLs) by New York State, most of the students came from homes in which their families spoke languages other than English, including Mandarin, Fujianese (mostly spoken in parts of the Fujian province in China), Spanish, Arabic and Mandinka (spoken in Guinea, Senegal and Gambia), even if they were not classified as MLL/ELLs.

One of the first things that Michelle shared was that she had decided to join the study group because over the years, she had noticed that many of her students were rejecting her home language practices after only a few years in school. Her students often didn't want to use their home languages in the classroom. Her Chinese and Chinese-American students often would take on American names and didn't want to say what their given names were to the class. Many of the families would complain to her that their children did not want to speak their home languages at home anymore, even though some lived with family members who only spoke their home language. Michelle was troubled by what she had observed: after only a few years in school her students had already learned that they needed to perform in English only and were rejecting their families' and communities' bilingual ways of knowing.

Before she joined the study group, Michelle had always encouraged her students to use their home languages among themselves and had partnered newcomers with students who shared their home language. She also often spoke Spanish with the children whose home language was Spanish when they needed help. However, she realized that using home language as a scaffold was not enough to counteract the hegemonic power of English. She wanted her students to be proud of their bilingualism. She realized that to ensure that her students' home and school language practices could build on each other, she needed to make changes to her instructional practices.

After joining the study group, Michelle began to design her lessons so that she could bring the translanguaging *corriente* to the surface with the support of the group. She strategically planned instruction to intentionally address some of her initial observations about her students. She wanted to connect her students' home and community language practices and identities to their language practices and identities in her classroom. In order to do so, she began by engaging her students with culturally and linguistically sustaining (Paris & Alim, 2017) texts (España & Herrera, 2020).

The book *The Name Jar* (Choi, 2003) tells the story of Unhei, a Korean girl who was anxious about starting school in America. On the first day of school, instead of introducing herself as Unhei, she tells the class that she will choose a name by the following week. Her new classmates decide to help out by filling a glass jar with names for her to pick from. On the day of her name choosing, encouraged by her new friends, Unhei chooses her own Korean name and helps everyone pronounce it. Michelle used *The Name Jar* to get the students to reflect through the character's journey about their relationships to their own names. She asked them to share what people called them at home and to create name plates with their names in the center, along with any drawings or words that they wanted to add, to display in the classroom.

I just really saw those students started to take a little more pride. Fatima[4] for example. She's from Gambia. She's the only one in our class [from Gambia], so she didn't even want to tell me that she spoke Mandinka at home in the beginning [of the year]. Anyway, she created a name card with her name, what her mom calls her and what it really means. It was really, really nice. There is also a boy in my class named James, and he is a Chinese speaker at home who would not say his name in Chinese [at the beginning of the year]. But he did write his name in Chinese, and finally he wrote the pronunciation and he started telling us and speaking up and saying words in Chinese in the class. It was a really nice shift, to see how much more comfortable he felt with his home language. (Michelle, interview, 29 May 2019)

This activity was an essential step into getting children to recognize her classroom as a space where students' school and home identities were in sync. Michelle also wanted to provide opportunities for students to develop linguistic practices for academic contexts, so over the course of the year, she used books in which authors used translanguaging to model for her students how their home language practices could become part of their school literacy practices, such as *The Ugly Vegetables* and *I love Saturdays and Domingos*. Using literature, she encouraged the children to recognize how bilinguals use their complex language repertoires to communicate with each other and why and how authors incorporate translanguaging as a literary device.

For one of the writing projects in her class, the students wrote short narratives based on personal experiences in which they described important moments in their lives. Michelle knew that one of the challenges was that most of her students hadn't had any literacy instruction in their home language. Nevertheless, she decided to encourage the students to try translanguaging in writing. She had read with the class books in which authors used translanguaging as a literary device and analyzed with the children the authors' use of language. During writers' workshop, she gave the students the option to sit at tables in which they shared home languages so they could help each other. She taught them how to use an online translation tool and bilingual dictionaries. Those students who had some literacy instruction in their home language helped others at their tables, becoming the experts. During one of our meetings, Michelle explained:

For the students who write in characters [or use a different alphabet], Arabic or Chinese, I showed them an example of how you can also spell them phonetically so that English speakers could read them and pronounce them. So for example, James, [he]would write in Chinese but then he would write the pronunciation. So he mixed in the characters with also the way you would pronounce them, which I thought was pretty advanced, right? For second graders. (Michelle, interview, 29 May 2019)

In teaching students about how transliteration could be used to reach multiple audiences, she fostered their metalinguistic awareness. Michelle helped the children to become more aware of their expressive potential, and encouraged the children to be cognizant of the linguistic choices they made in their work.

Michelle also wanted to make sure that she fostered a connection with the families. After going on a field trip with the students, she asked them 'How can you tell your parents about what you learned on this field trip?' The students translanguaged in their writing to write letters to family members about what they had learned (see Figure 8.1). Michelle shared:

> [Azuzena] who doesn't speak that much [Spanish] orally, she chose to write all in Spanish to her dad and talk about what we learned. So it's just really nice. I really also like the parent connection, and trying to involve parents more directly in the student learning, and discussing what they're learning at home. If you're only learning it in English, it might be hard to go home and translate, right? So that was really important. (Michelle, interview, 6 February 2019)

Michelle noted that having an authentic audience for this project inspired her students to add more details in their writing. It is important to note that Michelle gave students the option to choose how to use language in order to foster their agency. One of the key aspects of planning instruction from a translanguaging pedagogical stance is that it shifts the power dynamics of the classroom. Michelle, like many

Choose any of these questions to help you tell more about the trip:
- What did you learn?
- What was the most interesting part?
- What questions do you still have about life long ago in New York?

Figure 8.1 Rosa's letter to her mom and dad

other teachers, does not speak all of her students' home languages, so she provided opportunities for children to help each other by organizing her classroom so students could join a table and work with peers who speak the same home language. She also engaged families by creating assignments that position them as the main target audience.

At the end of the year, Michelle shared how, overall, she observed that her students became proud that they spoke languages other than English at home and were curious about each other's language practices. She also talked about how her students were more engaged in writing than in previous years, included more details in their stories, and were aware of the word choices that they were making, as they decided when and how to translanguage in their writing.

Nisa's 12th Grade Classroom

Nisa's 12th grade English Language Arts classroom at a High School in Brooklyn, New York, is large and bright, the walls lined with student-generated plot diagrams, character analyses and word walls. Over the course of our work together, however, the room shifted: the plot diagrams tackled not only assigned novels, but traditional folktales from a range of cultures, and the word walls shed their monolingual approach to include words from languages such as Arabic, Spanish, French, Mandarin and Haitian-Creole. This subtle change in her classroom's linguistic ecology reflected the substantive changes in her curriculum and pedagogy over the course of our year together. Nisa's work in the study group transformed her traditional novel unit into an opportunity for her students to demonstrate, share and extend their linguistic and cultural practices.

Nisa's enthusiasm for translanguaging stems from her own experience as an immigrant, refugee and multilingual learner. She is devoted to her students, all of whom share her immigrant background: all of the students at her school are immigrants or refugees, newcomers to the United States. Their previous educational experiences vary; some have little formal education before arriving in the United States in 9th or 10th grade, and some have attended private schools in their home countries. Eager to draw on her students' backgrounds through translanguaging, Nisa found a way to support her students to remain connected to their home countries and cultures and to recognize the inherent strength of their multilingual identities.

Nisa's students began the year by working on their personal statements for college. This exercise, an annual ritual in her room, encourages students to think about their personal histories. Many write about their home country and their journey to the United States, and when they write about their homes and families, Nisa has always encouraged them to include dialogue that reflects their language practices in those places. Though she hadn't called it translanguaging, as she began participating in the study group, Nisa quickly realized that this was precisely what she was encouraging her students to do: to draw on their full linguistic repertoires and to write authentically about their experiences using the linguistic tools that made the most sense to them.

Following this unit, Nisa's students read *The Hate U Give* by Angie Thomas. This popular and critically acclaimed young adult novel features a protagonist, Starr, who speaks openly about the 'code-switching' she practices as she navigates life in her Black community and her predominantly white private school. It is important to note that from a sociolinguistic perspective, the term code switching comes from a theoretical construct that assumes an individual accesses dual or multiple linguistic systems, as opposed to translanguaging theory which poses that individuals have a unitary competence and they use features of their repertoire according to the context in which they communicate (Otheguy *et al.*, 2019). However, Starr's experiences and her explicit description of how she 'code switched' in different contexts inspired conversations among students about how their language practices shift in different contexts and with different audiences. This, in turn, served as a springboard into the deeper investigation of language that Nisa took up in the spring semester.

Nisa already knew that she wanted her students to read Zora Neale Hurston's *Their Eyes Were Watching God* during the spring semester. At her school, teachers plan collaboratively across disciplines, and Hurston's novel dovetailed interestingly with the history teacher's scheduled unit on gender. Nisa realized, however, that Hurston's background as an anthropologist – her attention to African-American language and folklore traditions – also created a perfect opportunity to explore languaging practices more deeply.

Early in the unit, following a lesson on Hurston's work in anthropology, Nisa asked her students to take on the role of anthropologist in their own lives and within their own cultures. She shared an example of a folktale from African-American culture – that of Brer Rabbit – and then encouraged students to consider stories and folklore from their home countries. Following their enthusiastic brainstorm session of the many stories they've heard from family and friends, students selected groups and began to transcribe their stories.

This transcription process honored the oral tradition through which folk stories are passed down. Nisa told her students to try to capture the way that stories are actually told, drawing on all of their linguistic resources. This practice served multiple purposes: first, it encouraged students to recognize how language is always contextual, depending on audience and purpose; and second, it laid the foundation for reading Hurston's work, which relies on transcription of Black English in much of its dialogue.

In another lesson, Nisa introduced a quote from Hurston: 'No, I do not weep at the world—I am too busy sharpening my oyster knife'. Nisa contextualized the quote from them; many did not know what an oyster is, and this incited a discussion related to cultural context and language. After they analyzed the metaphor's potential meanings, students thought about metaphors in their home languages. Nisa recalled:

> If you were to explain this metaphor or to include a metaphor like this in your story, what would you do with it? Would you translate it literally and try to explain it? Or would you just replace it with a more familiar metaphor from your own native language? So, I thought that was a really good question that got them thinking. They're so used to just plugging thing into Google Translate, and then something coming back to them that doesn't make sense. We're trying to get at the root of that, right? Like, some things don't translate. Some things are culturally based, some things need a lot of context. So, what would you do, as an anthropologist, in this moment? As a writer, what would you do? Thinking about who is the audience? Right? Are they going to grasp this idea better if you just replace it with another metaphor or if you really explicate it? (Nisa, Interview, 24 May 2019)

Nisa's instructional design aimed to foster critical metalinguistic awareness – that is, students' ability to consciously reflect on the nature of language (García, 2017) – by studying and analyzing how language is used in their families, communities, schools and in society at large, as well as why it is used in these ways. This entailed helping students engage in critical analyses of how others may judge and interpret language practices in different contexts (García & Kleifgen, 2010; Paris & Alim, 2017).

Through these activities, students came to see that writing is always a creative act, and unsettled conceptions of 'standard written language' that permeate much of English Language Arts coursework in high school. Nisa's framing of her students as linguistic anthropologists provided a structure for their natural curiosity about their own languaging practices and cultural repertoires. Opening up the spaces for young people to tap into their entire linguistic repertoire can allow teachers to gain knowledge of their students as writers, thinkers, and above all as individuals (Ascenzi-Moreno & Espinosa, 2017).

Bringing the Translanguaging *Corriente* to the Surface

We began this chapter by discussing the purposes of bringing the classroom translanguaging *corriente* to the surface. In this section, we will examine how Nisa and Michelle navigated towards that.

Supporting students as they engage with and comprehend complex content and texts

Translanguaging can enable teachers to approach more complex content, allowing students to draw on their full linguistic repertoires as they are involved in interpersonal discussion or intrapersonal reflection. In Nisa's high school classroom, translanguaging pedagogy supported students in analyzing the complex narrative structure of *Their Eyes Were Watching God*. In Michelle's second-grade classroom, students read and analyzed how authors use translanguaging as a literary device and used them as mentors to write their own texts. Both teachers featured characters whose languaging practices opened space to discuss issues related to identity and language. Students engaged not only with difficult texts, but also with complicated issues that they were able to access by drawing on their full linguistic repertoires, such as the connection between their names, cultures and their identities and how speakers make different linguistic choices depending on the audience and context.

Providing opportunities for students to develop linguistic practices for academic contexts

In Nisa and Michelle's classrooms, students were supported in engaging in academic work. Nisa introduced her unit with a series of activities meant to draw students' attention to language features such as idioms, abbreviations, and metaphors. After Nisa introduced the idiom 'it's raining cats and dogs', students examined folk sayings from their own countries, noting that Puerto Ricans and Dominicans both said *Se está casando una bruja* (The witch is getting married) when the sun shone during a rainstorm. Other students chimed in: in Colombia, an old woman gets married during sun showers, and in Haiti, they say the devil is beating his wife. This activity spurred reflection on the origins of idioms, as well as the extent to which they can (or should) be translated into other named languages. Michelle's second graders also demonstrated metalinguistic awareness as they wrote their narratives, choosing whether and when to use translanguaging and/or transliteration as devices to reach multiple audiences with their work. In both classrooms, attention to audience and purpose shaped approaches to writing, and translanguaging allowed students to approach these issues with more nuanced orientations.

Making space for students' bilingualism and ways of knowing

Ultimately, translanguaging is not only about supporting students to achieve in traditional academic contexts; it also expands our notion of what counts as academic content in schools and invites critical inquiry into what forms of knowledge are traditionally sanctioned in classrooms. In making space for bilingualism, Nisa and Michelle also encouraged their students to practice metalinguistic awareness. During Nisa's lessons on idioms and folklore, for instance, students discussed words from their home languages that could and should be translated into English for an English-speaking audience, as well as those that did not have an easy translation. In Michelle's class, students wrote letters to their parents, describing a recent field trip. They were able to choose the languages in which they wrote, depending on which language would be most comfortably read by their audience.

Supporting students' bilingual identities and socioemotional development

In each classroom, students found ways to connect with their linguistic identities in a supportive and caring environment. Michelle used her observations of her students' relentlessness to share their names to inform her choice of what book to use in order to support her students in creating a bridge between their home and school identities and experiences. As the year progressed, her students showed growing pride in their linguistic practices.

Nisa's class was often filled with laughter as students learned English together and shared aspects of their home languages in groups. At the end of the school year, Nisa received some funding and was able to purchase books for her students; many asked, for the first time, if they could read in their home language. Their multilingual identities had a place in school.

Conclusion

We started this chapter with a reference to Ofelia García's banyan tree metaphor. Michelle and Nisa's work provide a window onto how two teachers who were new to translanguaging pedagogy grew their practices and shared their journey with colleagues as they nurtured each other's ideas. Their work was not done in isolation; as they finished the year, they shared it with their school communities and other CUNY-NYSIEB educators.

Nisa and Michelle's practices began to challenge the hegemony of English in their classroom and school community by making space for students' dynamic language practices and ways of knowing and for supporting students' socioemotional development. Like the banyan tree, the roots of this work need to expand in multiple directions as educators find their own ways to bring the translanguaging *corriente* to the surface.

In order to extend and grow this work, it is essential that translanguaging pedagogy be enacted with the goal of developing critical multilingual awareness. Many educators have embraced translanguaging scaffolds to support students' learning. However, in order to deepen and challenge ideologies of language deficiencies, it is essential that students and teachers regularly and collaboratively examine the ideologies that underlie the conventions of language in school and society. While educators are often working under time and curricula constraints, it is imperative that we create models for engaging students in metalinguistic reflection that provides spaces to examine their own language practices and those of their communities, as well as how they are perceived.

Post-Reading Discussion Questions:

(1) How did these two teachers leverage and extend their students' linguistic practices?
(2) What does it mean to bring the translanguaging *corriente* to the surface in your classroom context?

References

Aponte, G.Y. and Ascenzi-Moreno, L. (2019) A Professional Learning Community – Understanding, Validating, and Building on the Language Practices of Emergent Multilingual Learners (EMLLs) in Prekindergarten. New York, NY: New York State Education Department Office of Bilingual Education and World Languages. See http://www.nysed.gov/common/nysed/files/programs/bilingual-ed/resource-emergent-mll-professional-learning-community-a.pdf (accessed October 2020).

Ascenzi-Moreno, L. and Espinosa, C.M. (2017) Opening up spaces for their whole selves: A case study group's exploration of translanguaging practices in writing. *NYS TESOL Journal* 12 (1), 10–29.

Choi, Y. (2003) *The Name Jar.* Decorah, IA: Dragonfly Books.

CUNY-NYSIEB (2011) Principles and Practices. See https://www.cuny-nysieb.org/our-vision/ (accessed September 2020).

España, C. and Herrera, L. (2020) *En Comunidad: Lessons for Centering the Voices and Experiences of Bilingual Latinx Students.* Portsmouth, NH: Heinemann.

Fitcham, D.N. and Yendol-Silva, D. (2003) *The Reflective Educator's Guide to Classroom Research: Learning to Teach and Teaching to Learn Through Practitioner Inquiry.* Thousand Oaks, CA: Corwin Press.

García, O. (2017) Critical multilingual awareness and teacher education. In J. Cenoz, D. Gorter and S. May (eds) *Encyclopedia of Language and Education* (pp. 385–400). Cham: Springer.

García, O. and Ascenzi-Moreno, L. (2012) How to use this translanguaging guide: The descriptive inquiry process. In C. Celic and K. Seltzer (eds) *Translanguaging: A CUNY-NYSIEB Guide for Educators* (pp. 7–10). NY: CUNY-NYSIEB, The Graduate Center, The City University of New York.

García, O., Johnson, S. and Seltzer, K. (2017) *The Translanguaging Classroom: Leveraging Student Bilingualism for Learning.* Philadelphia, PA: Caslon.

García, O. and Kleifgen, J. (2010) *Educating Emergent Bilinguals: Policies, Programs and Practices for English Learners* (2nd edn). New York, NY: Teachers College Press.

García, O. and Otheguy, R. (2020) Conceptualizing Translanguaging Theory/Practice In CUNY-NYSIEB team (eds) *Translanguaging and Transformative Teaching for Emergent Bilingual Students* (pp. 3–24). New York: Routledge

Himley, M. and Carini, P.F. (2000) *From Another Angle: Children's Strengths and School Standards.* New York: Teachers College Press.

Martin, K.M., Aponte, G.Y. and García, O. (2019) Countering raciolinguistic ideologies: The role of translanguaging in educating bilingual children. *Les Cahiers Internationaux de Sociolinguistique* 2 (16), 19–41.

Otheguy, R., García, O. and Reid, W. (2019) A translanguaging view of the linguistic system of bilinguals. *Applied Linguistics Review* 10 (4), 625–651.

Paris, D.H. and Alim, S. (2017) *Culturally Sustaining Pedagogies: Teaching and Learning for Justice in a Changing World.* New York: Teachers College Press.

9 Bilingual Teachers Engage: Poetic Inquiry as a Site for Languaging Dilemmas

Carmina Makar

Native Tongues
Native is my tongue.
Raised in a small town, deep in the woods.
Bathed in coffee, not too sweet, simply just brewed.
From the ancestors of the Chibcha, and the airs of conquistadors,
my tongue grew with glee, infinite and free.
But by the age of ten, my tongue turned blue, red and white.
It was yanked from its land and dragged to be free.
Was it not free to thee?
In this new world my tongue was foreign.
My tongue became many things, and with it,
I too became many things, unwanted things.
Semilingual. Recessive Bilingual. Limited English Proficient.
English Language Learner.
It wasn't till the new world that my tongue and
I learned to appreciate one another.
To survive we had to be lovers. Lovers and warriors.
I became a knight, my tongue the sword, build to fight back,
hit them with words.
A weapon I would one day use to help other tongues.
Native are our tongues.
M. Camargo, 2019, study participant

Pre-Reading Discussion Questions

(1) How is bilingual education sometimes seen as both supportive of students' full linguistic repertoire and a system of oppression for them?
(2) Why do you think some bilingual speakers may feel conflicted about the ways they use their languages?

This study highlights the linguistic dilemmas expressed by a group of New York City teachers as they use poems to reflect on their bilingual selves. The poem of M. Camargo above, is one of many poetic artifacts analyzed in this study. In framing this analysis, I theorize the cases of these teachers by drawing on Ofelia García's lifetime work, honoring what I consider to be her landmark contributions to the field. I emphasize three areas of her scholarship: her sustained and lifelong commitment to bilingual and multilingual education; her efforts in pushing against deficit paradigms of bilingual children; and her theorization of translanguaging.

The chapter is organized as follows: first, I provide personal context for this inquiry, situating my knowledge and my experience of having Ofelia as my mentor; next, I describe the role of deficit paradigms in shaping our understanding of bilingualism in the United States; I follow this with a description of poetic inquiry as my methodological approach, and then discuss the case with a close reading of contributions. I end this chapter by highlighting the way in which Ofelia García's work has contributed to our current understanding of these issues, and looking at the ways we can expand on her work going forward. In this chapter, I choose to highlight translanguaging as a key premise in her scholarship, critically engaging with her work and underlining caveats and directions as we move forward in our theorizing of the concept.

Personal Point of Departure

I moved from Mexico to NY in 2005 to study bilingual education under Ofelia. This marked the beginning of our relationship. I credit Ofelia with my academic upbringing because her stance as an advisor and mentor strongly shaped not only the way I understand language and bilingual education, but the way I engage with research and the community at large. The opportunities I had to work by her side, as I assisted her research in schools – during her time at Teachers College Columbia University and then at the Graduate Center in New York – afforded me a personal view of her epistemology and practice. Very early on, I understood her work ethic to be centered around producing deeply transformative practices that included not only educators and students themselves, but also key stakeholders as policy actors. On a personal note, both in the United States, working with schools, and in Mexico, where we once conducted research, I witnessed Ofelia's deep commitment to carefully cultivating communities of practice, nourished over decades by her loving approach to research and teaching.

Ofelia's lifetime work cannot be understood in a vacuum. Her commitment to social justice, and her mission to show that bilingual children's languaging practices are powerful rather than deficient, undergird the spirit of her work across decades. Over the course of these years, I have found her role in shaping generations of scholars to be of particular relevance. In keen reflection of her spirit, her house has always been wide open. Cohort after cohort of students, many navigating the academic landscape for the first time, have been welcomed by Ofelia and her husband, Ricardo Otheguy, into their home. I owe them the deep understanding that scholarship, dialogue and community should always be accompanied by food, laughter and music. Ofelia's sustained work in the socialization and mentoring of emerging scholars is as much of a lifetime contribution as her theorization of language.

Deficit Views in Language Education

New York City is home to a diverse population of educational communities: multilingual families, students, teachers and administrators. According to the New York City Department of Education (NYCDOE), there are more than 176 named languages (Makoni & Pennycook, 2007) spoken in schools. This number is relevant if only to illustrate the breadth of the multilingual ecosystem in which these communities live and practice. The field of education of multilingual learners in the United States has been characterized by a dialectic history of language policies and sustained efforts to suppress students' dynamic languaging practices (García, 2009). These have ranged from declaring bilingual education illegal to the enactment of discrete measures barring students and parents from speaking languages other than English on school premises.

These efforts to annul the multilingual identity of diverse communities serve as an important backdrop to any discussion around bilingualism and bilingual education in the US. Historically, language has been used as a currency for nation building (García, 2009) and the United States is not an exception. Bilingual children have long been depicted as culturally and linguistically deficient. This flawed perspective has been entrenched in scholarly literature for decades, as revealed by Barbara Flores (2005) who, in a thorough review of educational literature, identified the development of categories to describe linguistically minoritized children over the span of 80 years. In her review, Spanish-speaking children were identified as being slow learners, learning disabled, culturally deprived, semi-lingual, limited-English speaking or at risk.

These paradigms reflect how diverse populations were measured against a white Anglo-Protestant middle-class standard. Tejeda and Gutierrez (2005: 270) described these as backlash practices, which have used race as 'the primary screening device for categorizing and marginalizing sectors of the population'. In keeping with this paradigm, she coined the term 'backlash pedagogy' to describe a pedagogy which, rather than harnessing diversity and difference as resources for learning, regards them as problems to be eliminated or remediated. Characterized by reductive notions of learning and literacy, backlash pedagogies necessarily prohibit the use of students' full linguistic, sociocultural and academic repertoire in the service of learning. In this way, 'backlash pedagogy becomes an institutionalized and structured response to diversity and difference' (2005: 266). Key to the premise of backlash pedagogies is the notion that they create surrogates, such as language, for the larger category of race. Linguistic difference – primarily language use – is at the center of backlash pedagogy. Gutierrez (2008) highlights the role of language in shaping racialized ideologies. This idea is expanded on by Flores and Rosa (2015) in their work on raciolinguistic ideologies, in which they describe the deep effects of the history of oppression, minoritization and racialization of diverse language practices.

Current deficit paradigms have consolidated themselves as a result of colonial internalization and have been deliberately employed by the nation state to naturalize social inequality.

Named Languages and Translanguaging

Drawing on Makoni and Pennycook's (2007) work on the 'disinventing and reconstituting of languages', García *et al.* (2017) refer to named languages as a product and invention of the nation state. The process of invention is a direct result of European colonialism. Since this view stems from an understanding of monolingualism as the norm, it then shapes the perception that standard views on bilingualism conceive a bilingual to be a monolingual in two languages. García (2009) refers to this process as Monoglossia, in which we look for 'either proficiency in the two languages according to monolingual norms for both languages, or proficiency in the dominant language' (García, 2009: 115). García argues that moving away from named languages is a way to fight the reproduction of nationalist ideologies that have perpetuated language minoritization efforts. It is also this focus on students' complete repertoire as one linguistic system that creates the need to conceptualize named languages. In translanguaging theory, these named languages are understood to be an invention.

As the teachers in this study reveal, if we consider languages as separate and autonomous entities, and bilingualism as simply additive (one language plus another equals two languages), we may endanger the language practices of minoritized bilingual communities. García (2009) has systematically emphasized that the language of bilingual students is not simply additive; it is dynamic.

Well-meaning policies or practices that use students' home languages in education without first reflecting on, and engaging with, the ways in which standard language and additive bilingualism have been used as instruments of oppression by making bilingual speakers feel they lack something or are deficient, end up perpetuating division and generating the kinds of conflict that the teachers in this study refer to when they reflect on their languaging practices. This is where translanguaging as a paradigm comes in. Conceptually, translanguaging took off in 2009, when Ofelia García drew from Cen Williams, who had coined the term to refer to a specific bilingual pedagogy and practice in which Welsh students alternated languages in different ways. García has since expanded the term to refer to 'the deployment of a speaker's full linguistic repertoire without regard for watchful adherence to the socially and politically defined boundaries of named (and usually national and state) languages' (Otheguy *et al.*, 2015: 283).

On This Study

This study draws on a project of poetic inquiry conducted with a group of graduate in-service teachers and undergraduate pre-service student teachers, enrolled in the programs of Bilingual Education and TESOL, at a large public college in New York, where I am a professor. The students were enrolled in a required course: Teaching Native Language Arts and Reading in Spanish. The analysis includes the poetic material of 33 students from three different cohorts that took the course in Fall 2018, Spring 2019 and Fall 2019. Each cohort, heterogeneous in composition, included pre-service teachers working in schools as part of their practicum, and in-service teachers earning their MA degree. Participants lived and taught in one of four boroughs in New York: Manhattan, Queens, the Bronx and Brooklyn. All participants self-identified as bilingual and spoke Spanish in the context of the class.

Study participants were tasked to write a free verse poem to 'reflect on their idea of being bilingual'. No further prompts were provided. Writing about being bilingual is something they are used to doing in the context of their program in Bilingual Education. The writing prompt was deliberately left open, and students had the freedom to write whatever they considered to be poetry. My analysis and discussion include the full corpus, but the narrative for this study could only accommodate a sample of the poems, chosen on the basis of representation.

Data analysis drew primarily on an inductive approach, using the principles of thematic analysis – coding text, examining the data for similarities and differences, creating categories of similar codes and generating themes to establish connections to the main drivers in the theories undergirding my understanding of language, bilingual education and translanguaging. I paid special attention to categories that could inform teacher practice and highlight educational implications. Limitations exist in the way these categories may highlight aspects relevant to my own practice and positionality, but I attempt to overcome these limitations by showcasing the poetic artifacts themselves, letting the participants' voices come through directly. I did not focus on figures of speech, such as metaphors or imagery, nor did I use specific literary devices as vehicles for analysis.

Poetic Inquiry as a Method

The use of poetry in research spans several decades. Its use across disciplines as a form of qualitative research has had multiple labels based on function: poetic transcription, ethnographic poetry, narrative of the self, research poetry, among others. In an attempt to unify these varied approaches, Prendergast (2009) coined the term 'poetic inquiry' to include several forms of poetry in research.

Since then, poetic inquiry has been used to refer to the use of poetry in any part of the research process: 'before a project analysis, as a project analysis, or as a product of research itself' (Faulkner, 2017: 201). Poetic inquiry is both a method and a product of research activity. Scholars interviewed by Faulkner gave a variety of reasons for their use of poetic inquiry: for its 'sustained and contemplative love of language' (Faulkner, 2017: 211); because citing poetry reveals 'truths that are not usually evident'; and because 'it's like the Matryoshka dolls; poetic inquiry goes further inside to the hidden, or waiting, treasure that the first, or second, glance does not give access to' (as cited in Faulkner, 2017: 219).

A common critique of the use of poetic inquiry has arisen around the definition and quality of the poetry in question: 'Poetic inquiry is not a welcome all for poorly constructed poetry; however, advocating for tightly bound definitions of work that is intended to be exploratory, evocative, and expressive would debilitate the field' (Cutts & Waters, 2019: 3). On this subject, Faulkner (2007) wrote, 'I am tired of reading and listening to lousy poetry that masquerades as research and vice versa' (Faulkner, 2007: 220). In this context, she suggests that researchers should consider why they are using poetry, what they seek to accomplish through the medium of poetry, and how they intend to use poetry in their studies. As a response to similar critiques regarding the purity of poetry as a genre, Leggo (2008) argued: 'I am concerned that some researchers put poetry on a pedestal as an object for awe-inspiring reverence. I like to stress that poetry is earthy, rooted in everyday experience, connected integrally to the flow of blood in our bodies, expressed constantly in the rhythms of our speech and embodied movement' (Leggo, 2008: 170).

As such, I align myself to the view that there are some generally accepted practices in the use of poetic inquiry, but there is no mandated paradigm on what constitutes poetry. One of the virtues of poetic representation, in whatever form that may be, is that it provides the researcher, as well as the reader, with a 'different lens through which to view the same scenery, and thereby understand data, and themselves, in different and more complex ways' (Sparkes *et al.*, as cited in Van Giessen, 2020: 155).

Analysis of Poetic Artifacts

At the core of the thematic analysis across the body of data lies what I have called a languaging dilemma. Students have expressed, with imagery, and in many forms, a continuous tension that inhabits their bilingual identity, their translanguaging practices, or their use of Spanish in varied contexts. These poems reflect an ongoing struggle to honor their language(s), while depicting uncertainty, confusion or shame in the use of one or both languages. Driving premises of this struggle include: (1) Language separation or division, feeling uncertain as to how or when they should use one or the other language or both, the perception that these languages are separate and that this separation is reinforced by school and community; (2) Language shame, feeling inadequate in one language or another, expressing the deep connections between their language and their origin, their or their families' immigration history, and the difficulties in navigating labels, expected proficiency benchmarks in one language or the other; and (3) Translanguaging ethos in which, almost by intuition, they recreate the need to see their languages as part of the same system.

I refer to their grappling with this process as a dilemma, for they seem to be torn between honoring a language that has clear connections to their home, families and communities, and the discursive forces that have shaped a hegemonic understanding of language use. While these students have been exposed to translanguaging theories and perspectives in their educational programs, the images that emerge in their poetic artifacts perpetuate a pre-existing conception of their languages as separate, and often at odds with each other. Embedded in this separation is the represented physical distancing of their languaging practices: Spanish is for home, English is for school. There is recurrent use of imagery depicting the embodiment of language: in their heart, their veins, their tongue, their mind. This visualization is often accompanied by a reference to the integrity of language, and to their languages as being 'split, divided, whole'.

The underlining premise of Ofelia García's conceptualization on translanguaging is that languages are not separate, they are a single unified system within which multilinguals engage. The depictions of separation in these poems undergird the importance of a translanguaging perspective. Separation is painful and thrusts multilingual speakers into a state of continuous tension – hence the dilemma I have described – in which they believe they constantly have to decide how and when to use which language. As can be seen in the poems below, the perceived separation does not operate in a vacuum, but comes instead as part of a hierarchy that puts languages at odds with each other.

I have included a series of poems and fragments to illustrate the analysis above. Their imagery is explicit and clear, so I have let these artifacts speak for themselves as you travel through the narrative. Some poems were in written in Spanish, I have provided literal translations in my attempt to honor the integrity of the original.

The race that will never be won
By S. Fuentes.

Like two lovers longing to meet,	*Like two lovers longing to meet*
Mi Español estrecha la mano	*My Spanish stretches it's hand*
Pero no lo alcanza	*It can't reach*
El ingles, siempre Adelante	*English, always Ahead*
Sin mirar atrás	*Without looking back*

Translate this for me
By A. Alqushi
Translate this for me
My Grandma would say;
Looking down at 10 year old me
Awaiting a reply.
My tongue forming the words
She wanted to hear.
An everyday practice,
Speaking one language and then another.
No more needing to stop and think
To search for the words that are always in the back of my mind.
The words that split me in half
But what makes me whole.

From these two poems above, we can highlight the imagery of running after English, and never catching up, as well as the awareness of language separation that split in half, but also makes us whole. We begin to see here the emerging awareness of the internalized relationship between these two, perceived as separate, languages.

Bilingual me
By N. Reyes

(..)
Bilingual since birth
The irony is I learned English where my Latin roots are rooted
Even though I was born in NY part of my heart will always be in DR

In my head it isn't two languages it is more like one mixed together
Sometimes I will start in English and finish in Spanish
However, it feels like I have both cultures playing tug of war

In the fragment above, I highlight the understanding that her languages are not two but one; and yet the idea of 'tug of war' further represents the tension between both languages. A recurrent theme across the corpus of poems was the intricate interconnection between family and community and the development and honoring of a language, as expressed in the following piece:

I owe it to my Grandma
By A. Martinez

Ma
Me
Mi
Mo
Mu
mamá, amo, ama,
Mi mamá me ama
'Vieja, mira lo que te traje'
I owe it to my grandma
As she sat down with me and modeled how to say each and
every word from that book
Nacho is the name

I owe it to my grandma
For welcoming me into the bilingual world

'Vieja, en la escuela puedes hablar en ingles, pero en casa tienes
que hablar en español'
'Woman, you can speak english in school, but at home you
have to speak Spanish'
{...}

I owe it to my grandma for welcoming me into the bilingual world
Where I can now welcome others
Gracias Mama.

The following poem further illustrates the impact of *othering* forces and how raciolinguistic ideologies shape their understanding of their languaging practices:

Oh Spanish
By M. Silos

Me acuerdo que era solo lo que sabía y pues amaba De las novelas a la música	*I remember it was the only thing I knew and loved From novels to music*

Hasta que fuiste me peor pesadilla	*Until one day you became my worst nightmare*
Un susto, ay como poder olvidar	*How scared I was, how can I forget*
El odio que sentía por ti	*The hatred I felt for you*
Porque a mi	*Why me*
porque yo	*Why did you have to be part of my life*
porque tuviste que ser parte de mi vida	
Si todos me miraban y pensaban que no era	*If everyone looked and thought it wasn't*
español y de repente que sabían que era español	*Spanish, and they realized it was Spanish*
me miraban de manera diferente	*They looked at me differently*
Porque tan o Fortunata ser español	*Why Oh Fortuna be in Spanish*
Tan cerca ser blanca pero a la misma vez tan lejos...	*So close to being White and at the same time so far*
(Eso es lo que sentía cuando crecí con el label de que no sabía English. De que era inferior a los demás.)	*(This is what I felt when I didn't know English, that I was less than everyone else)*

Mi Lenguaje No es Perfecto
D. Gomez

My language is not perfect
I know you're Dominican,
No hablas ingles. / You don't speak English
Are you dumb?
Am I dumb,
'How are you feeling today?'
I feel good.
But why you don't sound American.
How does an American sound?
You're grammar is horrible.
Does that mean I am horrible?
Tengo que cambiar, Tengo que entender, Tengo que ser mas Americana.
{I have to change, I have to understand, I have to be more American}

Español vives en mi
By A. Heimbu

Español, el idioma de mi tierra,	*Spanish you live in me*
Mi corazón te lleva adentro	*Spanish, the language of my land*
Vas clavado en mi sangre y en mi piel,	*You live inside my heart*
	You are forever in my skin and blood
Español, Español, Español!	*Spanish, Spanish, Spanish!*
Lengua tan exquisita y divina	*Such a divine and exquisite language*

Estoy en el medio de una lengua que	*I am in the middle of a language*
es la mía pero no lo es	*that is mine, but isn't*
no soy perfecta en ella	*I am not perfect in it*
tampoco en ninguna otra	*But neither in another language*
Una relación contradictoria, confusa	*A confusing, contradictory relationship*
Una relación a medias	*A relationship split in half*
Español mi lengua materna	*Spanish, my mother tongue*
Es un honor para mi.	*It is an honor for me*

The continued presence of perceived separation and hierarchy marks the impossibility of several languages coexisting dynamically in heart and mind. Of note is the continuous use of physical embodiment of the language in blood, heart, skin, veins as depicted in multiple poems.

Spanish
By V. Espino

Español · *Spanish*

Español	*Spanish*
No eres tan solo un lenguage,(sic)	*You are not only a language*
eres una forma de vida,	*You are a way of life*
eres parte de mi ser.	*You are part of who I am*
Te llevo como bandera,	*I carry you like a flag*
grabado como un tatuaje,	*Embedded like a tattoo*
a cada lugar que llego,	*Everywhere I go*
eres mi carta de presentacion.	*You are my presentation card*
Aunque compartas espacio	*Even if you share space*
con un nuevo lenguage	*With a new language*
en mi mente y en mi corazon	*In my mind and in my heart,*
siempre seras el primero.	*You will always be the first*

The power of language
By S. Pena

Florida born
American born
But feel lost in between and torn
Two Languages
Two cultures
Too much baggage
To handle
People still saddle up and paddle
To a country idolized by immigrants
Capitalist
Built on immigrants
Yet we do not have power
We are though as less

In America
Everywhere else we are more
I am more than just American

Cibaeña	*Cibaeña*
Caine es Carne	
Aiguna es alguna	*Mea\ is Meat*
Saiga es salga	*So\ is some*
Ta es esta	*Ou\ is Out*
Pote es frasco	*The\ is there*
Y jevi es bueno	*Ja\ is Jar*
	Go\ is good
Este es mi Español	*This is my Spanish.*
El Español del Cibao	*The Spanish of Cibao.*
El Español de Ciudad Corazon	*The Spanish of Ciudad Corazo*
El español de Santiago, RD	*The Spanish of Santiago, DR.*
El Español que es criticado,	*The Spanish that is criticized*
Porque la jente es pobre	*Because people are poor*
Porque somos del campo	*Because we come from the countryside*
Pero saben que mi jente	*But you know, my people*
Es pobre, humilde y trabajadora	*They are hardworking, poor and humble*
Y yo estoy orgullosa de	*And I'm proud of being a CIBAEÑA.*
Ser una CIBAEÑA	

While most poems depict the tension between Spanish and English, the poem above represents the varied tensions between Spanish as a colonizing language and other, minoritized, languages. This serves as a reminder to be continuously engaging in critical exploration of language hierarchies in the US context and beyond.

Querido acento
By J. Taveras

Querido acento,	*Dear Accent*
Tú eres la razón por la que siento miedo de hablar.	*You are the reason I am afraid to speak.*
Querido acento,	*Dear accent,*
Tú eres la razón por la que no comparto mis ideas.	* You are the reason I don't share my ideas.*
Querido acento,	*Dear accent,*
Eres lo que me hace sentir menos 'inteligente'.	*You are what makes me feel less smart.*
	Dear accent,
Querido acento,	* Sometimes I just want to get rid*
A veces sólo quiero deshacerme de ti.	*of you.*

Querido acento, Tú defines lo que soy.	*Dear Accent,* *You define who I am.*

Querido acento,
   Un día no me preocuparé por
ti porque lo más importante es
poder comprender, escribir y leer en
Inglés. Tu acento es una parte de mis
características de lo que soy.
	Dear Accent,
	   One day I won't worry about
	you because the most important
	thing is to understand, read and
	write in English. You are part of
	who I am.

Accent bias has been widely documented (Orelus, 2016) and as a practice of linguistic profiling perpetuates dangerous discriminatory practices towards students, as well as deep internalized feelings of inadequacy as expressed in the poem above.

Discussion and Conclusion

What the analysis of this body of poetic artifacts shows, in full, is how bilingual speakers grapple with the internalized hegemonic forces that police their languaging practices. Key among the findings is the depiction of a constant struggle between the students' perceived separate languages. This tension is expressed through the systematic use of descriptors such as war, separation, split, fight, division and feeling torn, among others. Their perception of how their languages exist as separate and conflicted entities reaffirms García's (2009) view on monoglossic language ideologies and the urgent need to further introduce translanguaging paradigms.

Ofelia García's lifetime work has been devoted to understanding how bilingualism and language policy operate across multiple levels, from the students and teachers she has worked with to the programs she has observed and the policies that inform them, in the United States and across the world. She has done this in pursuit of social justice and to advocate for the dismantling of minoritizing policies and practices. While translanguaging as a theoretical device is probably the most publicized aspect of her recent work, I view translanguaging as a critical synthesis of her work, the genesis of which began many decades ago with her systematic efforts to deeply and lovingly observe children and their ecosystems and actively advocate for the full use of the children's linguistic repertoire. Translanguaging is political because Ofelia's work has always been political in the many ways she has studied and advocated for historicizing our views on bilingualism, engaging in situated understandings of languaging practices across the globe, highlighting structural and social particularities for different ways of understanding language policy, advocating for different ways of knowing and producing knowledge and – critically – believing that educators are agents of social change. In that sense, translanguaging is the epitome of her critical approach to language education, decolonizing existing language hierarchies and liberating students from the monoglossic hegemony of language education policies.

The conceptual configuration of translanguaging will no doubt continue to evolve, both in Ofelía's own work and in the work of others who have explored and expanded its use and understanding across disciplines and geographical sites. As we continue to learn more about translanguaging, and to expand the concept empirically as a practice, as a pedagogy and as an epistemology, there are two areas I would like to highlight.

First, in the process of theorizing translanguaging, I would caution, in my role as a teacher educator, against a potential trend to position translanguaging in opposition to bilingualism or bilingual education. Standard, subtractive/additive approaches to bilingualism may reinforce monoglossic language ideologies by encouraging strict language separation, as García (2020), citing Kuhn and Neumann (2020) asserted: 'Bilingualism is more likely to push back translanguaging than to support it' (García, 2020: 16). However, extending this premise might result in blanket warnings for bilingual education. We owe much to the conceptual and historical legacies of those who fought for bilingual education, including García herself. In her words: 'Translanguaging does not negate the existence of bilingualism or multilingualism as a sociocultural concept, the importance of which, especially in the lives of members of minoritized communities, is most important. But it does negate the idea that named languages are linguistic objects that can be assessed separately' (García et al., 2018: 52). The participants in this study all decided to become bilingual teachers as a result of their own experience with bilingual education. Their loyalty to the education they received and the way it shaped their identity is an important marker of the distinction that must be made between bilingual education that negates full use of speakers' repertoire, and dynamic, transformative bilingual education that contributes to dismantling existing structures of vigilance and power. Having students understand – and be exposed to – current systems of power, the idea of named languages, and the colonizing structures that exist and operate in themselves, are healthy, pedagogical and socially just mechanisms to ensure that bilingual education in practice doesn't perpetuate monoglossic language ideologies and reproduce existing hierarchies of language hegemony. All this can happen while still honoring the legacy of bilingualism and bilingual education efforts in this country. In 'Doing and Undoing Bilingual Education', García and Tupas (2019) further explore the potential tension between current bilingual programs and practices and their potential for transformative or oppressive practice. This question merits further discussion and empirical practice as we move forward in our understanding of translanguaging in the context of diverse bilingual education paradigms. Turner and Lin (2020) suggest a potential direction in which this discussion could go, questioning the epistemological conflict between disrupting language hierarchies while continuing to retain the educational objective of learning a named language. They argue that named languages are external social constructions imposed on a speaker, but emphasize that the ways in which speakers appropriate these constructions are not the same. These are key questions that lie at the intersection of our understanding and the potential tension between standard bilingual education and translanguaging.

Second, translanguaging as a pedagogy has been questioned, with some (i.e. Jaspers, 2018) suggesting that it could potentially be exacerbating inequalities. In his piece on the limiting transformative power of translanguaging, Jaspers (2018) asserts that 'translanguaging scholars share a number of convictions with the monolingual authorities they criticize, that their transformative claims trade on causality effects that cannot be taken for granted, and that translanguaging, at least in some of its representations, is becoming a dominating rather than a liberating force' (Jaspers, 2018: 3). Some of Jaspers' concerns stem from his own empirical experience with the practice, which is bound to happen as the concept is expanded, interpreted and executed in different ways across diverse contexts.

However, variation in implementation of translanguaging pedagogies does not, in itself, dilute the transformative potential of the practice. As translanguaging continues to be promoted as a pedagogical practice and discussed in academic literature, those engaging in these practices require a deep understanding of translanguaging as a whole paradigm. This should go beyond seeing translanguaging as a fixed practice of moving from one language to another, and include instead a deep willingness to embark on a learning journey that begins by finding out more about how internalized mechanisms of colonial legacy have shaped our understanding of language(s), investigating which kinds of mechanisms of inclusion and exclusion exist in our particular language context, exploring what role raciolinguistic ideologies play in our understanding of language education and asking how our students navigate their languaging practices, etc.

This should become the first step of what García (2020: 16) has called the translanguaging stance, which is 'grounded in uncovering the colonial difference and the ways in which language, bilingualism and multilingualism have been used, and continue to be used, to minoritize and racialize conquered and colonized populations'. The second step of this journey should then involve thinking about the ways in which translanguaging pedagogies can support a dynamic view of bilingualism and help students deploy their full linguistic repertoire. This might require educators to serve as advocates within their current educational programs, upholding a commitment to dynamic bilingualism that reflects their translanguaging stance. By actively inhabiting the full spectrum of translanguaging, educators have the potential to turn it into a tool for reversing structural inequities. The journey into translanguaging is dialectic and calls for further efforts of guided communities, research, and dialogue around its conceptual understandings and pedagogical application. These recommendations relate not only to educators in the United States, but to educators worldwide who are engaging in language education.

Post-Reading Discussion Questions

(1) How can educators of language minoritized students engage in a dynamic understanding of translanguaging that includes critical awareness of the colonial matrix of power (Mignolo, 2005) while upholding its use as pedagogical practice?

(2) How can educators delink from the underlying oppression of named languages while honoring those named languages as social, not linguistic objects?

References

Camargo, M. (2019) Native tongues. Poem by study participant. February 2019, New York City.

Cutts, M. and Waters, M. (2019) Poetic approaches to qualitative data analysis. *Education Publications*. 145.

Faulkner, S.L. (2007) Concern with craft: Using ars poetica as criteria for reading research poetry. *Qualitative Inquiry* 13 (2), 218–234.

Faulkner, S.L. (2017) Poetic inquiry: Poetry as/in/for social research. In P. Leavy (ed.) *The Handbook of Arts-Based Research* (pp. 208–230). New York, NY: Guilford Press.

Flores, B. (2005) The intellectual presence of the deficit view of Spanish speaking children in the educational literature during the 20th century. In P. Pedraza and M. Rivera (eds) *Latino Education: An Agenda for Community Action Research*. Mahwah, NJ: Erlbaum.

Flores, N. and Rosa, J. (2015) Undoing appropriateness: Raciolinguistic ideologies and language diversity in education. *Harvard Educational Review* 85 (2), 149–171.

García, O. (2009) *Bilingual Education in the 21st Century: A Global Perspective*. Malden, MA: Wiley-Blackwell.

García, O. (2020) Singularity, complexities and contradictions: A commentary about translanguaging, social justice, and education. In J. Panagiotopoulou, L. Rosen and J. Strzykala (eds) *Inclusion, Education and Translanguaging* (pp. 11–20). Wiesbaden: Springer VS.

García, O. and Tupas, R. (2019) Doing and undoing bilingualism in education. In A. De Houwer and L. Ortega (eds) *The Cambridge Handbook of Bilingualism* (pp. 390–407). Cambridge: Cambridge University Press.

García, O., Johnson, S. and Seltzer, K. (2017) *The Translanguaging Classroom. Leveraging Student Bilingualism for Learning*. Philadelphia, PA: Caslon.

García, O., Menken, K., Velasco, P. and Vogel, S. (2018) Dual language bilingual education in NYC: A potential unfulfilled. In M.B. Arias and M. Fee (eds) *Profiles of Dual Language Education in the 21st Century* (pp. 38–55). Washington D.C. and Bristol: Center for Applied Linguistics and Multilingual Matters.

Gutierrez, K. (2008) Language and literacies as civil rights. *Counterpoints* 316, 169–184.

Jaspers, J. (2018) The transformative limits of translanguaging. *Language & Communication* 58 (January), 1–10.

Leggo, C. (2008) Astonishing silence: Knowing in poetry. In J.G. Knowles and A. Cole (eds) *Handbook of the Arts in Qualitative Research* (pp. 165–174). Thousand Oaks, CA: Sage.

Makoni, S. and Pennycook, A. (2007) *Disinventing and Reconstituting Languages*. Clevedon: Multilingual Matters.

Mignolo, W. (2005) *The Idea of Latin America*. Malden, MA: Blackwell.

Orelus, P. (2016) Accentism exposed: A critical analysis of accent discrimination with some implications for students' languages rights. In P.W. Orelus (ed.) *Language, Race, and Power in Schools: A Critical Discourse Analysis*. New York, NY: Routledge.

Otheguy, R., García, O. and Reid, W. (2015) Clarifying translanguaging and deconstructing named languages: A perspective from linguistics. *Applied Linguistics Review* 6 (3), 281–307.

Prendergast, M. (2009) "Poem is What?" Poetic Inquiry in Qualitative Social Science Research. *International Review of Qualitative Research* 1 (4), 541–568.

Tejeda, C. and Gutierrez, K.D. (2005) Fighting the backlash: Decolonizing perspectives and pedagogies in neocolonial times. In P. Pedrazza and M. Rivera (eds) *Latino Education: An Agenda for Community Action Research*. Mahwah, NJ: Erlbaum.

Turner, M. and Lin, A.M.Y. (2020) Translanguaging and named languages: Productive tension and desire. *International Journal of Bilingual Education and Bilingualism* 23 (4), 423–433.

Van Giessen, E. (2020) Reflexive poetry: A researcher's poetic personal narrative on social science research praxis. *New Sociology: Journal of Critical Praxis* 1 (1).

Part 3: Bilingual Community Education

10 Parental Voices in Bilingual Education

Li Wei and Zhu Hua

Pre-Reading

García, O. (2011) *Bilingual Education in the 21st Century: A Global Perspective*. Oxford: Wiley-Blackwell

May, S. (ed.) (2013) *The Multilingual Turn: Implications for SLA, TESOL, and Bilingual Education*. Oxford: Routledge.

Pre-Reading Discussion Questions

(1) What are the key agencies in the education of bilingual learners? What role can families and parents play in this context?

(2) In what way can translanguaging transform our understanding of bilingual education in the 21st century?

As García points out (2009: 151) 'All successful education relies heavily on parents and schools sharing the same values'. And translanguaging is about giving voice to the inherent minoritized bilinguals, which, in the context of education, must include the parents. This chapter makes the case for the parents' voices to be heard and taken seriously in implementing translanguaging approaches to teaching and learning in heritage language classes for children of immigrant and transnational backgrounds. We argue that this is important not simply because the parents are key stakeholders in education whose views should be taken seriously in any case, but because parents' own experiences with bilingualism and bilingual education can shape their views. We draw upon examples from the Chinese complementary schools in Britain. These schools are set up by the parents and the community to meet the needs of the families with regard to developing language and literacy skills in Chinese amongst the British-born children. While the school policy appears to focus primarily on the development of Chinese, translanguaging is common practice both in learning and teaching at the school and in building an extended social network. Nevertheless, the complementary schools are often perceived by the wider society as an example of minoritized communities wanting to insist on their own ethnic languages at the cost of English and to transmit these languages to the British-born generations. So how do the parents see the role of the Chinese complementary schools? How do they perceive translanguaging practices at these schools? What's more, how do the parents see their own children growing up in Britain?

Complementary Education and the Chinese Schools in the UK

First, a brief outline of the policy context of complementary schooling in Britain is necessary. Complementary schooling in the UK refers to language and literacy classes organized by minoritized transnational communities outside the normal school hours, usually over the weekend. Their primary aim is to teach the British-born children of these communities the heritage languages, especially the literacy in these languages. According to the National Resource Centre for Supplementary Education (NRCSE) https://www.supplementaryeducation.org.uk/, there are between 3000 and 5000 complementary schools offering some 100 different languages, from Albanian and Bengali to Vietnamese and Urdu. Many of them were set up in the 1950s amidst racial tensions and failures of the mainstream education system to understand and accommodate the needs of minoritized children. Li Wei (2006) reviewed the sociopolitical history of the complementary school movement in Britain and argued that the existence of these schools reflected a failure of the mainstream school system not meeting the needs of the immigrant and ethnic minority children and their communities.

The current Chinese community in the UK is developed from post-war migrants, the vast majority of whom came from Hong Kong in the 1950s. Most of them are Cantonese and/or Hakka speakers. Initially they were engaged in family-based catering businesses and other service industries. Since the 1980s, Chinese migrants from mainland China have been arriving in Britain. Most of them are educational transients who are in the UK for various levels of education. Some have stayed on. There are also professionals who take up jobs in Britain. UK immigration regulations determine that anyone wishing to settle in this country needs to have guaranteed employment. The 1997 return of sovereignty of Hong Kong to China triggered a small wave of new immigrants from Hong Kong. Again, they needed to have employment or substantial investment in order to gain settled status. Growth of the British Chinese community is mainly by the British-born generations. There has been a visible change of the hierarchy of the different Chinese languages in the Chinese community in Britain. The old community *lingua franca*, Cantonese, is being replaced by a new community *lingua franca*,

Mandarin or Putonghua. This is clearly influenced by the rise of China as a major political and economic world power (Zhu & Li, 2014). In the meantime, an intergenerational language shift from Chinese to English-dominant bilingualism/multilingualism has taken place. The majority of the British-born Chinese use English as their primary language of communication, even in the home setting.

Community language schools have been one of the three pillars of the Chinese diaspora worldwide; the other two being townsmen associations and community media. Wherever there is a Chinese immigrant community, there is bound to be a Chinese school. They are not only providing language teaching to the younger generations of Chinese heritage, but also a key social network connecting families who typically live in dispersed areas. In the UK, Chinese schools began to emerge in the 1970s and had a significant growth in number in the early 1990s. The UK Federation of Chinese Schools (http://www.ukfcs.info/) estimates that there are between 200 and 300 Chinese complementary schools of various sizes from about 30 pupils to 300 or 400 pupils, in all parts of England, Scotland, Wales and Northern Ireland.

The establishment of the Chinese schools must be seen as a major achievement of the community in their determination to support themselves. These schools receive little support from the local education authorities. They are entirely self-financed. Parents pay fees to send their children, and local Chinese businesses offer sponsorships and other support (e.g. paying for the hire of premises and facilities). Many of the schools use teaching materials provided free of charge by voluntary organizations and other agencies in mainland China, Hong Kong and Taiwan. The teachers are mainly enthusiastic Chinese parents and university students. In the last two decades, a pattern has emerged with four types of Chinese schools: (a) for Cantonese-speaking children from Hong Kong immigrant families; (b) for Cantonese-speaking children of Hong Kong immigrant families with particular religious affiliations (i.e. run by Christian churches); (c) for Mandarin-speaking children from mainland China; and (d) for Mandarin-speaking children of Buddhist families, mainly from Taiwan. Most of the schools run classes over the weekend for up to four hours. Parents play a crucial role in the schools – they pay, govern and teach. A typical Chinese complementary school in Britain looks like this: It rents its premises from a local school or education center. There is a temporary reception desk at the entrance for parents to speak to the teachers about any issues of interest. A sales desk or area is available for the children to buy snacks and drinks. Space is provided for the staff to have tea and coffee during break time and to have meetings. The children are grouped according to proficiency in Chinese. There are traditional Chinese dance, arts and sports sessions before or after the language and literacy sessions. Many schools also provide English language lessons for parents.

There are significant differences between the teachers' and the pupils' linguistic proficiency and preference: The teachers tend to be Chinese first language (L1) speakers; many of them have had a substantial monolingual experience as Chinese speakers, and their literacy level in Chinese is high; whereas the pupils have had limited and context-specific input in Chinese, have high proficiency in English, and use English as the *lingua franca* with their peers, including other children of Chinese ethnic origin. The children's English language proficiency in most cases is much more sophisticated than that of the teachers. What is happening in most of the Chinese complementary schools in the UK is rather similar to the situation Cen Williams (1994) described in terms of *trawsieithu* in Welsh revitalization schools where the input by the teacher and output by the pupils are often in two different languages. Li and Wu (2009) examined examples of how children manipulate the discrepancies in the language proficiencies and preferences in Chinese and English between themselves and their teachers to their own advantages in the classroom. When the teachers struggle to make the pupils understand something in Chinese, they often switch to English for explanations. Many teachers are keen to engage in co-learning (Li Wei, 2013) through translanguaging. They put themselves in a 'vulnerable' (Brantmeier, 2013) rather than authoritative position, open themselves up to pupils' bringing their own knowledge and skills into the learning process, and provide space for the pupils as well as themselves to maximize their bilingual potential by using whatever language they feel the most comfortable with.

It has to be said that we have been working with the Chinese complementary schools for more than two decades and have been promoting the idea of translanguaging, rather than an insistence on Chinese only, in the school context. The teachers are generally very happy to adopt a translanguaging pedagogy. They do recognize that the pupils are bilingual and multilingual British-Chinese, not monolingual Chinese in mainland China or Hong Kong. But some are concerned that the parents, who spend time and money to send their children to the Chinese schools, many of whom are running the schools behind the scenes, may not think that translanguaging would help to enhance their children's learning of Chinese, especially Chinese literacy. So what do the parents actually think?

Parental Voices

We have been studying the Chinese complementary schools in the UK since the 1990s through various projects. In particular, we carried out in-depth ethnographic observations in the Chinese schools in Newcastle, Manchester and London between 2005 and 2008. These were followed with further projects in Chinese schools in London in

2014 to 2016. As we said above, most of the complementary schools run for 3–4 hours over the weekend. Our ethnographic work was done during those hours, when we observed classes, talked to the teachers and the pupils, as well as the parents. We asked questions and listened to their views. None of these were formal, structured interviews. But our discussions with the parents focused on a number of themes: (i) their reasons to send their children to Chinese complementary schools; (ii) their beliefs in the importance of their children knowing Chinese especially Chinese literacy; (iii) their understanding of the children's identity; and (iv) flexible bilingual/multilingual approaches to learning as opposed to insistence on Chinese only at school and at home. Views on the first three themes were often voiced together. We will therefore discuss them together in the following. The fourth theme on translanguaging practice was the focus of our projects and will be discussed separately.

Language ideology and identity

The data below are from our work in the largest Chinese schools in London in 2014 and 2016, schools with over 300 pupils. We talked to more than 50 parents on different occasions during the fieldwork period. All the parents we talked to voiced strong beliefs that attending the Chinese school was beneficial to the children. This is not surprising because these are parents who chose to send their children to the complementary schools. But the reasons given by the parents differed. Some hold strong beliefs about the symbolic significance of the Chinese language, especially the writing system, as Parent A expressed:

> Parent A (Mother, Cantonese L1 speaker): (NB. Cantonese speaker's remarks are given in complex Chinese characters, and Mandarin speakers in simplified characters, followed by English translation in italics.)
> 要學中文啦。中國人不懂中文還叫Chinese嗎？你看有些小孩，連自己的名字都不識。在家裡也說外語，speak English all the time。我們沒有時間教他們啦。聽是可以的，但中文學校教他們writing。好難的，我們都不知怎麼教。小朋友在一起學比較好。
> *They should learn Chinese. How can you be Chinese and don't know the language? You see some children can't even recognize their own name (in writing). They speak English even at home. /speak English all the time/ We don't have the time to teach them. They can understand (spoken Chinese), but the Chinese school teaches them writing. It's very difficult to teach (writing). We don't know how to teach (writing). Children learn better together with other children.*

She links the ability to read and write Chinese, which has a logographic writing system, to 'being Chinese': one cannot be Chinese if one does not read or write the Chinese characters. Similar views seem to be very common amongst the Chinese and have been reported elsewhere (Li & Zhu, 2010). She also sees learning together with other children as beneficial.

Parent B sent her daughter to the Chinese school also to learn the Chinese characters. But she brought up another issue, which is to do with making Chinese friends and feeling connected with other Chinese people and the Chinese culture.

> Parent B (Mother, Mandarin L1 speaker):
> 在家她是跟我们讲中文的，所以听和说都没有什么问题。到中文学校主要是想让她学汉字了。她只能看很少的。其实也不只是学中文啦。平时都没有几个中国朋友，这里还是有点文化氛围的。她也交了些朋友挺好的。我们也交了些朋友的。
> *She does speak Chinese with us at home. So she has no problem in listening and speaking. We sent her to the Chinese school to learn to read and write the Chinese characters. She can understand very few of them. But in fact it is not just about learning Chinese. She has very few Chinese friends during normal school days. Here (the Chinese school) provides a cultural atmosphere. It is good that she can make some Chinese friends. We have also made some friends.*

When we further probed her about the 'cultural atmosphere' she meant, assuming that she had the cultural activities such as Chinese music, dance, painting, kung-fu etc. in mind, her response was very interesting:

> Parent B:
> 就是在这里啦，和其他中国人在一起，聊聊天，speak Chinese, drink tea。在中国人的圈里呀。
> *Just being here, with other Chinese people, chatting, (speak Chinese, drink tea), in a Chinese circle.*

She is not essentializing the Chinese culture with stereotypical activities. To her being in the presence of other Chinese people is sufficient to provide a cultural environment for her and her daughter's upbringing as a Chinese person.

Meeting other Chinese people and making friends seem to be a key motivation for lots of parents to want to send their children to the Chinese complementary schools, as Parent C says:

> Parent C (from southern China, speaking a number of Chinese dialects):
> 交朋友啦！学点中文，但主要还是交朋友。你看她们在一起还是说英语。It's OK啦。BBC都是这样的。在学校也没有什么华人同学。这里交朋友啦。她们一起组织活动。去年夏天她们和朋友家去度假，不用跟我们啦。挺好的。
> *Making friends (is why we want to send our daughters to the Chinese school)! Learning some Chinese, but most importantly, making friends.*

You look at them: they are all speaking English with each other. (It's ok.) BBC (British-born Chinese) are like that. They don't have any Chinese school mates. They can make friends here. They do things together. Last summer, she went on holiday with their friend's family. They don't need us anymore, which is good.

She accepts that even at the Chinese school, the British-born children tend to talk to each other in English. But like Parent B, Parent C believes that the Chinese school helps the children to make more friends with other Chinese and provides a social support network for them all, which is more important than simply learning the language.

Parent D, on the other hand, expresses a view that the Chinese language is useful for the children's future.

Parent D (father from Hong Kong, fluent in Cantonese, Mandarin and English):
中文當然有用啦。大陸經濟越來越好，歐洲不行呀。英國Brexit一塌糊塗。年輕人將來都沒有好工作。懂中文也許會有幫助的。去香港大陸工作也好啦，我們都可以。只要他們能找到自己喜歡的事就可以的。在這裡也可以給中國公司做事啦。我就在大陸公司作啦。所以我學普通話。

Chinese is of course useful. Mainland China's economy is getting better and better, whereas Europe is getting nowhere. Brexit has made a mess for Britain. It's going to be more and more difficult for young people to find good jobs. Knowing Chinese may help. They can go and work in Hong Kong or mainland China. We (parents) would be happy about that. As long as they can find something they like, it's fine. They can also work for Chinese companies here (in Britain). I'm in fact working for a mainland Chinese company. That's why I learned Putonghua.

Aspiration of future life has been found to be an important factor in transnational communities' choice and decision-making regarding language use and language learning (Zhu & Li, 2016). Parent D articulated a view that knowing Chinese could help to enhance his children's employment opportunities in the future, a view that is shared by many other parents we spoke to. He also set an example himself by learning Putonghua, the standardized national language in mainland China, to work for a mainland Chinese business, and further explained to us that he did not send his children to a Cantonese school because he felt Putonghua would be more useful.

A rather different reason was given by Parent E:

Parent E (Cantonese L1 speaker from Hong Kong):
他們是華人誰都看得出的。會不會受歧視？當然會的。你跟人家長得不一樣嘛！你又不會自己的語言，人家不笑話你嗎？都說華人孩子clever，你那麼clever連自己的話都不會讲，只会讲外语？

Everybody can see that they are Chinese. Will they be discriminated against? Of course they will. You look different from the others. If you can't even speak your own language, how can they not laugh at you? Everybody says that Chinese children are clever, but if you are that clever, how come you can only speak a foreign language but not your own language?

Whilst having generally been regarded as a successful immigrant community in the UK, the Chinese have experienced their share of racial discrimination. This mother is clearly aware of the discrimination and prejudice that is out there against the Chinese. She is also very much aware of the deeply rooted assumption of one-race-one-language in the British society, i.e. a Chinese person must know Chinese and English is always foreign or additional to the Chinese. Not knowing Chinese seems to be considered an embarrassment, even a shame, to the Chinese community.

School language policy and translanguaging pedagogy and practices

Turning now to the parental views of the language policy and practice in the Chinese complementary schools. The vast majority of the parents we spoke to seem to accept that the children are bilingual, and more importantly, British Chinese, not simply Chinese. They also accept, rather pragmatically, that the children's proficiency in Chinese is much lower than that in English. Translanguaging by the teacher in the classroom, therefore, was not regarded as a problem. The following was voiced by Parent B whose other comments we saw earlier.

Parent B:
有的老师是会用英语的，sometimes, it's OK。应为小孩子有的时候跟她们讲中文他们可能不会全能听懂，老师用英语解释一下也没关系啦。她们懂最好啦。
Some teachers use English in teaching. (Sometimes; it's OK.) Because sometimes when you speak Chinese to the children, they can't understand everything. It doesn't matter if the teacher explains it in English. It's best for them to understand.

Many parents say that whilst they want their children to learn to read and write Chinese, they would not expect them to have the same standard as the children in China.

Parent F (mother from mainland China):
在这里出生的孩子没有几个能读写汉字的，也不是在中国。 在中国他们就完蛋了， 定跟不上。在这里学一学简单的，差不多就可以，不是完全的文盲就好。

Very few of the children born here can read or write Chinese characters. But they are not in China. If they were in China, they would be finished. They can't follow the class. Here they can learn some basics. It's fine to know just a few, as long as they are not completely illiterate.

Like the other parents, this mother recognizes the difference between a British-born Chinese child living in Britain and children growing up in China. Literacy is clearly important. But the parents are not expecting their children to have the same standard as those in China. This quote also indicates that the parents are very much aware of the school standard in China and differences in pedagogical approaches, which the following quote confirms:

Parent G (father from mainland China):
我也说不好哪种教学方法好：英国的就像放野鸭子，中国的是填鸭。　其实他们并不一定能学到多少东西，但交了很多朋友，也有了华人感。教法不一定那么死板。
I can't say which pedagogy is better: the English way is like raising ducks in the wild, whereas the Chinese way is force feeding ducks. In fact they may not learn very much (in the Chinese school). But they make a lot of friends, and they gain a sense of being Chinese. Pedagogy shouldn't be so rigid.

When the Chinese school teachers give the children homework of copying characters repeatedly, many children and parents object, not only because they have little time other than the weekend to be devoted to the learning of Chinese, but also because they feel that it is an alien method in the British context as Parent G seems to be suggesting.

Many parents explicitly commented on the Chinese schools' teachers' teaching methods.

Parent H (mother from Hong Kong, Cantonese L1 speaker):
好多老師是中國留學生，好年輕呦。她們不懂得這些小孩子的學習習慣。教學方法比較和國內一樣。其實這樣不行的。他們不是中國小孩啦。大的環境不同嘛。
Many teachers here are students from China. They are so young. They don't understand the study habits of the children. Their teaching method is rather similar to those in China. It's not going to work. The children are not in China. The wider context is different.

Not understanding the children's study habits and needs is a concern that many parents have voiced about the teachers at the Chinese schools. They are indeed mostly young students from China who are clearly very good with their Chinese and eager to help with the overseas Chinese community. But their lack of knowledge of the cultural context, especially of the way children are taught and learn in ordinary schools in the UK presents a barrier in using the appropriate methods to teach the British

Chinese children in the complementary schools. Elsewhere Li (2013) discussed this issue in terms of co-learning in Chinese schools.

A few parents raised the issue of the teachers' English language proficiency.

> Parent I (father from mainland China):
> 有些老师英语很好，讲得很清楚。英语不太好的其实会有困难，学生的英语比老师的好，不好解释清楚。我儿子他们班里有两个广东小孩，父母是香港人，讲广东话。他们老师正好是广东人，有时跟他们讲广东话，给他们解释。我看挺好。
> *Some teachers have very good English. They explain very clearly. It's actually quite difficult if the teacher's English isn't very good. The students' English is usually better than the teachers'. It's not so easy to explain clearly (to the students if the teachers' English isn't good enough). There are two Cantonese-speaking kids in my son's class. Their parents are from Hong Kong, speaking Cantonese. As it happens the class teacher is a Cantonese speaker, and sometimes speaks Cantonese with them, explains to them (in Cantonese). I think that's very nice.*

This parent appears to accept that the teacher needs to explain in class in a language that the students understand and prefer. And the discrepancy in English language proficiency between the teachers and the pupils may put the teachers in a 'vulnerable' position in the sense defined by Brantmeier (2013). The parent also seems to think very positively of the dialect accommodation between the Cantonese-speaking teacher and the two Cantonese-speaking pupils. Translanguaging does enable the teacher to accommodate different linguistic needs of the pupils.

When specifically asked whether they had thought to insist on using Chinese only with and by the children, Parent J's response was quite typical:

> Parent J:
> They are British啦。在家裡他們也是講英語啦。 Bilingual啦嘛，英語華語都可以啦。堅持將中文也沒用的。他就不理啦，有代溝喔。
> *(They are British). They speak English at home too. They are bilingual. They can speak both English and Chinese. It's useless to insist on speaking Chinese only. They will ignore you, causing generation gap.*

Parents are clear about their children's identity as British Chinese and bilingual. They also seem to be concerned about a potential generation gap caused by differences in language proficiency and attitude. They therefore take a pragmatic approach to the issue of language use both at the Chinese school and at home.

While talking about the pedagogies in the Chinese complementary schools, the parents also comment on the practices of the mainstream schools that their children attend during the week. Like Parent G above, most parents are very aware of the different pedagogical traditions and approaches between the schools in Britain and those in China. Many feel that they do not have the opportunity to be involved in the running of the mainstream schools compared to what they can do about the Chinese schools.

> Parent H (father from Hong Kong):
> 中文學校是華人自己辦的學校嘛！這一點很重要，我們可以提意見。他們平常的學校不管我們的意見的。要贊助什麼活動的時候會找我們，平時不理我們的。家長會都是校長和老師在講，不會讓我們講的。其實有的時候他們老師教法有問題，可是我們也沒辦法，只能在家裡教小孩子學。有的時候又怕我們的方法不適合學校考試要求。（會不會以為家長不懂英語？）不清楚，有可能的。可能以為我們都不懂怎麼教。中文學校不一樣的。我們隨時可以提意見和建議。這裡的校長也是家長了，有的老師也是家長。和我們都一樣。大家都一樣，都有同樣的體會。
>
> *The Chinese schools are for the Chinese ourselves. This is a really important point. We can voice our opinions. The children's ordinary schools don't care about our opinions. They will contact us if they want sponsorship for some events. But ordinarily they just ignore us. At parents' evening, it is the head teacher and the teachers who will speak. We are not allowed to speak. In fact sometime there are problems with the teaching. But we can't do anything. We can only teach the children at home. Sometimes we are afraid that the way we teach (the children at home) won't meet the assessment requirements of the school. (Is it because they think the parents don't speak English?). I don't know, possibly. Maybe they think we don't know how to teach. The Chinese schools are different. We can make criticism and suggestions any time. The head teacher here is also a parent, and some of the teachers are also parents. We are all the same. Everybody is the same and has the same experience.*

It is clear from this parent's remarks that the Chinese parents feel neglected and detached by the mainstream schools that their children attend during the week, but much more involved in the community schools over the weekend. They can see the differences in pedagogical approaches and what they believe are problems with the mainstream schools' teaching. But they feel they can only voice their views at the complementary schools.

Conclusion

The parental voices that we have represented through the quotes in this chapter dispel a myth popular amongst the majority social groups that the minoritized immigrant communities prefer to maintain their ethnic languages at the cost of learning English and that the community language schools are set up simply to transmit the heritage language to the children's generation. Whilst the Chinese parents we spoke to do perceive high value in their children's learning of the Chinese language, they absolutely accept that the children are British Chinese and are bilingual. They have no problem with flexible use of languages either at the Chinese complementary schools or at home. They are very aware of the differences in language proficiency and preference between the generations and between the teachers at the Chinese schools and the children. They are also aware of the differences in pedagogical traditions between the mainstream schools and the Chinese complementary schools. Whilst all the complementary schools for the minoritized children in Britain are set up with the aim of maintaining their community languages, a one language only policy would neither be appropriate nor feasible. That is a clear message from the parents who themselves are key stakeholders of these schools. In the meantime, there are also important messages for the mainstream schools: there is much to be gained from listening to the minoritized parents' voices. More work certainly needs to be done to make their voices heard by the wider society.

Post-Reading Discussion Questions

(1) Why is it important to hear parents' voice in making decisions regarding bilingual education policy and practice?
(2) How can translanguaging contribute to the construction of bilingual learners' identities?

References

Brantmeier, E.J. (2013) Pedagogy of vulnerability: Definitions, assumptions, and applications. In R. Oxford, J. Lin and E.J. Brantmeier (eds) *Re-envisioning Higher Education: Embodied Pathways to Wisdom and Social Transformation* (pp. 95–106). Charlotte, NC: Information Age Publishing

García, O. (2009) *Bilingual Education in the 21st Century: A Global Perspective.* Oxford: Wiley-Blackwell

Hua, Z. and Li, W. (2014) Geopolitics and the changing hierarchies of the Chinese language: Implications for policy and practice of Chinese language teaching in Britain. *The Modern Language Journal* 98 (1), 326–339.

Hua, Z. and Li, W. (2016) Transnational experience, aspiration and family language policy. *Journal of Multilingual and Multicultural Development* 37 (7), 655–666.

Li, W. (2006) Complementary schools, past, present and future. *Language and Education* 20 (1), 76–83.

Li, W. and Wu, C. (2009) Polite Chinese children revisited: Creativity and the use of codeswitching in the Chinese complementary school classroom. *International Journal of Bilingual Education and Bilingualism* 12 (2), 193–211.

Li, W. and Hua, Z. (2010) Voices from the diaspora: Changing hierarchies and dynamics of Chinese multilingualism. *International Journal of the Sociology of Language* 205, 155–171.

Li, W. (2013) Who's teaching whom? Co-learning in multilingual classrooms. In S. May (ed.) *The Multilingual Turn* (pp. 177–200). London: Routledge.

Williams, C. (1994) Arfarniad o ddulliau dysgu ac addysgu yng nghyd-destun addysg uwchradd ddwyieithog. Doctoral dissertation, University of Wales, Bangor.

11 Translanguaging in Bilingual Community Education

Bahar Otcu-Grillman[1]

Pre-Reading Discussion Questions

(1) What is bilingual community education and what role(s) does it have in a named-language dominant society?
(2) Do young bilinguals translanguage in their own community's ethnolinguistic spaces? If so, how?

Introduction

This chapter discusses translanguaging practices in a bilingual community's educational settings, focusing on the findings of my doctoral dissertation Ofelia García sponsored at Teachers College, Columbia University between 2005 and 2009. Being a linguistic ethnography of a PreK-5 Turkish community school in New York, the dissertation investigated language maintenance and development and cultural identity formation in the research context. The chapter also draws on the theoretical understandings, Ofelia García, Zeena Zakharia and I, as co-editors developed together in *Bilingual Community Education and Multilingualism: Beyond Heritage Languages in a Global City* (2013).

Ofelia has a significant role in my completing this research, because she was the first person who encouraged me to pursue it. When I was invited to the Turkish bilingual community school in New York in the summer of 2005, I was impressed by the language choices and dynamics taking place there, and with Ofelia's encouragement, I selected this school as my research setting. I analyzed data I collected via participant observations, audio and video recordings, questionnaires and interviews through discourse analysis methods and revealed the discourses taking places in the school that are discussed elsewhere (Otcu, 2009, 2010). Among the findings was also translanguaging, which I briefly discussed in my dissertation. Ofelia had just conceptualized the term in her newly published *Bilingual Education in 21st Century: A Global Approach* (2009), and my findings then were preliminary. Here, I present the complete findings, discuss the results through the lens of translanguaging and reveal that translanguaging is a natural occurrence of ideologies and identities at play for effective communication and sustaining generational relationships in bilingual community education settings.

Bilingual Community Education

What we called *bilingual community education* (García *et al.*, 2013) has been given various names, such as heritage language or weekend programs, supplementary schools, ethnic community mother tongue schools (Fishman, 1980) and complementary schools in England (Creese *et al.*, 2008; Creese & Blackledge, this volume; Li & Zhu, this volume). As the assimilationist language policies in the US emphasize English in mainstream education at the expense of students' home languages, ethnolinguistic communities make extra efforts by founding their own bilingual community programs to teach their language and culture alongside topics like their history, geography and art forms. These schools mostly run by volunteers usually encounter considerable challenges such as young bilingual learners' resistance, funding and quality of instructors and teaching. Fishman's 1985 study identified 6553 such schools in the US attended by more than 600,000 children (Fishman, 2001), and it was the last major study of these US schools to date.

The specific cases of such schools examined by García *et al.* (2013) show that, although in Fishmanian sense, community language maintenance and development seem the most important goals of these schools, their activities are bilingual in nature and involve a community aspect. There were made two theoretical contributions:

(1) These bilingual community education spaces go beyond heritage and bilingual education by providing 'a context for American children to live the language other than English, not as heritage, but as life in an American present and a global future' (García *et al.*, 2013: 19). Rather than just focusing on the community language as a heritage language or strictly separating the use of two languages as in bilingual education, these schools support *dynamic bilingualism* (García, 2009) through varied and flexible language uses. García (2011) calls this feature *sustainable languaging*, because these schools indicate an American future of cultural and linguistic resources as opposed to reproducing a past heritage mostly full of pain and inequalities, and they are enriching as opposed to the isolating nature of bilingual education. This dynamic bilingual use is referred to as *translanguaging*

(García, 2009; García & Li, 2014), which is discussed further in the chapter.

(2) These educational spaces bring about new understandings of US ethnolinguistic speech communities as *diasporic plural networks*[2] with their fluidity, diversity and complexity. That is, they operate through local and global partnerships of various networks such as parents in the community, community-based agencies and homeland (foreign) governments.

Bilingual community schools are significant and reflect linguistic identities and ideologies (Creese & Blackledge, this volume; Otcu, 2009, 2010; Li & Zhu, this volume). Language ideology can be defined 'as a set of core beliefs and attitudes shared by individuals, as members of groups, regarding the use of a particular language in both oral and written forms' (Martínez-Roldán & Malavé, 2004: 161). It can be considered as a bridge connecting linguistic practices to broader sociopolitical structures (Blackledge & Pavlenko, 2001; García, 2009; Kroskrity, 2000; Woolard, 1998). The constant relationship between these micro- and macro-structures creates identities (Reyes, 2007) and develops certain beliefs and attitudes toward languages in language communities. Taking an ideological approach, Creese and Blackledge (this volume) state 'translanguaging is not merely a description of interactional contact, but an ideological orientation to communication and difference'. The Turkish school focused on in this study is considered to be a site where translanguaging is readily observed and language ideologies and fluid identities interplay. To understand these relationships, I now turn to the Turkish school context.

Research Context and Methodology

The Turkish bilingual community school has been operating for 50 years since its establishment in 1971.[3] The founder and sponsor organization, Turkish Women's League of America (TWLA), is the only official sponsor of the school. It operates voluntarily through donations from TWLA, as well as from the Turkish consulate, parents and donors. Until the Fall of the 2012–2013 school year, the school operated on the second floor of the ten-floor Turkish Consulate across the road from the United Nations in Manhattan. This second floor was a hall open to events of the Turkish community for free upon reservation. The hall would be transformed into a make-shift school setting on Saturdays via room-separating curtains creating classrooms. Since these were not real walls, voices from all grade level classrooms would mesh into each other, but somehow the students and teachers would continue their classes. In 2012, the Consulate building was vacated, because it was being replaced by a taller building. Ever since then, the school has moved to a different school building every year (and has operated remotely since Covid-19), and in that way, provided a real school environment to students. It takes place only on Saturdays from 10am to 4pm from October to June to provide complementary education to the elementary school-aged children of Turkish American families. There are no official holidays or breaks observed throughout the year. The school celebrates Turkish national holidays by preparing the students to perform on the celebration events by reciting poetry, reading essays and dancing modern or folk dances. By following the Turkish elementary school curriculum, they study Turkish language and literacy, Turkish literature, social studies, music, dance and visual arts. There are two benefits to the graduates: receiving a certificate, which may substitute for a Turkish elementary school diploma, and satisfying the foreign language requirement in the regular schools by receiving 3.5 credit points for having studied Turkish as a foreign language.

My dissertation, which took this school as a case study, was a linguistic ethnography (Creese, 2005, 2008; Heller, 1999). Data collection methods included audio and video-recorded participant observations, semi-structured interviews and a questionnaire administered to parents. By using Gee's discourse analysis methods (Gee, 2005), I found that the school's discourses were composed of four building blocks: (1) The semiotics of educational activities and routines: Discourses of semiotics and activity building, (2) Language choices, identities, and self-esteem: Discourses of relationship building, (3) Three Cs: Discourses of world building and (4) Discipline, status and challenges: discourses of political building. These are discussed in detail elsewhere (Otcu, 2009, 2010). In this chapter, I focus on the one-to-one semi-structured interviews with the focal students and on their recordings in the school setting, such as in the classroom during class sessions and while playing in the main school area (when room separators are opened to bring back the entire hall) during break times.

The focal participants whose data are analyzed here are five students: two in kindergarten, two in the third grade and one in the fifth grade. All focal students were US-born second generation Americans with at least one Turkish parent born in Turkey. One male and one female student in the kindergarten and third grades and one female student in the fifth grade wore a voice recorder like a necklace at all times; the recordings continued everywhere they went in the school. In this way, the sounds which were not clearly heard in one recording could be heard in the other one, because the two students were seated at the opposite ends of the classroom or the hall.

I transcribed all the interviews with the focal students and the naturally occurring speech recordings done in the school environment. The length of the recordings used and the focal children's detailed information can be seen in Table 11.1. Nicknames have been used to protect the children's privacy.

Table 11.1 Recordings from five children in an interview and in the school environment

Child-Age-Birth Place	Parents*	Interview Length (minutes)	Recording in school environment Length (hour:minutes:seconds)
Nur-4.5-US	M=TR, F=US	20:31	(02:24:05)
Eser-5.5-US	M=TR, F=TR	19:57	(04:28:07)
Kerem-11-US	M=TR, F=TR	17:43	(02:13:33)
Ceyda-12-US	M=TR, F=TR	14:36	(01:16:31)
Meltem-13-US	M=TR, F=TR	32:50	(02:00:03)

* M: mother, F: father, TR: Turkey-born Turkish, US: US-born American.

I analyzed the transcribed data with a colleague,[4] and by using qualitative methods, categorized the children's language use throughout the interviews and recordings in terms of translanguaging. Each and every occurrence of translanguaging data was counted and data tables were created. For the data tables, we normalized the data by calculating the absolute frequency of the abovementioned categories in terms of 15 minutes.[5] The results provided varied instances of translanguaging, which were categorized and listed as seen below.

(1) Ideology and identity-related remarks/positions: These are the kind of utterances that reflect children's feelings and beliefs about their bilingual and bicultural identities, of the linguistic ideologies that occur within the community school environment and of their language choices. They can also be explained by *positioning* (Davies & Harre, 1990), because the stakeholders build each other's identities within discursive practices via positions, i.e. a collection of beliefs that individuals have with regard to rights and duties to behave in a particular way. Hence, the terms 'ideology and identity-related remarks' and 'positional comments' are used here interchangeably. In a holistic sense, the positions we encountered among our data are a part of translanguaging in the school.

(2) Translanguaging: Some could argue that a more common term to describe bilinguals' using Turkish and English alongside each other could be *code switching*, which means 'to change in languages within a single speech event' (Saville-Troike, 2003: 48). However, we go beyond that stance following García (2012) and keep in mind that 'bilinguals have *one linguistic repertoire* from which they select features *strategically* to communicate effectively' (García, 2012: 1). As García states, translanguaging includes code switching and extends it to make it 'obvious that there are no clear-cut boundaries between the languages of bilinguals' (García, 2009: 47); therefore, bilinguals develop their own idiolects (Otheguy *et al.*, 2019), meaning their own individual language competence and linguistic practices.

Blackledge and Creese (2010) describe flexible bilingualism similarly 'without clear boundaries, which places the speaker at the heart of the interaction' (Blackledge & Creese, 2010: 109). Li (2011) mentions the transformative nature of translanguage when he notes that translanguaging creates a social space for the multilingual language user by bringing together different dimensions of their personal history, experience and environment, their attitude, belief and ideology, their cognitive and physical capacity into one coordinated and meaningful performance, and making it into a lived space (p. 1233). Li calls this lived space *translanguaging space* as a space for translanguaging and created through translanguaging (Li, 2011). We considered our participants' naturally occurring speech data as translanguaging, created in this space as well. The children used each language, English or Turkish, to convey a message, but it was in the bilingualism of the entire utterance that the full message was conveyed. In other words, without both languages, the meaning of the language was not clear (Blackledge & Creese, 2010). Following García's definition (2009) and the research of Blackledge and Creese on flexible bilingualism (2010), we determined the occurrence of translanguaging as follows.

Findings and Discussion

(1) Ideology and identity-related remarks/positions: The frequency analysis of the recordings and interview transcriptions rendered interesting results regarding the children's positions on the use of Turkish. Table 11.2 below clearly indicates that there are no instances of such comments in the recordings, whereas there are some occurrences in the interview.

Table 11.2 Number of occurrences of ideology and identity-related comments/positions in the total recording time and per 15 minutes

| | Ideology and identity-related remarks/Positions | | | |
| | Recording | | Interview | |
Children	Frequency	Frequency per 15 min	Frequency	Frequency per 15 min
Nur-4.5	0	0	4	0.02
Eser-5.5	0	0	2	0.01
Kerem-11	0	0	5	0.04
Ceyda-12	0	0	4	0.03
Meltem-13	0	0	8	0.03

The recordings reflect the children's natural environment in the school, such as the course of the lesson, recess times or time spent playing games with each other. In the recordings, there are no observed instances of the children focusing on their feelings and beliefs about their bilingual identities. On the other hand, there were questions in the interview about the children's bilingualism, bicultural and ethnic awareness. Since the children focused on and responded to those questions in the interview, their positional comments appear in the interview data rather than the recordings.

There seems to be a variety in the children's positional comments, even though a significant difference is not observed among them because of age. As the youngest of five participants, Nur, the little girl from K-grade, answered the interview question about what language she speaks at home. Her answer exemplifies her identity and translanguaging practices most beautifully:

(1) *İngilizce kardeşime, ve de Türkçe kardeşime. Ve de İngilizce babama, çünkü o Türk- Türkçe bilmiyo, çünkü Seattle'da born yaptı.*

English to my sister, and Turkish to my sister. And English to my father, because he isn't Turk – doesn't speak Turkish, because he was born in Seattle.
(Interview data, original in Turkish)

Nur also focused on having both Turkish and American identities as follows:

(2) **Bahar:** *Ee, bitirirken bi soru daha soruyum: Sence- sen mesela yeni birisiyle tanışırken Türküm mü dersin, Amerikalı'yım mı dersin, Türk Amerikalı mıyım dersin?*
Nur: *İkisi.*

Bahar: Err while finishing up let me ask another question: You for example, when introducing yourself to someone, do you say I'm Turkish, I'm American, or I'm Turkish American?
Nur: Both. (Interview data, original in Turkish)

Eser, a kindergartener boy who is one year older than Nur, explicitly shows his awareness of translanguaging although he uses the term 'mixing up Turkish and English'. While we analyzed translanguaging data below as they naturally occurred in the students' speech, we considered such cases regarding awareness of translanguaging as an indicator of awareness of bilingualism, hence a positional comment. Eser's other comments included his anecdotes of the times he spent in Turkey and descriptions of his friends there:

(3) **Bahar:** *Tamam peki mesela sen bu okula neden geliyosun?*
Eser: *Um çünkü galiba bazen İngilizce'yi ve Türkçe'yi um karıştırıyorum evde. Yani ama ama bazen ama Türkçe konuşmam lazım ama bazen İngilizce konuşuyorum.*

B: Hı hı anladım. Burda Türkçe'yi daha çok konuşuyosun di mi?
E: Hı hı.

Bahar: Okay, well for instance why are you coming to this school?
Eser: Err Because I guess I sometimes mix up English and Turkish at home.
I mean but sometimes but I must speak Turkish but sometimes I speak English.
B: Huh huh I see. You speak Turkish a lot more here, don't you?
E: Huh huh. (Interview data, original in Turkish)

A third grader, the boy Kerem's focus is also on his bilingual and
bicultural identity. While some instances of his identity-related comments
are on being different from his Turkish friends because he is an American,
he says that he is similar to them because they all do the same things. In
particular, playing soccer is an important pastime that he shares with
them in Turkey, and he loves it. In the following extract, Kerem indicates
his love of Turkey and his preference for Turkey over America. When
reading this piece, we should keep in mind that Kerem was seen speaking
English with his friends in the Turkish school at all times:

*(4) **Bahar:** Futbol seviyosun. Peki diyelim ki dünya kupası var. Futbol
yani o soccer olan futbol. Diyelim ki Amerika da Türkiye de finallere
kaldı. Ee hangisini desteklersin?*
***Kerem:** Türkiye.*
B: Türkiye'yi desteklersin. Tamam. Peki-.
K: (shows his face) A böyle yaparım yüzümde Türkiye var Amerika.
B: A bi yüzüne Türkiye'yi boyarsın bi yüzüne Amerika'yı.
K: Ve hangisi kazanmazsa ona çıkarırım.
B: Hangisi kazanırsa onu çıkarır mısın? (K: no) Kazanmazsa.
K: Kazanmazsa çıkarırım.
B: Çıkarırsın. Kazanan takımı tutarsın.
K: Daha tutarsın.
B: (laughs) Çok güzel. Yani bu durumda aslında ikisini de destekliyosun.
K: Evet.
B: Yani. En çok ama Türkiye'ye sevinirsin, öyle mi?
K: Çünkü Türkiye benim şehrim.

Bahar: You like football. Let's say there are World Championships.
Football I mean that soccer football. Let's say Turkey is in the finals. Err
which one do you root for?
Kerem: Turkey.
B: You root for Turkey, okay well-.
K: (shows his face) Here I do this there is Turkey and America on my
face.
B: Oh you paint Turkey on one side and America on the other side.
K: And whoever doesn't win, I remove.
B: You remove whoever wins? (K: No) Oh doesn't win.
K: I remove if it doesn't win.
B: You remove. You root for the winning team.

K: You root for more (sic).
B: (laughs) Very nice. In this case you root for both.
K: Yes.
B: Of course. But you'll be the happiest if Turkey wins, right?
K: Because Turkey is my city. (Interview data, original in Turkish).

In this excerpt, Kerem performs his bicultural identity in different ways. First, he indicates that he would paint both Turkish and American national teams' symbols on his face in a World Cup. Then, he says that he would erase the team which cannot win, so he would root for the winning team regardless of nationality. At the end, he mentions that Turkey's winning would make him the happiest, because Turkey is where he is from. Even though he uses the wrong word, *şehrim* (my city), instead of country or homeland or another concept he could not articulate, the entire excerpt is a display of his bilingual and bicultural identity.

Ceyda, a12 year-old girl from the third grade, is one year older than Kerem. She focuses on the use of her entire linguistic repertoire daily, reporting that she uses both languages depending on the context and addressee, and explicitly mentions her awareness of translanguaging. In the excerpt below, the interviewer starts asking if Ceyda has any friends in her regular school:

(5) **Bahar:** *Orda hiç Türk arkadaşların var mı?*
Ceyda: *Evet var ama Yunanlı ve böyle annannesi babannesi Türkiye'den, annesi falan. Ama babası Yunanistan'dan.*
B: *Hı hı. Türkçe konuşuyo mu o senle hiç?*
C: *Bazen konuşuyo-.*
B: *-Bazen. Niye öyle bişey yapıyo acaba?*
C: *Yani bazen tek ikimiz konuşmak istiyoruz, arkadaşlarımız duymasın (**B:** Duymasın!) Türkçe konuşuyoruz.*

Bahar: Do you have any Turkish friends there?
Ceyda: Yes I do, but from Greece and her grandmother is from Turkey, her mother and such. But her father is from Greece.
B: Huh huh. Does she ever speak Turkish with you?
C: She does sometimes-.
B: -Sometimes. Why does she do this, I wonder?
C: I mean sometimes we only want to talk to each other so may our friends not hear us
(**B:** May they not hear you!) We speak Turkish.
(Interview data, original in Turkish)

Ceyda's positional comment tells us about the function of the entire linguistic repertoire of Turkish American bilinguals in their lives. While the majority of the time, English is the language of choice among them, they may choose to speak Turkish for specific purposes in non-Turkish surroundings. Here, she reflects on the function of Turkish as a 'secret language' when she and her friend did not want to be understood by their friends who were monolingual in English.

Meltem, the 13 year-old girl from the fifth grade, reflects all of the aspects which the other students have mentioned. Meltem's interview data includes positional comments on the love of Turkish, using it daily, awareness of her translanguaging and its uses and being an American. In the following, she tells the reasons why she attends the Turkish school on Saturdays:

(6) *Ee ben okulu seviyorum. Gelmek istiyorum. Özlüyorum bazen. Böyle arkadaşlarımı özlüyom, ve öğretmenler yeni öğretmenler olcak onlarla buluşmak istiyo-yani ders çalışmak istiyom falan iyi yani. Türk benim dilim. Türkçe de öğrenmem lazım. Öğrenmem lazım değil istemiyosam ama istiyorum.*

Err I love the school. I want to come. I miss it sometimes. Like I miss my friends, and teachers, there will be new teachers, to meet with them – I mean I want to study and such. I mean Turk is my language. I also need to learn Turkish. I don't need to learn it if I don't want to, but I want to. (Interview data, original in Turkish)

Meltem owns her choice and takes the position that she attends the Turkish school because of her willingness rather than being obliged to do so by her parents. While in this excerpt, she focuses on her Turkishness (Otcu, 2013), she is observed speaking English to her friends and be a proud American most of the time. Some of Meltem's comments also pointed to the differences between the Turkish school and their regular schools. In the extract below, she was expressing her wishes about improving the Turkish school, making suggestions and complaining about the small space they have in their seats:

(7) *Kapı olsun. Kapalı olsun ve odamız insanı duymasın, bizi dersimiz olsun ve böyle table olsun. O zaman yanlarımızda böyle insanlar daha çok iyi oluyo, küçük yerde olunmuyo anlıyon mu? (B: hı hım) Küçük yerde düşüyo kitaplarım yoksa.*

May there be a door. May it be closed and may we not hear others in our room, us, let us have our lesson and may there be a table like this. Then it is much better, the people next to us, one cannot make it in a small place, do you understand? (B: Huh huh) In a small place my books fall down. (Interview data, original in Turkish)

Here, Meltem was pointing to the fact that there were no real classrooms in the Turkish school at the time of the research. Since the school was taking place as a makeshift school via room dividers in the

Turkish Consulate at that time, the noise from each classroom would distract and pose a challenge to the effectiveness of education in the school. Meltem, being the oldest of the focal participant students and as the daughter of a family highly involved with the school, makes certain observations on how to improve it. She justifies her suggestions by complaining that the seating space for them is very limited and causes her books to fall down.

The participants' identity-related comments and the participant observations show that the children in the Turkish school display fluid and hybrid identities. This display is obvious when their language choices are considered, despite the school language policies. The school's most important language policy is a Turkish-only policy. The adult stakeholders frequently warn students, 'Türkçe konu !' (Speak Turkish!). Students know they should speak Turkish to adults, but they contest this policy by translanguaging and speaking English to each other. Such language choices are explained by *performativity* (Pennycook, 2003), which questions pre-given identities and indicates performing identities via the use of language. Translanguaging theory explains such instances via *creativity* and *criticality* (García & Li, 2014) which is also observed in bilingual community education:

> Translanguaging, as a socioeducational process, enables students to construct and constantly modify their sociocultural identities and values, as they respond to their historical and present conditions critically and creatively. It enables students to contest the 'one language only' or 'one language at a time' ideologies of monolingual and traditional bilingual classrooms. (García & Li, 2014: 67)

While by speaking English among peers the children reject the adults' prescribing Turkish identities to them by being critical, they also speak Turkish to adults when necessary and accept their pre-given Turkish identities in creative ways. The findings below exemplify this situation further with regards to translanguaging.

(2) Translanguaging: According to the frequency analysis, there have been many instances of translanguaging in the children's speech. Table 11.3 shows that all of the speech data includes translanguaging, but there are more instances of translanguaging in the interviews than in the recordings.

The fact that there is more frequent occurrence of translanguaging in the interviews compared to the recordings may not be coincidental. In the recordings, which took place in the children's natural environments, we focused on data that included Turkish, to see translanguaging from English to Turkish. In their natural-speech data, the students were English dominant and spoke English to each other. The fact that the students did not translanguage much during the recordings may

Table 11.3 Number of occurrences of translanguaging in the total recording time and per 15 minutes

	Translanguaging			
	Recording		Interview	
Children	Frequency	Frequency per 15 min	Frequency	Frequency per 15 min
Nur-4.5	3	0.17	56	0.34
Eser-5.5	4	0.12	17	0.11
Kerem-11	1	0.06	40	0.29
Ceyda-12	0	0.00	4	0.03
Meltem-13	15	0.94	70	0.27

be because of their preference to speak English to each other and not needing Turkish, except for a few recorded instances.

In contrast to the recordings, the children were expected to speak Turkish to the interviewer. There were a few reasons for this expectation: (1) The children had known the interviewer for over a year as a person from the Turkish community who helped with the school. Since she was an adult and the adult stakeholders in the school speak Turkish to the children, the interviewer also established this relationship with the children from the first day in the school and spoke to them in Turkish. (2) The children's parents told them to speak Turkish with the interviewer during the interview. (3) The interviewer told the students that she prefers to talk to them in Turkish even though she also understands English. Because of these reasons, the children adhered to Turkish during the interviews. There are different levels of translanguaging observed, and Table 11.4 gives a few examples from both the interviews and recordings:

As seen in the table under word-level translanguaging, all participants' interviews show combinations of English word stems with Turkish affixes such as postposition, pronoun, modality, tense, plural, question and case markers.[6] Under utterance-level translanguaging, all children used an utterances in either language alongside each other. While we cannot be sure why the interview yielded more occurrences of translanguaging than the natural speech recordings, we predict that this may be because the students might have felt difficulty expressing themselves in Turkish and needed to convey meaning via use of their full *linguistic repertoire* (Gumperz, 1982), supplementing with their English. In other words, the children created their own idiolects (Otheguy *et al.*, 2019) and translanguaging space (Li, 2011) and made themselves as clear as possible. While doing that, they used their creativity in connecting the features, such as words and affixes, of both languages, as they needed.

Earlier in the chapter common challenges faced in bilingual community education settings, such as the resistance of young bilingual

Table 11.4 Word-level and utterance-level translanguaging

Children	Word-level translanguaging (from the interviews)	Utterance-level translanguaging (from the recordings)
Nur-4.5	*One hundred*'a kadar (up to one hundred); *shape*'ler (shapes); çocuk *bus (child bus); Sunday*'deler (on Sundays); *rocks* vardi (there were rocks); *recess*'e gidiyoruz (we are going to the recess)	Teacher: Bu kimin? Nur: Aa onun, sari sacli, *I mean*, onun onun. Teacher: Whose is this? Nur: Aa his, with blonde hair, *I mean*, his his.
Eser-5.5	*Time-out* zamanın (it's your time out); *baby sit*'sem (if I baby sit); *fifteen* aldin (you took fifteen); *box* çıkarıyo (He's taking out a box); *box*'in içinde (in the box)	There's a special note on on em in your- There's a special note em in your- *Defterinde özel bi tane not var, annene ver.* There is a special note in your notebook, give it to your mom.
Kerem-11	*Write* yapıyoruz (we're doing write); *sing* yapardım (I would do sing); *like* zor kelimeler (like difficult words); *well comics*'ler gibi (well like comics); burda *gym* var mı? (is there a gym here)	Ve uhm yüzüç yaşında öldü. (Friend asks clarification, Kerem whispers) *One hundred and three years. When he died.* And uhm he died at the age of one hundred and three…
Ceyda-12	*Cartoon*'lari seviyorum (I like cartoons)	N/A
Meltem-13	*Actual* günlerde (on actual days); *grammar*'da (in grammar); *chalkboard*'ları (the chalkboards); *related* dedemin (related to my grandfather's); *jewelry* yapıyorum (I am making jewelry); *tank top* giyiyorum (I am wearing tank top); temizlemiyo *mop*'ı (He's not cleaning the mop)	(To sister) I don't have. I have only one left. I want one. *Dur vericem.* (to Principal, in charge of water and food sales) *Su var mı, satıyo musun şimdi?* …Wait I will give you… Is there water, are you selling now?

learners, financing and quality of the education they provide compared to those of the regular schools in the United States were mentioned. Regarding these challenges, García *et al.* (2013) made specific recommendations to all stakeholders in the diasporic plural networks of bilingual community education. The overall recommendation was that 'policy-makers, educators, parents and communities have to be able to collaborate and trust each other if we are going to raise a generation of bilingual Americans' (García *et al.*, 2013: 309). Stakeholders in the diasporic plural network of the Turkish school such as parents, students, teachers, administrators, Turkish Consulate officials and members of the Turkish organizations within the Consulate building, all work collaboratively to support the school and provide an environment of sustainable languaging within the limited resources available to the school. The children in the Turkish school do not complain about such challenges or the schools' limitations and are in general content with the school once they arrive there. However, Meltem's comments, similar to her remarks above, and the children's talking about the differences between the Turkish school and their regular school in the interview indicate that they are well aware of the differences and challenges of attending a community-based school. Just as they contest the Turkish-only policy of the school by speaking English to each other and yet accept this policy and speak Turkish to the adults, they accept the difference of the Turkish school from their regular schools as a translanguaging space.

Conclusion

This chapter shed light on young Turkish American bilinguals' translanguaging practices by describing data from a Turkish community-based school in the US. There were two data sources in Turkish: interview data and naturally occurring data from recordings in the school environment. The participant children's data yielded the translanguaging data in terms of ideology and identity-related remarks, or positions, and translanguaging.

There were no instances of identity-related positional comments in the recordings, whereas there were some occurrences in the interviews. In terms of translanguaging, all of the speech data included it, but there were more instances of translanguaging in the interviews than in the recordings. Both identity-related comments and translanguaging data indicated the children's perceptions of their bilingual/bicultural identities and performance of their identities through their language choices, criticality and creativity (García & Li, 2014) and narration of their experiences in Turkey and in the US. Having hybrid and fluid identities, the students use their full linguistic repertoires actively in the Turkish school environment even though they are expected to speak only Turkish. While they contest the Turkish-only policy in the school by speaking English to each other, they also accommodate the adults' wants and wishes. The children speak Turkish to the adults; likewise, the adults try to help them as much as possible by letting them express themselves in the most meaningful way possible via translanguaging.

The findings discussed may be the result of the differences in the context of the children's Turkish use. During the interviews, they were conversing with only one interlocutor, the interviewer, and they were expected to speak Turkish. This fact may have put them in a challenging situation, which led them into more translanguaging as well as reflecting on their positional awareness on purpose. If this generalization is correct, we may conclude that the participant children use translanguaging for more efficient and meaningful communication in Turkish in one-on-one conversation situations. In other words, translanguaging supports their Turkish proficiency; they become successful meaning makers in Turkish and can use their full linguistic repertoires more efficiently with such support. Through translanguaging, they actively develop and use their own idiolects.

This chapter did not discuss the adult stakeholders' point of view regarding varying language needs of the students as it was previously discussed elsewhere (Otcu, 2013). In general, it was often observed that the adults accommodated the young bilinguals' languaging needs. For instance, kindergarten and the first-grade levels, where students' Turkish proficiency was lower, teachers translanguaged when giving instructions and calling numbers. In the fifth grade, where the curriculum became more academically demanding, the teacher translanguaged in order to make tasks better understood by the students. In other cases, the teachers, administrators or the parents simply let the students express themselves in the best way possible by using their full linguistic repertoires despite the school's Turkish-only policy. Focal students' parents reported different translanguaging practices in their homes. Some parents reported allowing translanguaging in the house, while some parents stated that they designate Turkish as the home language and English as the 'outside' language, to be spoken only outside the house. No matter what practice is used by the stakeholders, bilingual community schools like the Turkish school are significant translanguaging sites. With a lack of true bilingual education programs, community-based schools provide sustainable languaging and make sure that American children can have a bilingual/bicultural present and future despite all the challenges they face.

Post-Reading Discussion Questions

(1) What are diasporic plural networks and how can they ensure raising successful bilingual Americans?
(2) How are young bilinguals' criticality and creativity observed within bilingual community education?

Notes

(1) I am indebted to my friend and colleague, Maryam Borjian, for carefully reviewing a previous draft this chapter and joining me in the journey of co-editing this volume. Without her support, assistance, and beautiful writing, this volume would not have found life in its present form.
(2) For a brief discussion on the terms heritage, heritage language and bilingual education, please refer to (García et al., 2013).
(3) For a history of immigrations from Turkey to the US and sociolinguistics of the Turkish language, please see Otcu (2013).
(4) I am grateful to Prof Dr Deniz Zeyrek, my colleague and former advisor at Middle East Technical University, Turkey, for her valuable help in analyzing and interpreting these data.
(5) Normalization is a scaling method in which data points are shifted and rescaled so that they end up in a range of 0 to 1.
(6) Turkish is an agglutinative language with a general word order of subject, object and verb.

References

Blackledge, A. and Creese, A. (2010) Translanguaging in the bilingual classroom: A pedagogy for learning and teaching? *The Modern Language Journal* 94 (i), 103–115.

Blackledge, A. and Pavlenko, A. (2001) Negotiation of identities in multilingual contexts. *The International Journal of Bilingualism* 5, 243–259.

Creese, A. (2005) *Teacher Collaboration and Talk in Multilingual Classrooms.* Clevedon: Multilingual Matters.

Creese, A. (2008) Linguistic ethnography. In K.A. King and N.H. Hornberger (eds) *Encyclopedia of Language and Education, 2nd edition, Volume 10: Research Methods in Language and Education* (pp. 229–241). Springer Science + Business Media LLC.

Creese, A., Baraç, T., Bhatt, A., Blackledge, A., Hamid, S., Li, W., Lytra, V., Martin, P., Yağcıoğlu-Ali, D. and Wu, CJ. (2008) Investigating multilingualism in complementary schools in four communities. *Final Report for the ESCR for Project No: RES-000-23-1180.*

Davies, B. and Harre, R. (1990) Positioning: The discursive production of selves. *Journal for the Theory of Social Behaviour* 20 (1), 43–63.

Fishman, J.A. (1980) Ethnic community mother tongue schools in the USA: Dynamics and distributions. *International Migration Review* 14 (2), 235–247.

Fishman, J.A. (2001) 300-plus years of heritage language education in the United States. In J.K. Peyton, D.A. Ranard and S. McGinnis (eds) *Heritage Languages in America: Preserving a National Resource* (pp. 81–99). McHenry, IL: Center for Applied Linguistics and Delta Systems.

García, O. (2009) *Bilingual Education in the 21st Century: A Global Perspective.* Malden, MA; Oxford: Wiley–Blackwell Publishing.

García, O. (2011) From language garden to sustainable languaging: Bilingual education in a global world. *Perspectives. A Publication of the National Association for Bilingual Education,* Sept./Oct. 2011, 5–10.

García, O. (2012) Theorizing translanguaging for educators. In C. Celic and K. Seltzer (eds) *Translanguaging: A CUNY-NYSIEB Guide for Educators* (pp. 1–6). New York, NY: CUNY-NYSIEB.

García, O. and Li, W. (2014) *Translanguaging: Language, Bilingualism, and Education.* New York, NY: Palgrave Macmillan.

García, O., Zakharia, Z. and Otcu, B. (2013) Bilingual community education: Beyond heritage language education and bilingual education in New York. In O. García, Z. Zakharia and B. Otcu (eds) *Bilingual Community Education and Multilingualism: Beyond Heritage Languages in a Global City* (pp. 3–42). Bristol: Multilingual Matters.

Gee, J.P. (2005) *An Introduction to Discourse Analysis: Theory and Method.* London & New York, NY: Routledge.

Gumperz, J.J. (1982) *Discourse Strategies.* Cambridge: Cambridge University Press.

Heller, M. (1999) *Linguistic Minorities and Modernity: A Sociolinguistic Ethnography.* London; New York: Longman.

Kroskrity, P.V. (2000) Regimenting languages: Language ideological perspectives. In P.V. Kroskrity (ed.) *Regimes of Language: Ideologies, Polities, and Identities* (pp. 1–34). New Mexico; Oxford: School of American Research Press.

Li, W. (2011) Moment analysis and translanguaging space: Discursive construction of identities by multilingual Chinese youth in Britain. *Journal of Pragmatics* 43 (5), 1222–1235.

Martinez-Roldán, C.M. and Malavé, G. (2004) Language ideologies mediating literacy and identity in bilingual contexts. *Journal of Early Childhood Literacy* 4 (2), 155–180.

Otcu, G.B. (2009) Language maintenance and cultural identity construction in a Turkish Saturday school in New York City. Ed.D. Thesis, Teachers College Columbia University.

Otcu, B. (2010) *Language Maintenance and Cultural Identity Construction: An Ethnography of Discourses in a Complementary School in the US.* Saarbrücken: VDM Müller.

Otcu, B. (2013) Turkishness in New York: Languages, ideologies and identities in a community-based school. In O. García, Z. Zakharia and B. Otcu (eds) *Bilingual*

Community Education and Multilingualism: Beyond Heritage Languages in a Global City (pp. 113–127). Bristol: Multilingual Matters.

Otheguy, R., Garcia, O. and Reid, W. (2019) A translanguaging view of the linguistic system of bilinguals. *Applied Linguistics Review* 10 (4), 625–651.

Pennycook, A. (2003) Global Englishes, rip slyme, and performativity. *Journal of Sociolinguistics* 7 (4), 513–533.

Reyes, A. (2007) *Language, Identity, and Stereotype Among Southeast Asian American Youth: The Other Asian*. Mahwah, NJ; London: Lawrence Erlbaum Associates.

Saville-Troike, M. (2003) *The Ethnography of Communication: An Introduction*. Oxford: Blackwell.

Woolard, K.A. (1998) Introduction: Language ideology as a field of inquiry. In B.B. Schieffelin, K.A. Woolard and P. Kroskrity (eds) *Language Ideologies: Practice and Theory* (pp. 3–47). Oxford: Oxford University Press.

12 Bilingual Education: Making a U-Turn with Parents and Communities

Fabrice Jaumont

This personal narrative details the Bilingual Revolution and how the movement has encouraged the development of bilingual education among various ethnolinguistic communities in the United States in recent years. *The Bilingual Revolution* is also the title of a book I wrote in 2017 and for which Dr Ofelia García gifted me invaluable advice and guidance, as well as an incredible foreword, *Bilingual Education: Making a U-Turn with Parents and Communities*. With this brief personal narrative and the opportunity given to me to contribute to this volume, I wish to pay homage to the scholar and reflect on the importance and influence of Ofelia both on my academic and professional journeys. I also want to expand on Ofelia's precept that American society needs a U-turn for bilingual education, a return to its beginnings.

Ofelia *et Moi*

My introspection began soon after cleaning my closet and discovering an old certificate signed by Ofelia from when we participated in the International Symposium on Bilingualism and Biliteracy through Schooling in 1999. At the time, I was the director of Ecole Bilingue's Middle and Upper sections in Cambridge, Massachusetts – a private bilingual institution now called the International School of Boston with a French-American PreK3 to 12 curriculum. Hosted by Long Island University, the event featured scholars from all over the world, including Dr Joshua Fishman, who signed my copy of *The Handbook of Language & Ethnic Identity* with these words: 'Best wishes to you and to your work in the French-American school(s)'.

In retrospect, Joshua Fishman's inscription reads more like a premonition now, considering the number of French dual-language programs that I have helped create since. Thanks to Ofelia, whom I met for the first time then, the 1999 symposium was a way to connect with a community of peers. It left me recharged, inspired and forever changed.

Years later, while discussing my book with Ofelia in her office at the Graduate Center, City University of New York, I realized what a profound impact she had on people's lives, including mine. Who I was and what I had become had been defined by her. Recording a series of interviews and an episode of my podcast, *Révolution bilingue* together, we quickly found mutual ground in the idea that bilingual education starts with children and their families who were vested in their education. The belief that bilingual offerings positively transform and empower children, schools and communities in unprecedented ways continues to push me today. I am convinced that such programs not only help us preserve our linguistic heritage – as demonstrated in my research on French heritage language communities in the United States (Ross & Jaumont, 2013a, 2014) – but also raise a generation of young bilingual, bi-literate, multicultural and translanguaging citizens of the world.

The Desire of American Families

As an experienced author, Ofelia encouraged me to tell the story as it was, that of a grassroots movement that emerged from the dedicated involvement of motivated parents, educators and community actors willing to create and support dual language programs in New York City public schools. From a personal and scholarly perspective, I wanted to recognize the successes and setbacks of these programs in my writing through vignettes featuring parents and educators who initiated bilingual programs in their schools. This publishing process started with Ofelia's invitation to contribute a chapter for a volume she edited with Zeena Zakharia and Bahar Otcu. (Ross & Jaumont, 2013b; García *et al.*, 2013) I expanded these ideas in a book with the objective of encouraging every community's unique culture and promote linguistic heritage as an important part of the greater international mosaic of our society – helping communities re-engaging with public schools promoting a social, economic, and cultural sense of community and bridging gaps that continue to divide us. (Jaumont, 2017)

Ofelia acknowledged that books on bilingual education are usually for teachers. Historically, little attention has been paid to how families can help ensure that American public schools develop bilingual education programs for their children. She encouraged me to focus on 'the desire of American families to have their children schooled

bilingually, in English, but also in a language that has deep connections to them' (García, 2017: 1). And that, rather than starting with
government mandates and regulations and focusing only on those who
lack – lack English, lack years of residency, lack economic means – that
I propose that we start 'with the wishes of ethnolinguistic communities
(old and new) to bilingually educate their children' which she saw as a
'U-turn for bilingual education, a return to its beginnings' (García,
2017: 2).

In her own words, my work succeeded in recapturing:

> The promise of a bilingual education tradition and reminds us that
> all Americans – those with different racial identities, social class, and
> immigration history – have different linguistic and cultural practices. In
> this book, American parents whose children's heritages include linguis-
> tic practices that have traces of what are considered Arabic, Chinese,
> English, French, Japanese, Italian, German, Polish, Russian, and
> Spanish, understand these practices to be important. For these parents,
> a bilingual education is important not because of any connection to the
> past or foreign lands, but to recognize an American multilingual present
> and forge the possibilities of a more inclusive future for all American
> children. (García, 2017: 1–2)

Ofelia understood that I could play a role in educating all parents to
understand the benefits of bilingual education, as well as in supporting
parents of all backgrounds in organizing themselves, and that only
parents and communities could be change agents. She wrote that 'The
success of the American bilingual education tradition will rely on the
willpower of parents. But willpower alone is not enough' and thought
that my decision to give parents a roadmap of how to start and support
successful bilingual education programs was the right one: 'a roadmap
that can help them shape the path as they make a new road upon
walking, as they make, as Antonio Machado, the Spanish poet, says,
"*camino al andar*"' (García, 2017: 2). She encouraged me to focus on
a topic that was often absent in books on bilingual education: 'that of
the important role that parents of different ethnolinguistic backgrounds
have in shaping an appropriate education for their children in the United
States' (García, 2017: 1). Two years ago, this thinking led me to found,
with long-time friend and co-researcher Jane Ross, The Center for the
Advancement of Languages, Education, and Communities (CALEC), of
which Ofelia accepted to serve as an advisory council member. CALEC's
mission is to empower multilingual families and linguistic communities
through education, knowledge and advocacy.

We all agreed that American families with different ethnolinguistic
backgrounds were interested in developing bilingual education programs
for their children, contrary to popular opinion. And Ofelia understood
my calls for a revolution, 'a revolution led from the bottom up, by

families who appreciate the value of bilingualism because it is part of their American identity' (García, 2017: 1). Each day in CALEC's life I can see that parents' interest in bilingual education is increasing significantly as they discover what early exposure to dual-language programming can offer their children or what the cognitive, academic, social, personal and professional benefits may bring them and their community. They can see multilingualism and multiliteracy as assets, not only for their cultural virtues but also for their ability to produce 'citizens of the world'. There is no doubt in our mind that bilingual, if not trilingual, education should be accessible to every child in the United States and the world.

For this, a U-turn is necessary as we are constantly reminded that all Americans (of different ethnic identities, social classes and countries of origin) have multiple linguistic and cultural practices. In this U-turn, American parents whose linguistic heritage is imbued with Arabic, Chinese, English, French, Japanese, Italian, German, Polish, Russian and Spanish words, understand the importance of these practices. According to them, a multilingual education is not only a way to reconnect with the past, but also a way to recognize a multilingual American present and to forge a more inclusive future for all children.

The Promise of Dual-Language Education

Bilingual education means different things to different people. Some want access to English and the equal opportunity it provides. Others want to sustain their heritage and utilize dual-language education as a tool to do so. Others are interested in the benefits of multilingualism for cognitive development. Others are interested in the acquisition of a second, third or fourth language because of the professional opportunities and advantages it will yield. These perspectives all share the same goal: to create a multilingual society with greater access to languages and cultures. Yet, it is critical that we try to weave together these different perspectives, ensuring that more dual-language programs are created to generate greater opportunities for all children. Being bilingual is no longer superfluous nor the privilege of a happy few. Being bilingual is no longer taboo for immigrants who want so dearly for their children to blend seamlessly into their new environment. Being bilingual is the new norm, and it must start with our youngest citizens.

Over the last 20 years, linguistic communities in many cities in the United States have initiated and developed scores of dual-language programs in numerous languages, some of which have transformed schools and the education of our children in significant ways. In a sense, these programs have transformed both language education models and bilingual education models into a viable and desired solution for all families, bringing many benefits to our school communities whether they are in the United States or elsewhere in the world. These programs are more than just language courses. They allow children to better understand the cultures that surround them by offering them intercultural exchanges within the school. They strengthen and support our linguistic heritage and promote the value of cultural and linguistic diversity in all societies while fostering 21st century skills as well as empathy, tolerance, social cohesion. This is the U-turn that I have called for and which echoes Ofelia's words:

> A U-turn, returning the design of bilingual education to families and communities, reminding us that this is where it all started, in the 18th century, as well as in the 20th century. Our experience tells us that creating bilingual education programs from the bottom up is not easy. But it is an important struggle, one that has always been part of the American ethos and that is being reclaimed today by communities across the country. (García, 2017: 9)

Often it is said and written that 'it takes a village' to raise our children. Languages are part of our personal cultural identity and help create the fabric of our family, our friends and neighbors, and our communities in general. At this turning point in dual-language learning in the United States, and around the world, it is more important than ever to reach out to parents and communities and to value and respect their engagement in our cause.

Making the U-turn

Like many parents and educators, we are convinced that the cognitive, emotional and social advantages of being multilingual and multiliterate are a universal gift that should be given to every child because it can constructively change our schools, our communities and even our countries. In the context of the United States, as well as in my native country, France, monolingualism is the real obstacle to the development of society, which misses out on the enormous linguistic resource brought forth by its citizens. But dual-language education as fought for and advocated by parents and linguistic communities offers numerous advantages which are gradually being acknowledged by school authorities. As Ofelia confirms:

> These bilingual education programs do not find their children's linguistic or cultural practices suspect. They honor the communities' funds of knowledge. The book tells the story of real parents that organize the community and battle to change the direction of American education today. We see how the partnerships that the parents build are not solely among themselves or with powerful organizations, but with others and

other communities who have histories and experiences in the struggle. The greatest power it turns out is that of parents, interested and committed to the bilingual education of their children. This is not the usual parental participation or even engagement that the education literature talks about. This is about the leadership of parents who lead school change. The power dynamics are inverted, as it is the community itself that is in the driver seat, making the U-turn and leading the way. (García, 2017: 8)

In our increasingly interconnected, miniaturized and fragile era, schools around the world are striving to give young people the skills, abilities and sensitivities that will enable them to become autonomous, engaged and productive citizens. Dual-language teaching and learning and the so-called 'bilingual advantage' are resurfacing in schools, large and small, all over the United States. Parents and teachers are looking for an ideal of teaching or learning in two languages. However, it is also important to look to our past, and make this U-turn, this revolution, to understand the enduring importance of parents, families, and communities in education in general and in bilingual education in particular.

References

Fishman, J. (1999) *The Handbook of Language & Ethnic Identity*. Oxford: Oxford University Press.

García, O. (2017) Bilingual education: Making a U-turn with parents and communities. In F. Jaumont (ed.) *The Bilingual Revolution, The Future of Education is in Two Languages* (pp. 1–9). New York, NY: TBR Books.

García, O., Zakharia, Z. and Otcu, B. (eds) (2013) *Bilingual Community Education and Multilingualism*. Bristol: Multilingual Matters.

Jaumont, F. (2017) *The Bilingual Revolution: The Future of Education is in Two Languages*. New York, NY: TBR Books.

Ross, J. and Jaumont, F. (2013a) French language vitality in the United States. *Heritage Language Journal* 10 (3), 316–317.

Ross, J. and Jaumont, F. (2013b) Building bilingual communities: NYC's French bilingual revolution. In O. García, Z. Zakharia and B. Otcu (eds) *Bilingual Community Education and Multilingualism* (pp. 232–246). Bristol: Multilingual Matters.

Ross, J. and Jaumont, F. (2014) French heritage language communities in the United States. In T. Wiley, J.K. Peyton, D. Christian, S.C. Moore and N. Liu (eds) *Handbook of Heritage and Community Languages in the United States* (pp. 101–110). Oxford: Routledge.

Part 4: Language Policy and Language Ideologies

13 Translanguaging: An Ideological Perspective

Angela Creese and Adrian Blackledge

Preface

We are delighted to contribute a piece to this volume which celebrates the life and work of Ofelia García. We have so many memories of Ofelia's generosity and warmth over the years. Whether sharing fried fish on the beach at Cartagena, Colombia, inspiring doctoral researchers in Birmingham, UK, or providing a sumptuous meal in her beautiful apartment in Manhattan, New York, Ofelia's open heartedness, and open handedness, have been beyond compare. It is easy to see that her students, past and present, are deeply appreciative of her wisdom, guidance and profound investment as a teacher and advisor. Our only regret is that when we were Distinguished Visiting Fellows at the Advanced Research Collaborative, The Graduate Centre, City University, New York, our collaboration was cut short by the COVID-19 pandemic. But we did have some time together. Ofelia has always been our mentor, our colleague and our inspiration. We celebrate her immense achievement.

Pre-Reading Discussion Questions

In preparation for reading this chapter you might look at two of our articles, to understand our developing ideas around translanguaging as ideology. They are accounts of our research in heritage language schools in the UK, and they summarize our early work on translanguaging in educational settings:

Creese, A. and Blackledge, A. (2010) Translanguaging in the bilingual classroom: A pedagogy for learning and teaching. *Modern Language Journal* 94, 103–115.

Creese, A. and Blackledge, A. (2011) Separate and flexible bilingualism in complementary schools: Multiple language practices in interrelationship. *Journal of Pragmatics* 43 (5), 1196–1208.

(1) The first article develops the concept of 'classroom ecology'. What are the underlying ideological implications of using the metaphor 'ecology' when describing language classrooms? The second article argues that flexible and separate bilingualism are ideological practices. How might translanguaging be considered ideological?

(2) As educators we face dilemmas daily about the right linguistic approach to take with our students. What kinds of ideological dilemmas have you faced as either a teacher or learner in relation to language education?

Introduction

If our work on translanguaging has contributed anything to scholarship on language education, it is to point to the ideological significance of the term, and the variation around the practice which flows from it. We have been at pains to explain that monolingual, purist and separatist ideologies run alongside and constantly interact with flexible and multilingual ideologies in education and other settings. Drawing on Bakhtin's (1981) concepts of heteroglossia and polyphony, we have argued that standardizing forces and diversifying drives are never free from one another when it comes to language. Our ethnographic research has shown how teachers and students in heritage language schools manage contradictory ideologies in their classrooms and attend to the dilemmas they create. We saw that teachers and students were able to navigate ambiguities, and make sense of the disparate ideologies they indexed. For example, while at times a teacher in a Gujarati complementary ('heritage language') school insisted on strict attention to prescriptive language rules in answering examination questions, at other times the same teacher not only accommodated to local linguistic norms, but expected students to actively draw on these bilingual resources to get the classroom task done. Teachers in the complementary school endorsed a flexible language ideology *en route* to completing classroom tasks and activities, and incorporated the bilingual competence of their students as a resource to help them arrive at the standardized answer required by the Gujarati language curriculum. In our research it was evident that schools were not only aware of conflicting ideologies but used them productively for language learning. The same might be said of so-called monolingual classrooms where children speak a variety of non-standard dialects of English. In heritage language education teachers move between separate and flexible language ideologies to keep students engaged in classroom learning, while helping them to achieve a qualification in a minoritized language.

Through our ethnographic research we have described translanguaging as a practical response to social and linguistic ideological dilemmas. On the one hand teachers and students want to learn 'a language', while on the other they want to move beyond the restrictions that named languages impose. Translanguaging as a concept acknowledges the existence of languages, while simultaneously acknowledging that they are ideological inventions. Translanguaging can be understood as an ideologically informed practice which resolves this apparent paradox by working to reconcile dilemmas around communication in contexts of social and linguistic diversity. In this chapter we explore the ideological nature of translanguaging further.

We start with the 'trans' in translanguaging. For us, this is less about 'transformation' and more about 'trans-lation', by which we mean 'mediation' rather than the search for equivalence across different languages. We view translanguaging as a mediation resource for navigating ideological dilemmas around languages and other social phenomena. We might think of translation therefore, not only in terms of gaining understanding across different languages, but also as a mediating process which responds to conflicting ideologies. Viewing translanguaging as mediation is to acknowledge its role in the negotiation of different ideological positions about language. We take ideology to be 'the cultural system of ideas about social and linguistic relationships, together with their loading of moral and political interests' (Irvine, 1989: 255). An ideological perspective on translanguaging considers how people's values and beliefs about language come to shape the social context, and people's practices within it. In the UK's socially diverse cities, translanguaging is a process for mediating values and beliefs about language. Translanguaging is an ideologically informed practice which allows people to bring integrity to what is otherwise a seemingly conflicting set of ideologies. This is what we mean when we speak of flexible and separate bilingualism as simultaneously co-existent in many language educational contexts.

Ideology and Translanguaging

Bakhtin observed that language is always subject to opposing forces – centripetal and centrifugal – one attracting to an ordered center, the other urging diversification and change. Monolingual, bilingual or multilingual, this process of linguistic conformity and creativity, fixity and fluidity is in constant interplay. Those involved in education, and in language education in particular, face up to this dialectic daily. In our research, we found that teachers and students did not take up opposing views around standards and non-standard varieties of language, but rather recognized that both have a place in their bilingual lives. In the Bengali, Cantonese, Gujarati, Mandarin, Panjabi and Turkish heritage language schools we observed, teachers and students found their own way to live with these apparent tensions, often speaking about the balance directly, or negotiating the equilibrium in ways which made sense to them as the lesson took place. The following are examples from Gujarati and Panjabi schools, from our research in heritage language schools in Leicester and Birmingham.

Example 1: Field note extracts

- The teacher explains, 'Since this is a Gujarati school, I will mix English and Gujarati … if you don't understand, you can raise your hand and I will explain it'.
- The teacher tells her students that in class she speaks Panjabi 'most of the time', but she doesn't want them to struggle. 'If you don't understand, let me know. I want you to learn in a fun way'.
- The morning started from 9.30 and finished at 12, with an assembly held for children, parents and teachers at the start and finish of the morning. The headteacher was at her best, using Gujarati and English in her distinctive way, teasing and serious, including different participants at different times, in a talk which was for everyone. I don't know how she does it, but it is a joy to be part of.

Example 2: Classroom audio recording

Teacher:	bolwanu \<speak\>
Student:	shu bolwanu? \<speak what?\>
Teacher:	je discuss karyu hoi \<what you discussed\>
Student:	oh. etle we discuss it and then decide what we gonna say. Miss ame ek bijanu kaie ke ek ek? \<so we discuss it. Miss, do we speak about each other, or one by one?\>
Teacher:	tame decide karo ke kone bolwu chhe \< you decide who speaks\>

These examples illustrate the balancing act in which teachers and students constantly engage. All participants must reconcile a set of competing ideologies. Clearly evident is the requirement to pay attention to the prescriptive demands of the languages being taught and learned, while at the same time the desire to collapse language boundaries (if such things exist) to engage in identity performance, and complete learning tasks.

Ideology and Critics of Translanguaging

Critics of the 'multilingual turn' warn of the dangers of 'ideological complicities' (Kubota, 2016: 476) in the endorsement of what they see as neoliberal ideologies behind the multilingual and translanguaging turn. Because arguments for multilingualism and translanguaging tend to speak of individual repertoires in classroom practices, critics fear that structural entities like languages may lose their visibility, and their power to bring about change. This is seen as particularly troubling for the status of marginalized, minoritized languages, in relation to the hegemony of English. There is anxiety that if, as many translanguaging scholars argue, languages do not exist as intrinsic entities, they may not be defended, supported or sustained. Kubota (2016) sees this direction as foregrounding individual subjectivity over the collective needs of minoritized and marginalized people. She is troubled that proponents of multilingual approaches have lost their way, and become 'integrated into a neoliberal capitalist academic culture of incessant knowledge production and competition for economic and symbolic capital' (2016: 475). Kubota and Miller (2017) point to the gathering momentum in the academy for fetishizing concepts. Others have made similar points, not only about translanguaging, but about understandings of [super] diversity within applied linguistics. Reyes (2014) worries that the 'super-new-big' agenda is put forward by 'capitalist industries that set the conditions under which we are expected – or allowed – to study those worlds', rather than developing as a response to the needs of those we research (2014: 367). Pavlenko (2018) speaks of academic branding in an entrepreneurial climate. Jaspers (2018: 1), with specific regard to translanguaging, speaks of 'popular new concepts' with 'chameleonic capacity' that cover too much, but say very little. Jaspers' concern with translanguaging extends this 'discursive drift' to the concept of 'transformation'. He argues that while translanguaging adopts a discourse of equity and social justice, it is unable to effect real change in the structures of education and wider society.

Kubota, Jaspers, Reyes, Pavlenko and others give generously of their time and attention in critiquing developments in translanguaging, and more widely the 'multilingual turn', and diversity. They point out the dangers of 'neo-liberalizing paths' which fail to adequately respond to the systemic discrimination of disenfranchised groups. For Kubota (2019: 7) this is a tension between 'difference and sameness, or between individually conceptualized experiences of diverse subjects/agents and collectively understood group experiences'. For her, our energies should be focused on fostering collective solidarities, to bring about change. The multilingual and plurilingual turn is accused of being complicit in a 'neoliberal multiculturalism that celebrates individual cosmopolitanism and plurilingualism for socioeconomic mobility' (Kubota, 2016: 476).

Wherever we stand on the collective/individual continuum outlined by Kubota and others, we might find agreement in a need to narrow the theory/practice divide. It is the political and collective desire of many in our field that we continue to seek change in the iniquitous language ideologies of education systems and other social institutions, to improve the lives of multilingual, minoritized citizens. The tensional interplay between agency and structure, difference and sameness, individualism and collectivism, will not easily be resolved. Moreover, as Jaspers points out, drawing on Billig *et al.*, the dilemmas we face should not be seen as negative, but as facilitating. These tensions, according to Billig *et al.*, are what create a 'thinking society' (Billig *et al.*, 1988 in Jaspers, 2018: 6). In this research Billig et al specifically describe the dilemmas that teachers face in relation to the theory/practice divide:

> Teachers do not have the luxury of being able to formulate and adhere to some theory or position on education, with only another theorist's arguments to question its validity. They have to accomplish the practical task of teaching, which requires getting the job done through whatever conceptions and methods work best, under practical constraints that include physical resources, numbers of pupils, nature of pupils, time constraints, set syllabuses and so on. But these practical considerations inevitably have ideological bases, which define what 'the job' actually is, how to do it, how to assess its outcomes, how to react to its successes and failures, how to talk and interact with pupils, how many can be taught or talked to at once. (Billig *et al.*, 1988: 46)

In our research we have come to see translanguaging as a response to dilemmas about language and society. Translanguaging incorporates standardizing norms on the one hand, and diversifying practices on the other. We have observed this in heritage language classrooms. Empirical studies in translanguaging have predominantly emerged from educational research, as multilingual strategies and practices are proposed for successful learning. However, our ambition has been to expand translanguaging as a descriptive concept beyond its original remit in education, to consider its affordances in other social domains.

Translanguaging and Advocacy

Recently we have investigated translanguaging in social domains beyond education. One setting of particular interest has been that of community associations in inner city locations (Blackledge *et al.*, 2018). Community associations provide numerous services and activities to local groups. In our research we focused on one Chinese community center in a city in the West Midlands of England. The center provided various services to its users, often with few resources. These services included regular luncheon clubs and many other activities for elders, including dance and calligraphy. One well used amenity was the center's Advice and Advocacy service, which was available to Chinese heritage people from across the city who were seeking information about a range of topics. Many clients were concerned with claims for welfare benefits. Others were related to passport applications, insurance claims, school admissions, letters from doctors, electricity bills, council tax and so on. Many clients required support with more than one issue, as their challenges overlapped. Appointments with an advisor could be booked by clients as half-hour or hourly sessions. We conducted ethnographic observations in the Advice and Advocacy service provided by the center.[1] In the short extract here we represent translanguaging practices between an advisor and a client. We show how translanguaging allows the advisor to navigate between her roles as supportive listener and focused advocate. This was achieved through adherence to both language separation, and the seamless overlapping of linguistic resources.

Example 3: Advocating for the client

In this example, the client, X, requires help applying on her husband's behalf for Personal Independence Payment (PiP), a government welfare benefit which had recently been introduced at the time of our field work. In order to apply she must provide medical evidence of her husband's disability, and complete a PiP2 form, which ran to 33 pages on the computer, and asked claimants questions in English, in fifteen categories. The stated purpose of the form is to ascertain the type and level of need of the claimant. The meeting took place in the small office in the community center, which the advisor shared with another colleague. We are able to present only a tiny fraction of the hour-long interaction here. In the example we see the advisor move between the requirements of the PiP form, which represents the contingencies of the state welfare system, and the lived experience of her client, and her client's husband. We join the interaction here as it continues in relation to Question 3 ('Preparing Food') on the PiP form.

X is the client, A is the advisor. The interaction takes place in Mandarin.

> **X:** 他现在变老了，情况就更糟了
> 尤其是要他看医生的时候
> 两个星期前他有好几次要去诊所看医生
> 你知道吧？
> 他的血压有一百九十一
> < he's aging now and it's getting worse
> especially when he goes to see the doctor
> a couple of weeks ago he had to see the doctor several times
> you understand?
> His blood pressure is a hundred and ninety one >
> **A:** 所以他的血压高
> < so his blood pressure is high >
> **X:** 医生给他带那个东西的时候他还想打医生
> 把那个医生吓坏了所以我把他的病告诉医生了
> 好几个工作人员跑过来让他安静下来
> 但他就是和他们打架
> 他不想让那个血压计上身
> < when the doctor put the thing on him he wanted to hit the doctor
> the doctor got scared and I told him it's his illness
> several staff tried to calm him down
> but he just fought with them
> he didn't want the monitor on his body >

A: 他就是不懂周围发生什么事
你还没说完呢
我记下来两件事
一个就是他分不清味精和盐
我不知道数量，不知该放多少米，多少水
< it's just he doesn't know what's going on
you haven't finished yet
I've taken down two things
one is that he'll mistake weijing (food flavoring) and salt
I don't know how much I should put in like rice or vegetable
what else? what else does he not understand? >

X: um

A: 他知不知道饭熟了
要是煮米饭他知道吗
< does he know if the rice is cooked
when the rice is cooked, does he know that? >

X: 他不知道的
有时候正在烧饭的时候
他会跑到冰箱边上在里面乱翻找东西吃
他也不知道怎么关火
像我才有的一个很新的炉子
他不知道怎么用
他根本不知道该怎么用这个新的
< he doesn't
sometimes in the middle of cooking rice
he will go and rummage in the fridge and eat things from it
and he doesn't know how to switch it off
like the modern cooker I got recently
he doesn't know how to use it
he doesn't know how to use the new one at all >

The first task for the advisor is to render X's narrative into a formula that can be used on the PiP form. X's narratives veer away from the kind of focus the advisor needs to complete the form favorably on behalf of her client. The advisor makes clear that the questions on food preparation are not complete. She reads aloud in Mandarin what she has typed in English ('I don't know how much I should put in, like rice or vegetable'). If she is moving *between* languages here there is equally a sense that she is living *in* both languages, translanguaging as well as translating. The multilingual person is not someone who translates constantly from one language (or cultural system) into another, although this is something multilinguals are sometimes able to do. But to be multilingual is, above all, to be one for whom translation is unnecessary, because one lives in more than one language (Pratt, 2010). The advisor seeks further information, asking an open question ('what else does he not understand?'), which seems to temporarily silence the client. When the advisor rewords the question as a closed question ('does he know if the rice is cooked?'), with a far more limited range of possible answers, X resumes her narrative mode, and further information is unveiled, this time directly relevant to the section of the form in hand. Here we have another type of translation. Style is as important as content here, as how something is said, rather than only what is said is equally important. The way the advisor's question is worded is initially unsuccessful in eliciting further information. It is only when the question is further mediated that more information emerges: X's husband can become distracted while cooking, and eats from the fridge; X's husband doesn't know how to use the new cooker. Any process of transferring one section of language into another, which says the same thing in different words, is a process of translation. That is, any reformulation is a translation (Boase-Beier, 2011). The advisor acts as a mediator, gathering information and making connections, moving across language zones, putting languages and texts into circulation (Simon, 2012). Mediators are involved in activities of exchange that involve a range of activities which exceeds mere translation – they are multilingual authors, self-translators, often active in a variety of intercultural and inter-artistic networks, often migrants, who develop transfer activities in several geo-cultural spaces. The advisor's skill as a mediator facilitates X's narrative. Translation across cultural differences is at the heart of the advisor's agency and skill as she populates the template of the PiP2 form with elements of X's narrative for a particular purpose, and with a particular goal in mind.

While the interaction goes on beyond a full hour, and comes to a close as the allocated time ends, the advisor asks X whether she wants to add anything to this section of the form. She reassures X that she has typed in English everything that X has told her. At this point the advisor reads to X what she has entered in this section of the form. She reads aloud in Mandarin what she has entered in English. We might summarize the steps the advisor takes as follows:

(i)   translates X's narrative from Mandarin to English;
(ii) translates X's extended narratives into abbreviated, summary versions;
(iii) resemiotizes the spoken narratives into the format required by the computer-based form;
(iv) translates the requirements of the form, and by extension the requirements of the welfare benefits system;
(v)   translates the resemiotized English version of X's narratives into Mandarin.

As she moves through these steps the advisor renders X's narratives into the computer-based form as evidence. In doing so she resemiotizes them, changing them to a format that is relevant and legitimate. The advisor 'reads' in Mandarin what she has entered into the computer-based form in English. This version of X's narrative is a recontextualized version of the original. Moreover, because it is now in written (typed) form, and in English, it becomes the authorized version. Once the narrative attains the status of a literate artifact, inscribed in the language of the system, it gains legitimacy, and is privileged above other versions. Meanings presented in printed text are generally harder to challenge than spoken versions, not only because the writer is often not present to answer questions, change formulations or accept additions, but also because written registers are generally more abstract and generalizing than spoken ones (Iedema, 2003). The narrative told by X is not the same as that entered on the form. Its materiality changes with each iteration. So seamless is this process of multiple translation and resemiotization that the advisor hardly appears to 'translate' from one language to another at all. The multilingual person is not someone who translates constantly from one language (or cultural system) into another. But to be multilingual is, above all, to be one for whom translation is unnecessary because one lives in more than one language (Pratt, 2010). The advisor mediates all this, maintaining a convivial relationship with her client while keeping a professional eye on what counts as evidence according to the government department. The advisor's job requires her to keep languages separate while simultaneously working beyond their boundaries in order to get the task done. The task at hand is ultimately not about languages, but about social justice, as the advisor strives to achieve access to benefits for her client, and her client's husband.

Discussion

We found that the range of knowledge and expertise an advisor was required to draw on in the Advice and Advocacy service was extensive. She was a translator, but her role as a translator stretched far beyond the transfer of meanings from one language to another. She was legal advisor, counsellor, advocate, assessor and mediator. The role of advisor in the Chinese community center demanded that she navigated competing ideologies. She worked within the linguistic boundaries of Mandarin and English. English only was demanded by the PiP form. Mandarin only was the language in which the two women communicated. However, it was through translation and translanguaging skills that the advisor accomplished the practical task of offering advice and completing the form. The advisor made a series of practical considerations, which had an ideological basis, and which defined what the 'job' was. She was to be more than a sympathetic listener. Her re-narration and recontextualization of X's narrative, told first in Mandarin and now retold in English, for the purpose of accessing state welfare benefits for her client, shows an ideological commitment to work on behalf of those denied benefits dues to their lack of proficiency in English. But while A's ability to work across two languages was central to her achieving her goals, it was translanguaging which allowed her to complete the form in a way most beneficial to her client.

We believe our ethnographic focus on the advisor shines a light on the real, immediate, urgent and often hidden work undertaken by individuals in community associations. We refute arguments that the focus on an individual advisor's translanguaging practices is complicit in neo-liberalism. Certainly, the advisor does not fit the description of the 'plurilingual cosmopolitan', and nor is she a member of the 'socio-economic elite' as described by Kubota (2016). The advisor's work is a serious attempt to make a real difference to her clients' lives. But the fact that Advice and Advocacy service was held in the Chinese community center also speaks to the Chinese community's efforts to establish structural and communal support for an ethnic group which is too often excluded from the rights and benefits provided by the state in the UK.

Scholarship in translanguaging and social justice is very far from being a move to court popularity or follow fashion. Nor is it by any means bent to the will of multinational capital. Rather, when it is deeply rooted in rigorous ethnographic research it generates new knowledge about language practices in settings where some people may be marginalized, discriminated against and denied access to resources. Research in translanguaging looks locally, and brings ideological, political and economic contexts to the analysis of social practice. This is nowhere more evident than in the research of Ofelia García, who puts it this way:

> For me, translanguaging has always contained within it the seeds of transformation – transformation that can only come about by disrupting the naturalizations concerning language and language education that have kept minoritized communities disengaged and miseducated. Language education has always served as a way to support processes of minoritization, racialization and the perdurance of coloniality. Translanguaging is not solely a scaffold to learn the dominant ways of using language; and it is not solely a pedagogy for those who are least able to succeed. Translanguaging is a way to enable language-minoritized communities who have been marginalized in schools and society to finally see (and hear) themselves as they are, as bilinguals who have a right to their own language practices, free of judgement from the white monolingual listening subject; and free to use their own practices to expand understandings. (García, 2020: xix)

Ofelia García remains steadfast in her lifelong commitment to bilingual education. She refers to the systemic inequalities brought about by the hegemony of English, 'whiteness' and colonialism. From her early work she has been, and remains, inspirational in her ability to narrow the gap between theory and practice, engage with practitioners to improve the educational outcomes of students and take on powerful institutions which endorse harmful monolingual ideologies and exclude the everyday practices of bilingual learners. She is fearless in her ability to face resistance, speaking truth to power whenever and wherever she is able. Hers is a recognition that practice must lead theory, and not the other way round. Translanguaging is not merely a description of interactional contact, but an ideological orientation to communication and difference. In her warm, inclusive and engaging manner Ofelia García has reshaped the landscape of bilingual education, second language teaching and learning and education pedagogies more widely. We owe her a huge debt of gratitude.

Post-Reading Discussion Questions

After reading this article you may wish to read more about translanguaging in non-schooling settings. These two readings focus on translanguaging and the arts, and translanguaging in a library setting:

Moore, E., Bradley, J. and Simpson, J. (eds) (2020) *Translanguaging as Transformation: The Collaborative Construction of New Linguistic Realities*. Bristol: Multilingual Matters.

Creese, A. and Blackledge, A. (2019) Translanguaging and public service encounters: Language learning in the library. *Modern Language Journal* 103 (4), 800–814. *https://doi.org/10.1111/modl.12601*

As you read, you might consider the following questions:

(1) How is research on translanguaging extended beyond educational settings in these two texts?
(2) How can a translanguaging for social justice agenda be developed in contexts beyond education?

Note

(1) A comprehensive representation of our linguistic ethnography of the Advice and Advocacy service is published as Blackledge, A. and Creese, A. (2021).

References

Bakhtin, M.M. (1981) *The Dialogic Imagination. Four Essays*. (Translated and edited by M. Holquist). Austin, TX: University of Texas Press.
Billig, M., Condor, S., Edwards, D., Gane, M., Middleton, D. and Radley, A. (1988) *Ideological Dilemmas: A Social Psychology of Everyday Thinking*. Thousand Oaks, CA: Sage Publications, Inc.
Blackledge, A. and Creese, A. (2021) *Interpretations – An Ethnographic Drama*. Bristol: Multilingual Matters.
Blackledge, A., Creese, A. and Hu, R. (2018) Translating the City. *Working Paper 34*. (http://www.birmingham.ac.uk/generic/tlang/index.aspx) Visited 10th October 2020.

Boase-Beier, J. (2011) *A Critical Introduction to Translation Studies* London: Continuum.

García, O. (2020) Foreword: Co-labor and re-performances. In E. Moore, J. Bradley and J. Simpson (eds) *Translanguaging as Transformation: The Collaborative Construction of New Linguistic Realities* (pp. xvii–xxii). Bristol: Multilingual Matters.

Iedema, R. (2003) Multimodality, resemiotization: Extending the analysis of discourse as multi-semiotic practice. *Visual Communication* 2 (1), 29–57.

Irvine, J.T. (1989) When talk isn't cheap: Language and political economy. *American Ethnologist* 16, 248–267.

Jaspers, J. (2018) The transformative limits of translanguaging. *Language & Communication* 58, 1–10

Kubota, R. (2016) The multi/plural turn, postcolonial theory, and neoliberal multiculturalism: Complicities and implications for applied linguistics. *Applied Linguistics* 37 (4), 474–494.

Kubota, R. (2020) Confronting epistemological racism, decolonizing scholarly knowledge: Race and gender in applied linguistics. *Applied Linguistics* 41 (5), 712–732.

Kubota, R. and Miller, E.R. (2017) Re-examining and re-envisioning criticality in language studies: Theories and praxis. *Critical Inquiry in Language Studies* 14 (2–3), 129–157.

Pavlenko, A. (2018) Superdiversity and why it isn't: Reflections on terminological innovation and academic branding. In B. Schmenk, S. Breidbach and L. Kuster (eds) *Sloganization in Language Education Discourse* (pp. 142–168). Bristol: Multilingual Matters.

Pratt, M.L. (2010) Response. Translation studies forum: Cultural translation. *Translation Studies* 3 (1), 94–110.

Reyes, A. (2014) Linguistic anthropology in 2013: Super-new-big. *American Anthropologist* 116 (2), 366–378.

Simon, S. (2012) *Cities in Translation: Intersections of Language and Memory*. Abingdon: Routledge.

14 Multiple Actors and Interactions Are at Work: English Language Policies in Post-Revolutionary Iran

Maryam Borjian

Foreword

The ideas discussed in this essay first emerged as the theme of my dissertation at Columbia University's Teachers College, where I had the privilege to work with Ofelia García as my academic mentor and doctoral advisor (2005–2009). At the time, globalization was a fashionable term and very popular across academic disciplines. In the field of educational linguistics, many books had been written on the theme of linguistic globalization and its impact on language education policies and practices worldwide. It was there that García offered a course on this topic that greatly resonated with me and my interest in language policy and political economy. As I now write these words many years later, I remember that instead of asking her students to read selected sources with a single, repetitive theoretical lens on the part of their authors, a lens in tune with her own view, García did the exact opposite. She went beyond the left and the right of theoretical spectrum and brought all sources with all views and approaches to her classes. Thanks to her highly inclusive and welcoming pedagogical style, we were able to read across theoretical lenses and academic disciplines to be able to shape our own ideas and form our own views. Although the Americas have served as the main research settings of García's research, her inclusive pedagogy and her global outlook, as evident in all her research, made García a key figure in shaping the minds of many scholars, whose research settings went way beyond the Americas to include many other parts of the world, including Iran, the subject nation of the present study.

Pre-Reading Discussion Questions

(1) Where do you place English in terms of its global status within the system of world languages today?
(2) How has English gained its current status/position at the international level?

Introduction

Whether English is perceived as a 'global language' (Crystal, 1997), as one of the most important 'world languages' (Ammon, 2013), a 'killer language' (Skutnabb-Kangas, 2003), a 'lingua Frankensteinia' (Phillipson, 2008), a 'thief' or a 'hydra' (Rapatahana & Bunce, 2012), there is no doubt that it is the most powerful language of our time. It has been 'on the move' and tirelessly 'in motion' (Pennycook, 2012), traveling through time and space (both geographical and virtual) and across borders (social, political, cultural and economic), finding itself new homes or adopted homes. It can be found everywhere and anywhere: both in expected and unexpected places.

The question as to whether English and the Anglo-American cultural norms are randomly diffused or systematically disseminated has triggered controversial responses in the field of language studies of the past three decades or so. Some scholars (Crystal, 1997; Graddol, 1998) attribute such diffusion to the will and desire of endogenous forces (or local borrowers), whom, in their quest for economic growth and competitiveness in the global market economy, borrow the global norms and implement them locally. Others (Phillipson, 2008; Rapatahana & Bunce, 2012; Skutnabb-Kangas, 2003) draw upon the Marxist notion of 'hegemony' to direct attention to the role of exogenous forces (or global lenders). Through this lens, the trajectory of the flow of the global norms is always one-way: from the English-speaking nations of the West to the rest of the world, which is said to be due to the unequal distribution of power (military, economic and political) that exists between the Center nations of the global North and the subjugated nations of the global South. There are still others (Canagarajah, 2005; Pennycook, 2012) who draw upon the postmodern notions of 'relativity', 'flux' and 'fluidity' as a means of giving agency to the local borrowers as well as to confirm the existence of national and regional variations of global norms. Arguing that the local actors are not passive entities to be manipulated by global forces, these scholars give power to the bottom-up forces of the global South for appropriating/localizing the global language as a means of fitting their own local contexts.

Instead of gazing at the local from afar and from behind a thick curtain, blurred by distance, a global imaginary, or a grand theoretical narrative, I argue that the local is not a homogenous entity to be examined through a single theoretical lens. Every local context has its own locally situated condition, which correlates directly to the socio-logical characteristics (sociocultural, political, economic, historical, etc.) of that particular context. Instead of having a single theoretical lens and going to the field to collect data to prove our theory-driven, already-proven conclusions, case studies with a multi-dimensional framework are needed to capture the multiplicity of actors and the complexity of interactions between the local and global forces. My reason for this position stems from my past research on the theme of English in post-revolutionary Iran (Borjian, 2013), in which none of the above-mentioned theoretical lenses can alone explain the strong position and popularity of English in today's Iran.

Post-revolutionary Iran is a nation whose English was localized as a means of both resisting the global and safeguarding the local. The localization movement began some four decades ago, after the country's 1979 revolution, which put an end to the country's secular monarchy and replaced it with a religious theocracy: the Islamic Republic of Iran (IRI). Since then, Iran has turned away from its western allies to follow an anti-western and anti-imperialist ideology. It was within such a climate that English became 'the language of the foes', 'a tool of Westoxication' or 'a plague from the West', with the power of emptying the minds of the local people of their own values and replacing them with those of the western nations.

Today, four decades later, this revolutionary past is still present and its reverberations can be felt. The billboards of Iran, alongside all other public spaces, bear large images of the leaders of the revolution alongside the pictures of the martyrs of the revolution and the martyrs of Iran-Iraq War (1980–1988), whose deaths are blamed on the unjust global imperialism and capitalism. Above, below and all around these images, there are anti-American slogans, shouting the anger of a nation's politicians at the enemy other: the United States of America and its western allies. These public images, signs and words, together with the localized English textbooks, are meant, among others, to preserve a past, a rather forgotten past, frozen in 1979 Iran, and to bring it back to reality and to the collective memory of Iranians. Typically young, educated, urbanized and secular, majority of Iranians are detached from this revolutionary past. They rather long for a different version of Iran and a different version of English education: a form of Iran that is not isolated from the international community, and a form of English that is not deviated from the international English.

As a result of these diverging interests between the forces from above and those from below, a duality exists at the heart of English education in today's Iran: one the localized English that is used in state-run schools, and the other the global form of English, or its Anglo-Americanized form, that is used in private language institutes. Of the two forms, the latter is in vogue and most popular among Iranians.

The Framework

Ofelia García (2009) is an advocate of a multi-dimensional conceptual framework that is both 'recursive' and 'dynamic'. In her view a recursive-dynamic theoretical framework supports the multiplicity of actors and the complexity of interactions. Viewing language education policy as a heterogeneous site as opposed to a homogenous whole, elsewhere, García *et al.* (2013: 33) call for a framework through which 'differences and tensions' among stakeholders and their motives and interests can be seen as 'the ordinary condition' of language policies.

This paper can be seen as a response to García's call. Using post-revolutionary Iran (1979–present) as the subject nation, I will examine the country's English education over the past four decades to reflect on the multiplicity of actors and interactions, which have set the stage for the current presence and popularity of the global English practices and norms in today's Iran. In doing so, I will examine the contributions of three sets of actors, namely: (1) national forces or those who operate at the nation-state level (e.g. government officials), (2) sub-national forces, those who operate below the nation-state level (e.g. private sectors) and lastly (3) supra-national forces who operate above the nation-state level (e.g. international organizations). By situating English within the country's broader sociopolitical, economic and historical context, I will go beyond the country's English education to reflect on reasons that have led to the current position of English in the country.

English: The Language of Westoxication

One set of powerful policy actors in almost all nations are politicians and government officials. In the field of comparative policy, the term policy 'emulation' or 'import' is used to refer to a process in which politicians or state officials copy policy lessons taken from elsewhere as a means of reshaping, modifying, or fundamentally revising their existing policies (Bennett, 1991). Yet, during radical political changes within a country, politicians may drop their references to foreign policy lessons or use them in a disparaging manner to distance themselves from foreign influence or the previous regime (Steiner-Khamsi, 2004). Such a distancing can be seen in Iran after its 1979 revolution, in which English was perceived as a tool of Westoxication by the country's politicians.

The term Westoxication (*gharb-zadegi*, in Persian) emerged in Iran long before the country's 1979 revolution. In fact, the term was first coined by Jalal Al-e Ahmad, a prominent Iranian leftist-Islamist writer and social-political critic who has been most praised (or blamed) for his 1962 book *Occidentosis: A Plague from the West*, in which he harshly criticized Iran's modernization reform under the Pahlavi dynasty (1925–1979). Entirely disregarding the positive impact of modernization – e.g. the construction of modern infrastructures, free education, free healthcare, women's emancipation from religious laws, to name but a few – Al-e Ahmad perceived modernization as a form of Westoxication that had weakened the country's Islamic values. A decade and half later, when Khomeini took control over the country as its supreme leader, he embraced Al-e Ahmad's Westoxication thesis and declared:

> The poisonous culture of imperialism [is] penetrating to the depths of towns and villages throughout the Muslim world, displacing the culture of the Koran, recruiting our youth and masse to the service of foreigners and imperialists. (Khomeini, 1981: 195)

Driven by the uncontested power of religion and bent upon the ideology of creating an Islamic image of the country, the IRI politicians used the Westoxication thesis as the basis of their policies. The outcome was notable in the field of English Education. All foreign experts and teachers (majority of them Americans) were expelled from the country. All foreign-run English language institutes were shut down, one after another. The two most notable of such institutions were the British Council (*Irān-Ingilis* in Persian) and Iran-America Society (*Iran-Āmrikā*), each with branches throughout the country. Although the former had a brief comeback (for more see, Borjian, 2011), the latter never had a chance to return; it was nationalized and became a state-run institute with a new name: Iran Language Institute (*kānoun-e zabān-e Iran*).

Another strategy for eliminating Westoxication was the localization strategy with its two underlying principles of purification and Islamization. Whereas the former purified the content of the locally produced English textbooks from the 'unwanted' western cultural elements, the latter replaced those elements with the so-called local values, which were entirely religious. As a result, a new form of English was born; a form in which the yesterday 'Jacks', 'Joes' and 'Marys' of New York or London all disappeared from school textbooks and were replaced by new characters: 'Mohammad', 'Ali' and 'Fatima' who were all pious Muslims who dressed modestly, prayed daily and read the Koran constantly.

With all these measures taken, there are pieces of evidence to suggest the IRI politicians were not against English. The first evidence concerns the former Iran-America Society, which was nationalized after the revolution but it maintained its pre-revolutionary status as the most important English language institute in Iran, having many branches throughout the country. The institute continued using its pre-revolutionary American English textbooks with little or no modifications. Although labeled as a nationalized Institute, in reality, it functioned as a private institute and charged students tuition and other fees for its English classes, which was a source of revenue for the revolutionary government. Another piece of evidence was a speech made by Khomeini in the early years of revolution. Instead of eliminating English fully, in this speech, he emphasized the importance of learning English in this way:

> In the past, there was no need for learning a foreign language. Today, however, learning foreign languages should be included in school curricula. (Khomeini quoted in Birjandi & Soheili, 2000: 1)

Following this speech, he issued a decree, asking for a local publisher to be created and funded by the government for the purpose of creating homegrown English textbooks for local use. In response to his call, SAMT was established in 1985. Although the English textbooks produced by this publisher (and other state-run publishers) were labeled as homegrown, localized English textbooks, in reality they were reprinting American and British English books with some modifications, like appropriating the cultural aspects of these books to fit the revolutionary ideology of the state (for more on SAMT and its books, see http://samt.ac.ir).

Within such circumstances, where were the country's sub-national forces – those that operate below the nation-state level? There was no participation on their part back then. The 'purification' principle of the Cultural Revolution that took place in Iran between 1980 and 1982 broke the back of the country's professional and elite networks. Some professors and educators were purged from their posts, some left their positions voluntarily, some were imprisoned and some others left the country permanently (on Iran's Cultural Revolution and its similarity with Chinese Cultural Revolution, see Sobhe, 1982). During this time, the private sector did not exist in the country either. All private-run institutions (just like their foreign-run counterparts) were either shut down or taken away from their owners and were given to the government. In the absence of sub-national forces (and also supranational forces), the IRI government enjoyed its absolute monopoly over the country's education and English education.

English: The Language of Privatization

By the late 1980s, the fervor of the revolution had already faded away. The prolonged Iran-Iraq War (1980–1988) left the country's economy in a state of turmoil, which suffered from mass destruction, a high rate of unemployment and inflation. In addition, the population explosion in Iran throughout the 1980s, due to abandoning Iran's pre-revolutionary Family Law, brought a high demand for employment and education that could not be met by state-run agencies. The death of Ayatollah

Khomeini in 1989 and the rise of pragmatic-cleric politicians to power, headed by Hashemi Rafsanjani (IRI President between 1989 and 1997), set the stage for the country's politicians to look abroad for successful policy lessons to emulate as a means of tackling the country's multiple problems. But where exactly did they look for such successful policies?

Against all expectations, the IRI politicians neither looked at other Muslim nations nor at other post-revolutionary countries with a similar anti-capitalist track record, like post-revolutionary Cuba (Corona & García, 1996). Their reference society was rather an international bank, the World Bank, whose biggest share-holder is the United States of America, labeled as 'the Great Satan' by the IRI's politicians. The World Bank is not just in the business of lending long-term loans to developing nations, but it is also in the business of lending its best policy lessons to loan-borrowing nations. Between 1991 and 1993, the World Bank resumed its loan-lending to Iran (Weiss & Sanford, 2008). In return of the borrowed loans, Iran accepted to implement the World Bank's 'structural adjustment policy', an offshoot of the neoliberal, macro-economic policies, which favored privatization and decentralization of state-run agencies. The privatization policy aimed to reduce the presence of government and government subsidies by transferring ownership from the public to private sectors in order to produce economic benefits.

Borrowing both loans and policy lessons from the World Bank could have been a source of controversy for a country whose leaders had been known for their anti-imperialist and anti-capitalist slogans. In order to reduce the controversy, no explicit reference was made to the origin (the USA-UK) of policy privatization. But there was another problem too. The World Bank's privatization policy demanded school privatization, another controversial policy for a country whose leaders had claimed their unconditional support for deprived and dispossessed people. Yet, rapid increases in the school-age population throughout the 1980s doubled the country's population, whose educational needs could no longer be met by state-run schools only. Consequently, a law was passed that permitted the private sector to invest in education sector, but again no explicit reference was made to the World Bank or the origin of policy privatization. This led to the rise of the so-called 'non-profit' private schools (madāres-e qeyr-e entefā'i), which, in reality, charged students high tuition fees. Thus, starting from the early 1990s, private schools became a norm in the country (Mehran, 1997).

Since the World Bank tends to be in favor of lending long-term loans for promoting English as the language of economic growth in developing countries, in search of any explicit or implicit references to English, I examined the country's First and Second Development Plans (implemented in 1989–1994 and 1995–1999, respectively). Although a significant amount of data was found on the improvement of the quality of education, perceiving higher education as a source of 'human capital' and a tool for economic growth, all the neoliberal jargons used in the World Bank's policy documents, there was no reference to English in the country's First and Second Development Plans.

The next sets of policy documents that I examined were the regulations issued by the Supreme Council of the Cultural Revolution, in charge of overseeing the country's macro educational laws and regulations. Among the regulations issued between 1989 and 1997, two were directly related to English but none of them was in favor of promoting the language. The first regulation (No. 306 issued on 6 April 1994) decreased the number of required English courses in universities (English courses were reduced from 14 to 10 credits) and the number of years of learning English in schools (reduced from 7 to 6 years). The second regulation (No. 294 issued on 16 November 1992) called for more allocation of funds to SAMT, the local publisher, for producing more localized English textbooks.

But English-related policy transfers cannot be examined only by looking at the actions of top government officials. As the insights of language policy analysts (Canagarajah, 2005; García, 2009; Spolsky, 2004) suggest, it would be misleading to refer to those in positions of authority (i.e. top-down forces like government officials) as the sole decision makers because many other people and forces influence language education policies and practices. Such forces may not hold governmental positions, but they can use their funds, power and/or voices to pull policy outcomes in directions they desire.

The most important set of sub-national forces that emerged in Iran in 1990s as the consequence of the World Bank's policy privatization were private language institutes. Unlike their counterparts in public schools, private language institutes were permitted to offer their own chosen curricula and textbooks as long as they complied with the broader rules and regulations set by the government. In order to attract fee-paying students, the private English language institutes looked abroad for best English practices, textbooks and teaching materials. The result was the importation of Communicative Language Teaching methodology, English textbooks and audio-visual products from various English-speaking nations, especially the UK and the US – e.g. *Headway* and *Interchange* among many other English textbooks entered Iran throughout the 1990s. Since Iran did not sign the international copyright law, the private language institute could pirate, reprint and reproduce foreign English books and materials with no penalty.

To prevent the wholesale borrowing of foreign materials, the Ministry of Culture and Islamic Guidance – in charge of supervising and approving the content of all books in the country – issued a decree, which required all private English language institutes to send a copy of their pirated/reprinted foreign textbooks to the ministry to get approval before using them in classrooms. The ministry was concerned only about trivial matters, like 'inappropriate' terminologies or pictures that were not in tune with the Islamic laws: e.g. terms like boyfriend, girlfriend, wine and alcoholic beverages would be replaced by brother, sister, milk and tea, or a headscarf would be drawn on women's hair to follow the strict Islamic dress code for women.

This suggests that the IRI officials were not only aware of the wholesale borrowing of American and British English textbooks by the private sector, but they were also involved in the process. It was striking for me to learn through my interview with the director of the Kish Language Institute – one of the largest English language institutes in the country, which was most credited for bringing the best practices and the latest American/British English textbooks to Iran in the 1990s – was not truly a private entity. It was rather a state-run agency, which falsely represented itself as a private Institute only to attract fee-paying students; students who had found the localized form of English offered in public schools of little or no use for preparing them for international English exams, job or study opportunities abroad (for details on my field notes on this topic, see Borjian, 2013).

English: The Language of Knowledge Economy

The next phase of borrowing both loans and policy lessons from the World Bank began in 1997 under another clerical president, Mohammed Khatami. During his eight years in the office, he prepared his twin development plans, namely the Third and Fourth Five Years Economic, Social and Cultural Development Plans (implemented in 2000–2004 and 2005–2009, respectively). In both plans, he called for economic reconstruction in a broader context of social, cultural and educational domains. It was a call for a further expansion of policy privatization. What was new, however, was the emulation of the World Bank's another economic policy, namely 'knowledge economy' (for more on the four pillars of the World Bank's knowledge economy, see http://web. worldbank.org/).

In addition to the World Bank, starting from the year 2000, Iran's social and economic reform was influenced by various developmental agencies of the United Nations. Available resources, both technical and financial, were mobilized to assist Iran to implement a systematic reform. Soon scores of collaborative projects between the IRI government and various developmental agencies of the UN were launched. The result was the emergence of many reports, including *United Nations Common Country Assessment (CCA) for Iran* (August 2003), *United Nations Development Assistance Framework (UNDAF) (2005–2009) for Iran* (September 2004), *The First Millennium Development Goals (MDGs) Report: Achievements and Challenges* (November 2004), to name but a few.

What all these reports had in common was their consistency in offering Iran a 'reform package', that emphasized the need to build the capacity for a knowledge-based economy through expansion of information technology, proactive international collaboration, improvement of national capacity in 'applied sciences', increasing 'national scientific research capacities', 'information technology' in universities, among others. The reform package that was offered to Iran was not country specific. It was rather part of the 'global reform package' or 'traveling policies' (Steiner-Khamsi, 2004), which had traveled across the entire Middle East, Central Asia and post-Socialist countries throughout the 1990s. Iran was, in fact, a late adopter of the global reform package.

The following excerpt may capture the type of educational reform (in accordance with the principles of knowledge economy) recommended by the international organizations to Iran, which read:

> Quality education creates economic growth … . Iran is facing the problem of students with degrees that leave the country each year because of the lack of appropriate infrastructures in universities and research centers as well as a lack of dynamic links between university and industry. It is important also to mention the missing link between industry, universities and research. The technological gap between Iran and advanced countries will be widening if this country doesn't reinforce its innovative capacity through quality education and appropriate fundamental and applied research capacities. (The First Millennium Development Goals Report for Iran, 2004: 13)

The impact of such a policy was notable on Iran's English education. The Fourth Development Plan 2005–2009 was the first policy document in which English was mentioned explicitly. For the first time in the history of the IRI rule in Iran, the modernization of English curricula became an explicit policy goal. Section D of Article 52 of the Fourth Development Plan of the country declared:

> With the purpose of … enhancing quantitative and qualitative development of the public education, government is charged with the responsibility … of enhancing necessary reform in the educational tutoring programs, deepening and improving teaching of mathematics, science, and English language. (Article 52, Section D, Law of the Fourth Economic, Social and Cultural Development Plan of the IRI, 2005–2009)

Starting from the early 2000 with the support of the local government and the technical and financial assistance of the international organizations, universities and schools began to equip themselves with computers and internet communication. Within a short period of time, major universities offered e-journals, e-books and e-databases, the majority of them in English. This digital revolution brought changes within the country's education system, including reducing the state's absolute monopoly over the content of the private-run, and to a lesser extent, the state-run school curricula and textbooks.

The move from a teaching-based education to a research-based education equally empowered the position of English. University professors and graduate students were now required by the government to publish their research in the international journals (the majority of them are in English). According to the 2008 report of the *International Comparative Performance of the UK Research Base,* Iran substantially increased its share of world papers, showing a 10-fold increase to almost 7000 papers in 2007.

The desire for a knowledge-based economy continued even further during the presidency of Mahmoud Ahmadinejad (2005–2013) and his successor, Hassan Rouhani (2013–present). Such desire is evident in the following speech delivered by Ali Asghar Fani, Rouhani's Minister of Education in 2015, who said:

> Currently a total of 401 student research centers are active in the country … and we have planned to increase the number of centers to 752. A research-oriented country requires preparing schools and students for research. (IRNA, 2015)

Other government initiatives included revisions of homegrown English school textbooks, revised twice: in 2003 and 2010. Whereas the 2003 version brought minor changes in the content of the locally produced English textbooks (e.g. slightly decreasing the overtly ideological tone of the textbooks), the latter, used Communicative Language Teaching (CLT) methodology, i.e. added communicative language skills (listening and speaking) to the content of the locally produced English textbooks, which had taught grammar, vocabulary and reading (for more on textbook revisions, see http://eng-dept.talif.sch.ir/).

While the government officials and the international organizations were busy in the borrowing-lending and implementing the global reform packages in Iran, sub-national forces were busy too. Private English language institutes were expanding their operations throughout the country. There was no official estimate on the exact number of such institutes. However, based on the estimate provided by an official from the Ministry of Culture and Islamic Guidance, whom I interviewed in 2008, as well as another estimate provided by Tehran Times in 2012, it can be said that the number of private language institutes in Iran rose from 2200 in 2003 to 5000 in 2012. What is noteworthy is that some of these language institutes – e.g. Kish, Shokouh, Simin and Iran Language Institute (i.e. the former Iran-America Society) – have more than 100 branches throughout the country. This limited estimate may show both the widespread nature of the private sector involved in English education and the popularity of learning English among Iranian students.

To the list of sub-national forces that reinforced English language policies and practices (albeit indirectly and implicitly) in post-2000 Iran, we should add the fee-paying students. There were several reasons why youth in Iran showed substantial interest in attending private English language institutes. One reason could be the low quality of locally produced English textbooks and curricula that were used in the public schools. These books (at least prior to Iran's 2010 school textbook reform initiative) promoted little more than reading and grammar skills. Due to the absence of communicative language skills, it was unsurprising to learn that less than 5% of Iranian students graduating from public schools in 2012 could speak English (Tehran Times, 2012). Secondly, students were motivated by job prospects and the ability to pass the international English exams (such as IELTS, TOEFL, etc.) as a means of finding a job, studying abroad, or leaving the country permanently for a decent level of freedom. Thus, many Iranian students attended private language institutes to learn the type of English that would increase their social and economic mobility at the international level. This is what Spolsky (2004: 85) regards as 'the quest for empowerment'. This quest is evident in the results of the IELTS Exam (a.k.a. International English Language Testing System), as shown in Table 14.1.

IELTS is an exam required for migration to or admission to universities in the UK, Canada, New Zealand and Australia. It is assessed on a 9-band scale and reports scores both overall and by individual language skills. As the data illustrates, Iranian students ranked the highest in their overall performance in the Middle East region. This performance, especially in speaking skill, is notable if we take into account the condition in which Iranian students learn English, i.e. no official-bilateral student/teacher-exchange programs between Iran and English-speaking countries, absence of the international English language teaching centers in Iran, the existence of many international sanctions against Iran, to name but a few. None of these constrains existed in the neighboring countries, yet Iranian students performed better than their other Middle Eastern counterparts.

Table 14.1 Mean band IELTS Score for the Most Frequent Countries or Regions of Origin (Academic Training), 2012

Countries	Listening	Reading	Writing	Speaking	Overall
Iran	5.9	5.9	5.7	6.3	6.0
Kuwait	5.3	4.9	4.8	5.7	5.2
Oman	5.3	5.1	5.1	5.8	5.4
Qatar	5.0	4.7	4.6	5.5	5.0
Saudi Arabia	4.8	4.7	4.7	5.6	5.0
UAE	4.8	4.6	4.7	5.3	4.9

Source: http://www.ielts.org

To the list of Iranian sub-national forces that have contributed to the promotion of English in Iran, private press and publishing houses should be added. Since foreign publishers have not been permitted to operate in Iran since 1979, on the one hand, and since the local publishers have been permitted to reprint, reproduce and even pirate foreign English textbooks, on the other hand, the local publishers have been very active in importing English teaching materials and textbooks to the country for their own economic gains.

Conclusion

The expanding role of English, and English education, has received much scholarly attention over the past three decades or so. This has, in turn, led to a vibrant debate among scholars on how and why English has gained its powerful position in the world. Instead of taking a side or favoring a view over another, this paper went beyond the theoretical lenses and examined English education policies in post-revolutionary Iran to understand the who, how and why of the current popularity of English, especially its Anglo-Americanized form, in today's Iran. Based on what was discussed in the paper, several concluding remarks can be made.

Firstly, the IRI politicians have displayed ambivalent attitudes towards both the West and the English language. On the one hand they called English the language of Westoxication, but on the other hand they did not eliminate it from school curricula. On the one hand they closed all foreign-run English language institutes, but on the other hand they took control over those institutes and offered English (not the localized but the Anglo-Americanized form to fee-paying students).Whereas they claimed unconditional support for the disposed people, they privatized schools unaffordable by the disposed families. They claimed to be against the West, but they turned to the West for technical and financial assistance. Although they promised international organizations to privatize state-run agencies, they falsely labeled their own institutes as private English language institutes. Whereas they called for a mass production of localized English textbooks, they both initiated and highly encouraged a wholesale borrowing of English practices from English-speaking nations. The reasons for such conflicting actions were multiple. The Westoxication thesis and the localized English textbooks were used as strategies to signify the country's emancipation from the western cultural and linguistic hegemony only to please their supporters at home. The implementation of policy privatization and knowledge economy was to tackle the country's multiple social and economic problems to have stability in the country. Yet, the representation of state-run language institutes as private entities was surely for economic gains.

Excluding the state-run educational organizations that falsely represent themselves as private entities, the rest of Iranian sub-national forces have been fragmented groups, populated by small private companies like private publishers and private language institutes. These private institutes have limited capital, resources, and opportunities. In non-democratic countries where everything is controlled by the government, the sub-national forces may not have much power. In the case of Iran, such forces are not allowed to initiate or make policies. Regardless of their limited power, Iranian sub-national forces have used every platform given to them to pull policy outcomes in directions they desired. This tendency was evident in actions of the private English language institutes and private publishers that looked abroad for innovative ideas, best practices, teaching materials and textbooks to improve the teaching and learning English in the country. The motive for such actions was mostly economic. Students were another set of sub-national forces who contributed (albeit indirectly) to the popularity of the Anglo-Americanized form of English in Iran. This was done mainly by showing interest in the type of English they wanted to learn; the type that was not offered in public schools but rather by private language institutes. Their motives were more personal, like finding better opportunities inside or outside the country.

Lastly, on supra-national forces, they have had no representatives in Iran over the past four decades. In the realm of English education, Iranians have been fully in charge of their own English education. It would, however, be inaccurate to assume that supra-national forces have had no role to play in strengthening English education in Iran. The content of the neoliberal reform packages of policy privatization and knowledge economy, which were lent to Iran by the international organizations throughout the 1990s and 2000s, were after all global. It is true that these policies were mostly economic, but they set stage for English to strengthen its position in Iran. Due to Iran's oil-based economy, however, it would be misleading to assign absolute agency to the international organizations. Iran is not a 'loan-dependent' nation, whose implementation of the global policies could be explained only by the 'loan conditionality' of the international finance organizations. Regardless of the existence of many international sanctions against Iran, the country has been able to survive thanks to its oil-driven economy. As such, borrowing policy lessons from abroad and implementing them locally were done voluntarily by the country's politicians as a means of tackling the country's internal problems.

Post-Reading Discussion Questions

(1) In this paper, we examined some reasons for the popularity of English in Iran. What are other reasons for the popularity of English in other parts of the world?
(2) We also focused on the role of various actors who have strengthened English education in Iran. Who are the actors who have strengthened English in countries that you know?

References

Ammon, U. (2013) World languages: Trends and futures. In N. Copland (ed.) *The Handbook of Language and Globalization* (pp. 101–122). Malden, MA: Wiley-Blackwell.

Bennett, C. (1991) What is policy convergence and what causes it? *British Journal of Political Science* 21 (2), 215–233.

Birjandi, P. and Soheili, A. (2000) *The 8th Grade English Course Textbook*. Tehran: Organization for Educational Research and Planning.

Borjian, M. (2011) The rise and fall of a partnership: The British Council and the Islamic Republic of Iran (2001–2009). *Journal of Iranian Studies* 44 (4), 541–562.

Borjian, M. (2013) *English in Post-Revolutionary Iran: From Indigenization to Internationalization*. Bristol: Multilingual Matters.

Canagarajah, A.S. (2005) *Reclaiming the Local in Language Policy and Practice*. Mahwah, NJ: Lawrence Erlbaum.

Corona, D. and García, O. (1996) English in Cuba: From the imperial design to the imperative needs. In J. Fishman, A. Conrad and A. Rubal-Lopez (eds) *Post-Imperial English: Status Change in Former British and American Colonies, 1940–1990* (pp. 85–110). Berlin: Mouton de Gruyter.

Crystal, D. (1997) *English as a Global Language*. Cambridge: Cambridge University Press.

First Millennium Development Goals Reports: Achievements and Challenges (2004) Tehran: United Nations and the Institute for Management and Planning Studies in Iran.

García , O. (2009) *Bilingual Education in the 21st Century: A Global Perspective*. Malden, MA: Wiley-Blackwell.

García, O., Zakharia, Z. and Otcu, B. (eds) (2013) *Bilingual Community Education and Multilingualism: Beyond Heritage Languages in a Global City*. Bristol: Multilingual Matters.

Graddol, D. (1998) *The Future of English*. London: British Council.

IRNA (2015) Iran to open some 50 Nano research centers. See http://www.irna.ir/en/News/81425287/ (accessed May 2015).

Khomeini, R. (1981) *Islam and Revolution: Writings and Declarations of Imam Khomeini (1941-1980)* [Translated and annotated by H. Algar]. Berkley: Mizan Press.

Mehran, G. (1997) Education in postrevolutionary Persia, 1979–1995. In E. Yarshater (ed.) *Encyclopædia Iranica* (Vol. VIII, Fascicle 2). Santa Ana, CA: Mazda Publishers.

Pennycook, A. (2012) *Language and Mobility: Unexpected Places*. Bristol: Multilingual Matters.

Phillipson, R. (2008) *Linguistic Imperialism Continued*. Hyderabad: Orient Black Swan.

Rapatahana, V. and Bunce, P. (eds) (2012) *English Language as Hydra: Its Impacts on Non-English Language Cultures*. Bristol: Multilingual Matters.

Skutnabb-Kangas, T. (2003) Linguistic diversity and biodiversity. The threat from killer languages. In C. Mair (ed.) *The Politics of English as a World Language: New Horizons in Postcolonial Cultural Studies* (pp. 31–52). Amsterdam: Rodopi.

Sobhe, K. (1982) Education in revolution: Is Iran duplicating the Chinese Cultural Revolution? *Comparative Education* 18 (3), 271–280.

Spolsky, B. (2004) *Language Policy*. Cambridge: Cambridge University Press.

Steiner-Khamsi, G. (2004) *The Global Politics of Educational Borrowing and Lending*. New York, NY: Teachers College, Columbia University.

Tehran Times (2012) Retrieved 20 March 2015 from: http://www.tehrantimes.com/component/content/article/94791.

Weiss, M.A. and Sanford, J.E. (2008) *CRS Report for Congress: The World Bank and Iran*. See http://www.fas.org/sgp/crs/mideast/RS22704.pdf (accessed August 2015).

15 Reimagining Language Policy through the Lived Realities of Bilingual Youth

Sarah Hesson

Pre-Reading Discussion Questions

(1) How was the language policy determined in different spaces you have been part of, such as school or work? Were you part of the decision-making process?
(2) Does the kind of language you use change in different contexts or with different people? If so, how do you choose your language practices?

Introduction

This chapter foregrounds the perspectives of bilingual Latinx adolescent youth in reimagining school and classroom-level language allocation policy in ways that center the language practices and lived realities of youth. At the core, this approach is grounded in Dr Ofelia García's conception of translanguaging and dynamic bilingualism (2009), and our shared belief that children's and communities' language practices must be at the center of pedagogical and policy decisions. The data from this chapter draws from my dissertation research study, which sought to explore bilingual Latinx middle schoolers' experiences of language as a means of generating individual and collective critical understandings of the connections between language, race, ethnicity and power. The study took place in an after-school program at a K-8 dual language bilingual school in New York City in 2015, and Dr García guided my work as my dissertation advisor. Data collection methods centered on interactive activities during the after-school sessions, as well as individual interviews before and after program participation.

Using García's theory of dynamic bilingualism, I outline four lessons from youth based on their reported language use and perspectives on bilingualism and translanguaging, then consider the implications of these lessons for language allocation policy, suggesting an approach to language policy that is grounded in both dynamic bilingualism and youth's lived realities. The first two sections focus on bilingualism, including youth's views on translanguaging and the ways youth describe using language, noting the use of qualifiers such as 'mostly' and 'usually' that suggest the use of translanguaging in many contexts. The third section focuses on youth's reported difficulty in speaking monolingual Spanish and notes that most refer to instances of speaking only Spanish as 'having' to do so, in contrast to monolingual English, where the qualifier 'have to' is absent and they simply 'speak'. The fourth section examines youth perspectives of the language dynamics within the after-school program itself, and theorizes on what might have shifted the dynamics, and to what effect. These findings carry important implications for school and classroom language policies for multilingual youth.

Translanguaging

Translanguaging provides a theoretical framework to understand the flexible and dynamic language practices used by transnational, multilingual US communities. The theoretical basis for translanguaging moves away from an understanding of language as a system of structures, to consider instead how language emerges from use. Rather than 'language', which implies a fixed, static body of knowledge, the term 'language practices' highlights the way in which speakers shape and define language through use, and how language itself is embodied in the users of those practices (García & Li, 2014). When speakers engage in language practices, they are languaging; they are actively creating and recreating language as they use it. Translanguaging, then, can be understood as this process of communication and meaning-making between speakers who use multiple language practices.

García (2009) writes, 'For us, translanguagings are *multiple discursive practices* in which bilinguals engage in order to *make sense of their bilingual worlds*' (2009: 45, emphasis in original). Thus, for bilinguals, dynamic bilingual interactions, in which speakers use multiple languages to communicate, are natural and often essential to sense-making. Rather than seeing the separation between languages as natural and inevitable, and seeing languages as self-contained systems that individuals possess, García's concept of translanguaging recognizes that bilinguals do not *have* separate languages, but rather *use* multiple language practices in dynamic ways. Though for purposes that range from practical to political, societies label languages such as 'English' or 'Spanish' as distinct, static entities, in practice, bilinguals use language fluidly and dynamically (García, 2009; Mignolo, 2012).

To speak of languaging is not just to be descriptive of the reality of multilingual communities, it is also to speak back to hegemonic linguistic and cultural practices. Mignolo writes:

> The celebration of bi or pluri languaging is precisely the celebration of the crack in the global process between local histories and global designs … and a critique of the idea that civilization is linked to the 'purity' of colonial and national monolanguaging. (2012: 250)

Thus, Mignolo asserts the rightful place of translanguaging, or bi or pluri languaging as he calls it, in the nation-state, as well as challenges the elevated status of 'pure' colonial languages such as standard English or Spanish.

For Mignolo, bi or pluri languaging is also intimately tied with the fruitful border thinking that is generated by, and also generates, the unique positionality of 'the new mestiza' as conceived by Gloria Anzaldúa (1987). Mignolo attributes Anzaldúa with the idea of 'bilanguaging as a fundamental condition of border thinking' (Mignolo, 2012: 253). In other words, translanguaging plays a key role in the development of the identity of the new mestiza, and the fruitful generation of ideas that accompany this unique positionality. Without translanguaging, it might be impossible to explore, name, embrace or resist aspects of life, and of self, in the borderlands.

Creating opportunities for multilingual youth to engage in the world multilingually and to develop multilingual voices is distinct from opportunities to develop multiple languages separately from each other. Further, situating multilingual language practices in the borderlands while elevating the status of these practices in school has the potential to transform school from a place to learn any given language, to a place where youth in the borderlands have opportunities to see who they are, where they are, why they are, and to fight injustice in their lives. Starting with the location of youth and their language practices rather than the abstract idea of language, school becomes a place ripe for critical analysis and change.

Translanguaging as resistance

Linking language practices to the agenda of the nation state, and recognizing which language practices are valued, upheld and officially sponsored, and which are deemed inadequate, is essential to viewing the act of translanguaging as transgressive, especially in the context of schooling. Mignolo (2012: 273) writes, 'While the nation-state promotes love toward national languages, bilanguaging love arises from and in the peripheries of national languages and in transnational experiences'. Mignolo goes on to describe bilanguaging love as 'love for being between languages, love for the disarticulation of the colonial language and for the subaltern ones, love for the impurity of national languages … '

(2012: 274) and further connects the idea of bilanguaging love to Freire's idea that rebellion by the oppressed is an act of love and 'grounded in the desire to pursue the right to be human' (Freire, 1993: 38 as cited in Mignolo, 2012: 274).

Mignolo's idea of bilanguaging love, Freire's assertion of basic human rights and Anzaldúa's description of the borderlands and the subjectivity that living in that space creates, all provide a useful frame for thinking about translanguaging as an act of resistance to cultural and linguistic domination and an assertion of self in the context of schooling. Pratt calls spaces of diverse cultural interaction 'contact zones', and recognizes that they often take place 'in contexts of highly asymmetrical relations of power ... ' (Pratt, 1991: 34). Many dual language bilingual schools are contact zones in that they serve diverse student bodies including white and students of color. Further, US educators are disproportionately white. These two factors shape the context of schooling for multilingual youth of color. Using youth's full linguistic repertoires creates space for multilingual youth, as well as new opportunities to address unequal power relations and cultural and linguistic hegemony.

Further, 'all language learning is cultural learning' (Heath, 1983: 145–146); this relationship is critical to understanding the importance of the ways that schools ask youth to use, or not use, their language practices, and how these choices can lead to more or less liberatory educational spaces. Watson-Gegeo (2004) affirms this idea in two critical tenets of language socialization, that 'language and culture are mutually constitutive and socially constructed' and that further, 'all cultural activities across different contexts are socio-historically marked' (2004, as cited in Baquedano-López et al., 2010: 342). Thus, there is more at stake when learning a new language than simply memorizing a new code of communication; as speakers acquire new ways of communicating, they do so in social contexts that further shape their identities and positions in varying contexts. Likewise, choosing which language practices to use in a given context carries greater significance than just practicing that language; the linguistic features chosen situate and contextualize the communication. A sentence said in English then repeated in Spanish does not communicate the same message twice, but rather each communication carries with it the weight and context of those language practices for both the speaker and the listener. The same sentence spoken using translanguaging practices communicates a different meaning still. In the classroom, this has implications for how children and adolescents are socialized into ways of languaging to 'generate culturally meaningful ways of thinking, feeling, and being in the world' that will afford them sociolinguistic interactions that dynamically resist the reproduction of social inequality (Watson-Gegeo, 2004, as cited in Baquedano-López et al., 2010: 342).

'It's Not a Standard Language but It's Still a Language'

This section focuses on data collected in an after-school session aimed at exploring youth's articulated understandings of translanguaging, and their reflections on their own language practices. In this session, participants identified translanguaging as a common everyday practice in which they engaged, but did not view as appropriate for 'official' use.

I first asked youth to define 'standard English' or 'standard Spanish', then asked if they had heard of Spanglish (the word youth used to identify translanguaging), to which they responded yes. I followed up with the questions, 'Is Spanglish a valid way of talking? Is it just as acceptable as speaking standard English?'.

Isabel responded,

Not like at school and stuff, no … . In school they're trying to teach you like how to correctly speak these two languages, like let's say, they're trying to teach you how to speak Spanish correctly, and then English correctly, but when you mix those together, it's not correct but it's still a language; it's not standard, it's not a standard language, but it's still a language. (Field notes, 8 June 2015)

Isabel explained the practice of translanguaging as a valid way to communicate, but that it was limited in the context of school. Her description of the school 'trying to teach you like how to correctly speak these two languages' demonstrated her understanding of the school's focus on standardized language forms, rather than the socioculturally situated practices that she recognized may not be standard, but are nonetheless still a language. Monica responded to the same question,

Ok, so my mom says that Spanglish is nothing, that it's the wrong way to say it … so whenever my mom says, whenever I speak like Spanglish … my mom says no, you cannot tell me like that, either you're speaking Spanish or English. (Field notes, 8 June 2015)

Monica's home experiences mirrored Isabel's school experiences; while both participants used translanguaging, they both received the message that the practice was not as acceptable as using a standard language form.

I followed up by asking why they thought others had a negative view of mixed language practices. Isabel theorized,

Well I'm pretty sure they have that negative view because … to some people it's not a language, so then to that person, that says it, they're just like oh yeah you know what, they're just speaking like that cause they don't know the language. Like let's say you go to like Brazil or something, and you know a little bit, you know a little bit of Portuguese, and then you're from here, so then you'll, you know you'll stick in some English words, and then they'll be like oh yeah they just don't know how to speak it, but then you still know it, you just you're so comfortable with English, that when you're speaking Portuguese it just comes naturally. (Field notes, 8 June 2015)

Isabel emphasized how natural it is for multilingual people to use their full linguistic repertoires when they communicate.

The data from the session above shows, on the one hand, the insecure place of translanguaging in institutional or official capacities, and on the other, the very secure and real place that translanguaging had in youth's lives. Despite official messages from home or school, youth recognized that while translanguaging may not be standard, it was 'still a language'. This finding carries important implications for dual language bilingual programs; while these programs strive to build on the language practices of their students, the findings here suggest that strict language policies that separate the two languages are not consistent with the way youth typically use language. Further, the way youth describe translanguaging practices as 'nothing', 'not a language' or 'not correct' based on their own or others' views demonstrates their understanding that socially, translanguaging is viewed as inferior to standard language forms. Bilingual programs, then, must consider the messaging to youth and the impact on youth's sense of self and belonging when considering the policy on using translanguaging in school.

Translanguaging Is Not a Balanced Act

The findings above are further corroborated in the following section, in which participants described their language practices using qualifiers such as 'mostly' or 'usually', showing a measure of linguistic flexibility in their interactions. When asked how participants used language, many reported using both English and Spanish with other bilinguals, including family, friends and classmates, usually with an emphasis on one language or the other.

Monica reported that with her sister, 'we usually speak English and Spanish' with an emphasis on English, while with her parents, she spoke ' ... mostly in Spanish but like my dad is usually we speak both', and with her friends 'we'll usually speak both languages' with an emphasis on English, except when they make a concerted effort to practice Spanish (Entry interview, 27 May 2015). At Sunday school, Monica reported usually speaking Spanish, while in school there was a greater emphasis on English, though,

... we will usually speak both languages. And either Spanish or English, but when it's like English, English week, we speak English but when it's

Spanish week, we usually speak a little bit English, cause like sometimes we don't know the words in Spanish so we say it in English. (Entry interview, 27 May 2015)

Joanna also reported speaking a mix of English and Spanish at home, with an emphasis on Spanish. 'I speak a lot of Spanish. Um I sometimes speak English with my mom, when it's like about what we're gonna eat' (Entry interview, 13 May 2015). Conversely, she reported mostly speaking English with her friends, but using Spanish in certain scenarios,

With Angie when I argue with her and she gets like really annoying I would scream at her in Spanish … . With Yanetsy I would like not really scream at her because then she would pretend to cry. So I'll just like say really annoying stuff to her in Spanish. (Entry interview, 13 May 2015)

Diana similarly described using 'mostly' English with her brother, '… with my brother we mostly talk English because he understands more English than Spanish' (Entry interview, May 27, 2015). When asked how she used language with friends, Diana said, 'With my friends I just use English because since our domain language is English and we understand more than Spanish we talk mostly that' while with her father, 'I speak more Spanish with him because since he's still learning [English] … ' (Entry interview, 27 May 2015).

Isabel described usually speaking English with her mom and brother,

So I usually speak English with my mom and my brother, but my mom wants me to speak more Spanish with her, but I speak a lot of Spanish when I'm with my father because a lot of them don't know English so I have to speak Spanish. (Entry interview, 20 May 2015)

She further reported mixing the languages more in contexts that required more Spanish than English, including speaking to a Spanish-dominant friend and when completing a lesson in Spanish (Entry interview, 20 May 2015).

Edwin likewise described bilingual language practices with friends and family, explaining that he used 'Spanish … and English too' at home, while with friends, he used 'English … with Spanish' (Entry interview, June 3, 2015). Talking about school, Jorge reported, 'I get to speak both languages, not only English or Spanish, but both. Like in my house I speak both languages too' (Entry interview, 18 May 2015).

The findings above demonstrate that translanguaging is not a balanced act. Qualifiers such as 'usually', 'mostly', 'sometimes', 'both' and 'too' indicate that youth use translanguaging to communicate, usually with an emphasis on one language or the other depending on the context. The youth consistently describe language practices that are language-dominant ('mostly English', 'usually in Spanish') rather than monolingual. This finding suggests that translanguaging is not a balanced act composed of 50% linguistic features of one language and 50% from another. Instead, translanguaging happens with shifting emphases, and for shifting purposes. Which language was emphasized depended on the given context, not just their own linguistic ability; youth described making linguistic choices based on factors such as audience (e.g. English-dominant siblings), place (e.g. church) and purpose (e.g. conveying feelings). Some youth reported using both languages with people who also knew both languages, such as siblings, though in many of these instances they identified an emphasis on one language or the other. Other youth reported using translanguaging to aid communication in Spanish-dominant contexts where they felt less comfortable. In other instances, youth made deliberate shifts in their language emphasis because parents requested that they practice Spanish, or to practice Spanish with friends.

In these contexts, Spanish or English was not spoken exclusively, but rather was the language of emphasis. Just as subway passengers shift their weight from one foot to the other to maintain their equilibrium while standing on a moving train, we might think about youth shifting their linguistic 'weight' from one set of language practices to the other based on contextual factors; and yet just as the whole body is engaged in the act of standing, so is one's entire linguistic repertoire engaged in communication even as the emphasis may shift from one 'language' to another. Further, maintaining equal weight on both feet would not allow for necessary movement, but shifting weight as needed creates flexibility, and in this imbalance is where youth report finding their linguistic equilibrium. Designing school language policy that offers youth opportunities to use and hone these practices could have a powerful impact on the ways multilingual youth engage with school, and the ways schools support multilingual youth and community language practices.

On 'Having to' Speak Spanish

In this section, I examine youth's articulated attitudes towards Spanish-dominant versus English-dominant contexts. Most participants expressed difficulty in speaking predominantly in Spanish and referred to these instances as 'having to' speak Spanish, in contrast to English-dominant contexts, where the qualifier 'have to' was absent and they simply 'spoke'. Six of 11 participants, in the entry interview, described *having to* speak Spanish in certain contexts, in contrast to simply *speaking* English. Three additional youth described challenges they had in completing their work during 'Spanish time'. At the same time, many participants expressed enthusiasm for these challenging pedagogical spaces, and saw the structured school policy that mandated Spanish use as creating more opportunities for them to develop Spanish language skills. However, nearly all participants described using both languages in these Spanish-dominant spaces in school, challenging the notion that they are Spanish-monolingual spaces as the school's language policy intended.

Table 15.1 outlines the instances in which participants described 'having to' speak Spanish (bold emphasis mine).

Table 15.1 Participant descriptions of speaking Spanish

Participant	Response in entry interview
Isabel	With family: ' … I speak a lot of Spanish when I'm with my father because um a lot of them don't know English **so I have to speak Spanish**'. With friends (corrects herself when describing speaking English): 'Um with Julia, **I have to speak Spanish sometimes**, but with most of my other friends, **I have to speak -I speak English** … ' (20 May 2015).
Diana	With her mom: ' … since she doesn't know that much English, **I have to translate to, for her**, when it's some business, or when she doesn't, when she needs me to translate it for her'. With family in general: 'Well they um mostly use Spanish so when they talk Spanish, **I also have to talk Spanish** because they don't know that much English' (27 May 2015).
Monica	With friends, 'try to' and also 'have to' speak Spanish: ' … we always **try to speak Spanish**, like because Susana wants to get better in her Spanish, and Niya, **so we always have this like week that we always have to speak Spanish**, so yeah, so we help each other'. With her mom: ' … with our mom, **we have to speak Spanish** so yeah' (27 May 2015).
Luz	At home, at the dinner table: ' … the people that are there talk Spanish, **so we have to talk in Spanish** or sometimes me and my sister like to talk by ourselves and talk English' (20 May 2015).
Yanetsy	In school during 'Spanish time': ' … **you would have to speak** … well not, like when the teacher is leaving everyone speaks English, but like in class like when you answer questions **you have to … say it in Spanish**' (27 May 2015).
Chris	In school: '**Sarah**: How do you use language at school? Like in the classroom. **Chris**: Uhh, it depends, like. **When we have to talk Spanish, we talk**, or if it's English week then we talk' (18 May 2015).
Jorge	Not of his own speech, but when speaking of teachers: '**Sarah**: … when it's Spanish time, do people sometimes speak in English at the tables? **Jorge**: Yeah, to each other. But when the teacher's asking them, they speak Spanish, cause **the teachers all have to, the teachers also have to speak Spanish**' (18 May 2015).

Seven of 11 participants referenced 'having to' speak Spanish, six of them in reference to themselves, and one (Jorge) in reference to teachers. The other four participants in the program did not use the construction 'have to', but three reported difficulties in completing schoolwork during 'Spanish time'. Tyler reported that he must respond in Spanish at times during the school day:

Sarah: And how do you like use language in school, will you always follow the rules of the language?

Tyler: *No.* [A bit emphatically]. [Sarah laughs]. Like in Spanish like if I'm speaking to my friend I'll speak English, but if the teacher asks me a question in Spanish I must respond *in* Spanish (Entry interview, 11 May 2015).

Tyler also explained that his vocabulary is smaller in Spanish than in English, 'Yeah cause English it's like I can use so many words, then in Spanish, I have like not a small vocabulary, but not as big as English' (Entry interview, 11 May 2015).

When asked if she found language harder in certain situations, Joanna responded, 'When I'm explaining a Math problem, it's like really hard in Spanish 'cause I don't know what to say and I barely speak Spanish, I rarely say Math stuff in Spanish, like um saying equations and stuff' (Entry interview, 13 May 2015). Angie also reported a tendency to speak more English than Spanish amongst peers, including during 'Spanish time':

Sarah: And how about in school, do you use the language according to the day or the class?

Angie: Um no. Well what what we used to do for like years like for example let's say it's writing and uh and it's English time … and everybody speaks English, but when it's Spanish time, people speak English to themselves, but when but when the teacher's like oh this kid come up and show this, the kid's speaking in Spanish, and explaining everything, translating the thing that they said in English to the teachers, but in Spanish. (Entry interview, 20 May 2015)

When asked if the same happened during 'English time', Angie reported that students stuck to English. When asked why she thought that was, she responded,

Because um a lot of these people were born in the English people environment, New York, and a lot of people wanna learn English, sometimes, some people, so they just speak English so they can train about it. And people who already know English just wanna speak English just because. They just feel like it. It's more comfortable for them. (Entry interview, 20 May 2015)

The only participant who did not use the language described above or report difficulties during 'Spanish time' was Edwin, who was the only participant in the after-school program from the self-contained special education classroom. Significantly, in that class, the teacher did not follow the same strict language policy that the general education classes in the school followed. When describing his language practices in school, Edwin simply reported using both languages in all his interactions –at school, with family and with friends.

In sum, while most participants felt stretched by Spanish-dominant contexts, they simultaneously valued those contexts as opportunities to use Spanish-dominant language practices. In the context of this study, a middle school dual language bilingual setting in which the majority of youth were US-born or had been in the US since a very young age, most participants felt less comfortable in Spanish-dominant settings, as evidenced in their description of 'having to' speak Spanish while simply 'speaking' English. Despite this challenge, most participants reported valuing Spanish-dominant spaces in school, even though the strict language policy sometimes felt forced or stretched them beyond their comfort zone. These findings point to the need to rethink language policy in dual language bilingual programs (1) to meet the needs of youth, (2) to accurately reflect the language use in those spaces and (3) to more effectively counter English hegemony in bilingual schools.

Reflecting on Language Use in the After-School Program

The findings in the section above show that while youth sometimes found themselves in Spanish-dominant contexts that challenged them linguistically, many saw value in the practice of creating Spanish-dominant spaces. Youth reported learning more Spanish and being stretched to practice Spanish in a way they may not have otherwise.

It is in this context that I now turn to reflect on the language dynamics of the after-school program itself. I told participants at the beginning of the program that there was no official language policy during the after-school program, or rather, that the policy was that they could use whatever language practices they wanted. This was a point that I brought up throughout the program as well. However, while some participants used Spanish-dominant language throughout the program while talking in small groups and occasionally in whole group discussions or interviews, the space was decidedly English-dominant. In participants' exit interviews, I asked them (in English), 'How did you feel being able to use whatever language you wanted during the program?' As a follow-up question, I asked them how they would have liked a language policy that mirrored the stricter school language policy. In asking these questions, I was curious to know how participants felt about having greater linguistic freedom.

When asked about language use during the after-school program, Jorge responded that the open language policy of the program was 'good', but when asked if he thought alternating languages would have been better, he responded,

> Yeah, that would be kind of better ... so like one week of English could be good, so then and one week of Spanish would be, too. So people can practice their, their like, they can pronounce the words correct in English or in Spanish. (Exit interview, 26 June 2015)

At the beginning of the program, when asked how he felt going to a bilingual school, Jorge responded, 'I get to speak both languages, not only English or Spanish, but both. Like in my house I speak both languages too' (Entry interview, 18 May 2015). Jorge was the only participant who described 'getting to' speak both languages. For Jorge, then, the free-form policy may have led to potentially missing out on the opportunity to participate in more Spanish-dominant spaces that could have been carved out through intentional policymaking.

Diana, when asked how she felt about the language policy in the after-school program, said, 'Well ... I talked mostly in English because well, English is my main language and um, and I was born here ... And also because most of us in the class also knew more English' (Exit interview, 25 June 2015). When asked if she would have preferred an alternating language policy in the after-school program, Diana said, 'Maybe because well, since I know a lot of Spanish and also English it might be preferable to me but for others it might not be' (Exit interview, 25 June 2015). Diana's responses suggest that linguistic proficiency ('English is my main language'), identity ('I was born here') and others' preferences ('it might be preferable to me but for others it might not be') were all factors she considered when making linguistic choices. In the case of the after-school program, Diana explained why the group spoke English in part by noting that most participants were more comfortable in English. In discussing an alternative, she recognized that using Spanish more may have been preferable to her but not to others. This complexity is indicative of the borderlands that Diana navigated as she made linguistic choices, and highlights that linguistic choices are not simply synonymous with linguistic ability.

Monica's response to the questions about the after-school program's language policy demonstrated her use of both languages, as well as her recognition that others may not be as dexterous in both languages. An excerpt of her exit interview transcript (25 June 2015) is below:

Sarah: How did you feel being able to use whatever language you wanted during the program?

Monica: It felt good. Like, mostly, like, Diana, she mostly speaks Spanish. So we will be like talking English and then talking Spanish, so it could be just like back and forth.

Sarah:	Would you have felt different about the program, you think, if we were doing, like one day English, one day Spanish? Like that?
Monica:	Yeah, I'd feel different. Like, cause mostly, like everyone speaks English. So yeah, they mostly don't speak Spanish.

[In response to asking whether she spoke mostly English during the program]:

Monica:	Like, we spoke with different, well, we mostly speak, spoke, um, English and Spanish, so yeah, but I will mainly speak with a group of like, Diana and, and my sister and Jorge we'll speak Spanish.
Sarah:	Mm-hmm (affirmative).
Monica:	So yeah.
Sarah:	Mm-hmm (affirmative). So in the program, you were finding like if you and Diana and Jorge and your sister were speaking, you would speak mostly in Spanish?
Monica:	Yeah.

Monica's description of the way she and some of the other participants used Spanish during the program suggests that Spanish-dominant speech was marginalized by the flexible language policy, as they tended to use English-dominant speech in the large group, but preferred Spanish-dominant speech when working in a smaller group. This suggests that in this program, no language policy translated into a de facto English-dominant policy in part due to the perception that the group was more comfortable with English-dominant practices. This is an important factor in considering how to shift language policy towards more flexible practices while ensuring that English does not overpower minoritized language practices. Especially as programs are increasing in popularity among monolingual English-speaking families, the issue of English-dominant language practices overpowering Spanish-dominant ones needs further investigation and understanding.

At the same time, while the policy was *de facto* English-dominant, the flexibility built into the language policy of the program provided opportunities for Monica and others to use their full linguistic repertoires, particularly during small group work. This finding might guide larger conversations about language policy in bilingual schools; encouraging translanguaging more in English-dominant spaces within bilingual programs could be a powerful way to resist English hegemony and to ensure that Spanish-dominant and more balanced bilinguals have as many opportunities as possible to access their full linguistic repertoires.

In contrast to Monica, Diana and Jorge, who felt as comfortable in Spanish-dominant contexts as they did in English-dominant ones, Yanetsy reported feeling less comfortable in Spanish-dominant situations, but nonetheless supported the idea of an alternating language policy rather than the open language policy that was enacted. First, Yanetsy explained that the open language policy, 'was pretty good because I don't really speak Spanish that much. Because I, like I don't really understand it that much anymore … ' (Exit interview, 26 June 2015). However, when asked how she would have felt if we had an alternating language policy like in school, she responded (Exit interview, 26 June 2015):

> Yanetsy: I think it would've felt different because it's almost like, we're doing everything bilingual, so then it's like we have one whole week just English and then one week of Spanish, and then there's like there's more, probably more interesting things going on in different languages.
>
> Sarah: Mmm, so in a way you think it would have been better to do one week English, one week Spanish?
>
> Yanetsy: Yeah.

In reflecting that there are 'probably more interesting things going on in different languages', Yanetsy recognized the ways that cultural knowledge and understandings are inextricably bound to language practices (26 June 2015). Thus, her response points to the ways in which being an English-dominant space potentially limited the content of the conversation. Becker notes that learning a new language is tantamount to learning 'a new way of being in the world' (1995: 227). Likewise, Yanetsy's observation suggests that consciously creating Spanish-dominant spaces in school is a powerful way to connect to youth's cultural practices, family histories and ways of being in the world.

Some participants, like Yanetsy, felt that Spanish-dominant spaces in school were challenging but useful for reasons ranging from accessing culturally and linguistically embedded knowledge to developing their linguistic repertoires and providing them an important skill. Others reported feeling just as comfortable in Spanish-dominant spaces, and therefore reported that they would have preferred to have a language policy in the after-school program that mirrored the alternating model of the school. The fact that these participants chose English-dominant practices in the large group and that some switched to Spanish-dominant practices in the small group demonstrates youth's sophisticated and seamless ability to modulate their linguistic choices based on various contextual factors. School language policy that pushes educators and youth to use language in ways that stretches beyond the social context, for the purpose of developing and maintaining language practices, is valuable based on youth's responses outlined here, yet it will require thought, planning and flexibility to execute in a way that simultaneously values youth's linguistic and cultural practices and identities.

Though participants did not mention this as a factor contributing to their language choices, in reflecting on my own identity as an English-dominant white US-born woman, I also recognize that my identity, coupled with my own comfort in English and tendency to introduce activities in English more than Spanish, undoubtedly influenced youth's language use throughout the program. Teachers and other adults in positions of power or authority have the unique opportunity, and responsibility, to use that power in ways that will lead to more equitable educational opportunities for youth. In this case, had I consistently used both English and Spanish-dominant practices, the language dynamics may have shifted, but more importantly, the reflections and explorations of youth may have shifted as well.

In the data above, youth reported mostly English-dominant practices during the after-school program, and those who did use Spanish-dominant practices did so in a small group. At the same time, participants recognized the value of and expressed a desire for Spanish-dominant spaces, for many reasons ranging from the knowledge that might emerge in such spaces to their own comfort level. Thus, protecting 'Spanish time' in bilingual programs can be understood not as protecting the language, but as protecting youth's opportunities to engage with Spanish-dominant language practices, and in doing so to explore the knowledge and understandings that emerge from such a space. Further, understanding such a space as Spanish-dominant and not Spanish-only, opens up new possibilities for engaging all multilingual youth.

Conclusion

In this chapter, I examined youth's articulated understandings of translanguaging, their description of language-dominant rather than language-only spaces, and their qualification of 'having to' use Spanish in Spanish-dominant contexts, while at the same time expressing a desire to protect Spanish-dominant pedagogical spaces. Below I consider some implications of these findings, particularly for crafting language policy in bilingual programs.

First, findings indicate the need for school language policy to delineate 'language-dominant', rather than 'language-only' spaces. 'Language-dominant' spaces would provide the structure needed for students and teachers alike to engage meaningfully, plan accordingly, and protect minoritized language practices. Though it has been well established that bilinguals are not two monolinguals in one (Grosjean, 1989), many bilingual programs still approach language policy through the lens of teaching two languages rather than the lens of engaging multilingual youth while maintaining and building on community language practices. Engaging exclusively in monolingual spaces (in this case, either monolingual Spanish or monolingual English) potentially impacts not only how educators and researchers think of multilingual youth, but how youth make sense of their own identities and language practices. A language-dominant, rather than language-only, policy would open new possibilities for engaging youth and institutionally recognizing and valuing youth's language practices.

Second, findings suggest the need for youth to be partners alongside educators in creating school and classroom language policy. Carol Boyce Davies said:

> Taking space means moving out into areas not allowed ... *in which the dancer negotiates the road*, creating space, as in the Trinidad verbalized, 'give me room'. In this particular context, the dancer is able to negotiate among a variety of other dancers; his/her own particular dance space. (Davies, 1998, as cited in Henry, 2011: 274, emphasis in original)

Creating space as Davies described is as much about the process as the end result; it is a constitutive act that transforms the actor through participation. In this context, including youth in decision-making around school language policy not only improves language policy, but just as importantly, it recognizes youth as essential partners in this work, and gives youth the opportunity to create space and feel the power in doing so. Youth engagement in school and classroom language policy could include:

- Dialogue on existing language policy.
- Youth input on school language policy micro-structures to be used within already-decided macro-structures.
- Community forums throughout the school year to talk about language practices and to collectively commit to multilingualism.
- Space in the curriculum for the local history of bilingual education.
- Research projects in which youth study the multilingual histories of their own communities and articulate their own present and future desires for their community.

Lastly, creating a dedicated space to listen to multilingual youth and foster critical metalinguistic awareness should also be considered an essential component of a strong language policy and any program oriented towards educational equity. The findings of this study are significant because they are based on the experiences and analyses of multilingual youth. Any program serving multilingual youth would greatly benefit from the input of the youth it serves. Thus, a significant implication of this study is that creating and learning from spaces that center youth voices is essential to designing equitable and liberatory language policy. Just as Dr García conceived of translanguaging by studying the language practices of communities, the best way to serve multilingual youth is by listening to youth themselves, and letting their perspectives, experiences and language practices guide the creation of more equitable language policy.

Post-Reading Discussion Questions

(1) Reflect on a collaborative approach to language policy-making. How might you engage youth in creating and maintaining school and classroom-based language policies? What benefits and challenges might arise in the process?

(2) In the school setting, what is the difference between a language-*dominant* space and a language-*only* space? What are some possible educational benefits of creating a school language policy with language-*dominant* rather than language-*only* spaces?

References

Anzaldúa, G. (1987) *Borderlands/La frontera: The new Mestiza* (1st edn). San Francisco, CA: Spinsters/Aunt Lute Books.

Baquedano-López, P., Solís, J. and Arrendondo, G. (2010) Language socialization among Latinos: Theory, method, and approaches. In E.G. Murillo Jr., S.A. Villenas, R. Trinidad Galván, J. Sánchez Muñoz, C. Martínez and M. Machado-Casas (eds) *Handbook of Latinos and Education* (pp. 329–349). New York, NY: Routledge.

Becker, A.L. (1995) *Beyond Translation: Essays Toward a Modern Philosophy*. Ann Arbor, MI: University of Michigan Press.

Davies, C.B. (1998) Carnivalised Caribbean female bodies: Taking space/making space. *Thamyris: Mythmaking from Past to Present* 5 (2) n.p.

Freire, P. (1993) *Pedagogy of the Oppressed* (2nd edn). New York, NY: Continuum.

García, O. (2009) *Bilingual Education in the 21st Century: A Global Perspective*. Oxford: Wiley-Blackwell.

García, O. and Li, W. (2014) *Translanguaging: Language, Bilingualism, and Education*. New York, NY: Palgrave Macmillan.

Grosjean, F. (1989) Neurologists beware! The bilingual is not two monolinguals in one person. *Brain and Language* 36, 3–15.

Heath, S.B. (1983) *Ways with Words: Language, Life, and Work in Communities and Classrooms*. Cambridge: Cambridge University Press.

Henry, A.M. (2011) Feminist theories in education. In S. Tozer, B.P. Gallegos, A.M. Henry, M. Bushnell Greiner and P. Grover Price (eds) *Handbook of Research in the Social Foundations of Education* (pp. 261–282). New York, NY: Routledge.

Mignolo, W. (2012) *Local Histories/ Global Designs: Coloniality, Subaltern Knowledges, and Border Thinking* (2nd edn). Princeton and Oxford: Princeton University Press.

Pratt, M. (1991) Arts of the contact zone. *Profession* 91, 33–40.

Watson-Gegeo, K.A. (2004) Mind, language, and epistemology: Toward a language socialization paradigm for SLA. *The Modern Language Journal* 88, 331–350.

16 American Jewish Summer Camps as Translanguaging Thirdspaces

Sharon Avni

> After _birkat_ (Grace after Meals), meet in front of the _chadar_
> (dining room) for _peulat erev_ (evening activity).[1]
> Staff member, Camp Tel Yehudah, Summer 2015
>
> I was late for _omanut_ (arts and crafts) because I had to
> get something at the _mirp_ (infirmary).
> Camper, Camp Tel Yehudah, Summer 2015

Pre-Reading Discussion Questions

(1) What do you know about Jewish summer camps in the United States?
(2) What is the relationship between American Jews and Modern
     Hebrew?

Introduction

To the outsider, this seamless mixture of Hebrew and English may
appear to be the linguistic stock of bilingual communities. However,
in the case of American Jews, the use of Hebrew is quite surprising
given that the vast majority do not speak Modern Hebrew and can
only decode and recite _lashon hakodesh_ (sacred language), a term that
subsumes varieties of biblical and rabbinic Hebrew, as well as Aramaic.
Nonetheless, for two months every summer in Jewish camps across the
United States, Hebrew – in all of its varieties – is interwoven into the
fabric of the camping experience. To better understand this hybridized
multilingual phenomenon and its meaning for American Jews, this
chapter positions summer camp as a translanguaging thirdspace – a
liminal site that 'does not merely encompass a mixture or hybridity of
first and second languages', but which 'invigorates languaging with
new possibilities from a site of "creativity and power"' (García & Li,

212

2014: 25). More specifically, this chapter argues that translanguaging practices at American Jewish overnight summer camps reveal a richness of linguistic creativity that disrupts the asymmetries of power associated with nationalistic language ideologies, on one hand, yet remains tethered to existing language hierarchies rooted in these ideologies, on the other. Seen in this way, translanguaging practices at American Jewish summer camps offer an innovative perspective into the potential reach and limits of local language practices as a site of disruption and transformation.

Background to American Jewish Camping

While summer camping emerged in American culture in 1860s (Paris, 2008), overnight (also referred to as residential or sleepaway) Jewish camping can be traced back to the immediate aftermath of World War I. At that time, Jewish communal leaders started sending Jewish youth living in crowded and unsanitary cities to rustic sites during the summer months with coreligionists for fun and games, some Jewish learning, and much needed fresh air. Within a few decades, these vanguard overnight camps inspired dozens of other overnight camps across the United States to open their doors, reaching a crucial decade of exponential growth between the late 1940s and the 1950s (Sarna, 2006). From the start, community leaders imagined summer camping as a liminal and transformative space; camps were located outside of the boundaries of school and family life, were limited to the summer months, and were located in remote places that were cut off from the outside world. Combined, these conditions meant that camps could offer an immersive experience that differed markedly from other forms of Jewish education occurring during the rest of the year. After World War II and the devastation of the Holocaust, Jewish leaders shifted their focus to ensuring a strong Jewish community in the United States (Prell, 2007). Jewish educators saw that the totalizing nature of overnight camps could be a primary site of Jewish learning and socialization, a trend that has largely continued up to the present time (Sales & Saxe, 2004). Today, American Jewish overnight camping is a summer ritual for over 200,000 campers and staff members each summer at over 200 camps that represent Judaism across the ideological and religious spectrum.

Hebrew was a part of Jewish camping from the start, though up until the 1920s, it was mostly restricted to the variety of biblical and liturgical Hebrew referred to as *lashon hakodesh* (sacred language). As camps took on more ideological and educational objectives, camp leadership mobilized Modern Hebrew to create communal bonds and affirm Jewish values. Camps like Massad, established in 1941 in Pennsylvania, for example, viewed Modern Hebrew as an effective tool for not only promoting identification with the nation-building project in Palestine, but also as an integral component to strengthening bonds between Jewish communities living in disparate lands, thereby ensuring a Jewish future in North America. The quest for an indigenous American Judaism led Massad leadership to enforce a Hebrew-only policy at camp, necessitating them to create a camp Hebrew dictionary, which included neologisms for words that did not yet exist in Modern Hebrew, such as baseball. While Massad was extreme in its Hebrew orientation, camps established in the latter half of the 20th century also looked to Modern Hebrew as a vehicle for reaching a broad range of ideological and educational goals.

Some of these vanguard camps provided immersive Hebrew contexts, as well as daily Hebrew lessons, as part of the camp schedule. However, the American Jewish community's changing political and cultural orientations over the decades, along with market-driven dynamics operating in the youth summer programming, resulted in a paradigmatic shift. It moved from a focus on Hebrew acquisition to a new model, 'Hebrew infusion' – a set of spoken and written practices in which Hebrew is integrated into the everyday camp experience through songs, blessings, signage, games, and routinized interactions (Benor *et al.*, 2020). As a result, the primary goal of using Hebrew in contemporary camps is to strengthen campers' connection to being Jewish, and not on developing linguistic competency. Benor *et al.* explore how campers and staff members use Camp Hebraized English, a hybridized variety that includes Jewish life words (i.e. words used in other Jewish communal settings such as *shalom* and *Shabbat*), Modern Hebrew (i.e. Hebrew spoken in Israel), textual Hebrew (i.e. prayers and liturgy), camp words (i.e. words used across Jewish camp contexts like *chadar ochel* [dining room]), and camp jargon (i.e. words developed and used only in specific camps) in varying degrees, which provide an insider code for the local camp community. This chapter extends this analysis by viewing camp language practices through a translanguaging lens, and provides a unique opportunity to explore translanguaging outside of the classroom and school setting. It frames summer camping as a translanguaging thirdspace that offers an alternative lens through which to view the rebalancing of the 'trialectics of spatiality–historicality–sociality' (Soja, 1996: 57), which are so central to both the notion of thirdspace and the contemporary Jewish camping experience. Adding language practices to this mix, this chapter advances translanguaging scholarship as a distinctive phenomenon that 'gives rise to something different, something new and unrecognizable, a new area of negotiation of meaning and representation' (Soja, 1996: 61).

As sentences in the epigraph of this chapter demonstrate, Camp Hebraized English is socially recognized as indexical of camp life. Simply put, these language practices constitute the camp experience. As one camper quipped, 'this is just how we talk at camp'. Seen through the lens of language socialization paradigm, new camp participants are socialized *into* specific uses of Camp Hebraized English, and *through* this register to act and interact in culturally appropriate ways in the camp context (Ochs & Schieffelin, 1984). At the same time, these hybridized language practices socialize camp members to take interactional stances, which in turn come to be ideologically associated with Jewish peoplehood – a social category that signifies Jewish collectivity, and specifically a sense of unity and solidarity that transcends religious and political difference, cultural practices, and geographic distance (Pianko, 2015). Hence, translanguaging works in creating overlapping local, national and transnational Jewish identities.

The Performance of Bivalency

At the core of García's argument is that translanguaging theory pushes past the tendency of seeing languages as discrete linguistic codes that function independently of each other. Rather, it argues that by deploying elements indexically linked to more than one language within the same utterance, speakers can invoke multiple identities simultaneously. Drawing on Bakhtin's concept of simultaneity in language, Woolard's notion of bivalency – the 'simultaneous membership of an element in more than one linguistic system' (Woolard, 1998: 6) – is a site where speakers can strategically play and manipulate the boundaries between languages and the social values they represent. García and Otheguy (2019) underscore the bivalent nature of translanguaging, writing 'when speakers language they are deploying a unitary linguistic repertoire, that is, a single aggregation of lexical and structural resources' (2019: 9) that disrupt the discreteness and the hierarchies in which languages are placed. This phenomenon is at work in the Word of the Day skit – a common activity found at many camps. Part-performance, part-slapstick, and part-language acquisition, this ritualized daily event occurs when all campers gather together in one physical space, usually following a meal in the dining room or during the morning flag-raising ceremony. The skit loosely follows a particular dramatic arch in which several staff members help each other understand a Hebrew word in terms of an English equivalent, with the catch (or comedic success) based on the words' homophony, not on their referential meanings. Though these skits were not done at all camps, nor done exactly in the same way at different camps, the example here encapsulates many of their characteristics.

> **Counselor 1**: I need to bring my *teek* to the ropes course in the woods. I want to have it with me.
> **Counselor 2**: I don't know what you mean. Why would you need a tick? We need Hebrew man to help us solve this problem.
> *(Counselor 3 runs in wearing an Israeli flag as a cape and a baseball cap with USA written on the lid)*

Hebrew man: There is no need to be confused. *Teek* means bag. *Teek*, tick, tick *teek*.
Laughter
Counselors and campers (singing): *Ivrit, Ivrit, Ivrit daber Ivrit* (Hebrew, Hebrew, Hebrew speak Hebrew) .
(Observation, Camp Tel Yehudah, 29 July 2015)

To understand the humor in this skit is to recognize that *teek* (bag) and tick (bug) sound the same when spoken in an Israeli accent because Hebrew phonology does not distinguish between the short and long [i] vowels of English. That is to say, when an Israeli says the word *teek* to English-speaking Americans, it sounds like tick. As a result of homophony, there is a misunderstanding, which Hebrew man resolves through metalinguistic commentary. Often repeated from year to year, the words chosen in these skits draw from a litany of combinations that include: *mazleg* (Hebrew: fork)/ma's leg (English) and *bayit* (Hebrew: home)/buy it (English). The skit often ends with the audience joining the performers in singing the Word of the Day ditty, and the campers quickly resume with other activities or announcements.

On the surface, Word of the Day skits are impromptu jocose rituals, hastily arranged several minutes before the performance, and not perceived as deeply educative or meaningful events. After witnessing enough of these skits each summer and over the years, campers know that the featured Hebrew words are not chosen for any instrumental or communicative goals, but rather because they work homophonically. As one camper attested, 'Nobody is going to learn Hebrew from these skits' – a comment that underscores not only the diminutive way in which campers perceive these skits, but also the arbitrariness of the words chosen. If the campers see in these skits a camp tradition equivalent to the eye-rolling jokes told at family events, they likewise understand their role in these ludic rituals. They embrace the farcical nature of the word play, laughing the loudest when the equivalency of meaning is most exaggerated or when pronunciations need to be stretched to make the use of both languages work, and look forward to the day when they can be a staff member taking part in this aesthetic experience.

Word of the Day skits can also be understood as translanguaging performances that take advantage of linguistic repertoires, along with their ideological attachments, to temporarily suspend boundary making, and in doing so, create, display and negotiate social identities. The origin of the Word of the Day skit is unclear. However, the refrain *Ivrit, Ivrit, Ivrit daber Ivrit* (Hebrew, Hebrew, Hebrew speak Hebrew) that at many camps still functions as the opening or closing bookend of this performance, harks back to a nationalistic trope, which saw the revernaculization of Hebrew, a language which had not been spoken for thousands of years, as critical to the success of the Zionist project that envisioned the establishment of the Jewish homeland in Israel. Just like the land of Israel was perceived as uncultivated soil on which a new national culture could emerge, Modern Hebrew was seen as the vehicle through which this new nation could be revitalized, linguistically unified, and symbolically connected with its national past, even if it required coercive and oppressive hegemonic language policies against the use of other home languages (Zerubavel, 1995). When campers and staff sing this song as part of this skit, they are knowingly or not, echoing a nationalistic ideology that called for Jewish nationalism through linguistic uniformity (Spolsky & Shohamy, 1999).

This ideology, however, is turned on its head in the camp performance. There are almost no traces at the vast majority of contemporary camps of the impulse to create a Hebrew speaking community; that is, Hebrew is no longer taught explicitly as it once was and camps are no longer Hebrew-speaking environments. The fact that these short skits are often the only overt Hebrew teaching events at camps downplays their symbolic force and turns an ideological *cri de coeur* into a site of humor and verbal play. As Jaffe notes, comic performances involving multilingual repertoires achieve success by defying the dominant view of languages as fixed and bounded codes which signify single identities, and allow 'multiple identities – and even multiple ideologies of identity and value – to coexist in a single event of experience' (Jaffe, 2000: 57). The role of Hebrew man (which at some camps is called Mr. Hebrew or *Mar Milon* (Mr Dictionary) is itself a cultural reframing of the notion of the New Hebrew man. This archetype was central in the Zionist narrative of rebirth and renewal, in that it symbolized the aesthetics of toughness (Pieterse, 1993: 39) – the negation of the image of the weak, passive, and submissive image of the exilic Jew. Yet at camp, Hebrew man, a symbolic artifact of Jewish strength, self-reliance, and pride is inverted and rebranded as an almost comical superman figure that swoops in, not to carry on his shoulders the weight of building a new nation, but to resolve a language misunderstanding. As the mediator between Hebrew and English (and arguably between Israel and the United States), this character is endowed with the authority to resolve linguistic ambiguity, yet he literally wears his syncretism on his sleeve. He is armed for battle with the Israeli flag as a cape, but wears a baseball cap –the quintessential symbol of America's pastime - with the unabashedly patriotic USA written on the lid.

As translanguaging performances, Word of the Day skits offer the potential to reimagine and upend the supposed boundaries between languages, their speech communities, and their associations with nationalist ideologies. Their social effect is a direct result of bivalency, which serves as an 'important denial of the boundary identifying force of the two languages' (Woolard, 1998: 70). Put another way, Word of the Day skits are a distinctive form of translanguaging that draw from

Hebrew and English simultaneously and only take on meaning when the two languages are put side by side. Seen in this way, Word of the Day skits mobilize linguistic repertoires that blur boundaries between the languages and the communities that speak them, demonstrating that one language or community is not privileged over the other, and that in fact, Hebrew only makes sense in light of English, and vice versa. In blurring these 'fixed language identities constrained by nation-states' (García & Li, 2014: 21), Word of the Day skits reimagine a social identity based in simultaneity, and in the process carve out the potential of creating a local identity that is neither wholly American or Israeli – but rather a blended construction requiring both to co-exist and thrive.

Translanguaging and Linguistic Creativity

Translanguaging word play at American Jewish camps casts aside nationalistic ideologies as closed systems where everything 'holds together nicely and neatly' and exposes them as 'constantly emergent open systems with fuzziness, leaks, inventions, constructions, negoti-ation, and imaginations' (Sherzer, 2010: 10). Camp Hebraized English – a register that combines different varieties of Hebrew (liturgical, Biblical and Modern) as well as localized camp jargon – is replete with creativity, and this ingenuity creates a localized American Jewish identity that does not look to Hebrew spoken in Israel for its legitimacy.

To recognize the extent of the creativity within Camp Hebraized English is to first revisit the tightly knit ideological connection between the revitalization of Modern Hebrew and the success of nation-state of Israel. Much of this ideology was born out of the fear of the linguistic diversity of Jewish communities that made their way to British Mandate Palestine from disparate areas around the world. Without a common language, Zionist ideologues feared this multilingualism as a Tower of Babel – a symbol of Jewish fragmentation, weakness, and ineffectiveness (Halperin, 2015). Replacing the varying diasporic languages spoken by the Jewish immigrants with Hebrew was crucial in the nationalistic project of building a strong and resilient Jewish community, whose home was in Israel and in establishing the new nation-state as the cynosure of Jewish life. This process cemented the triangle of associations between people (Jews), place (Israel) and language (Modern Hebrew). The revitalization of Hebrew therefore shows how language comes to be seen as an object with certain attributes and as the property of the group that speaks it in a particular geographic territory. Indeed, that Modern Hebrew is also referred to as Israeli Hebrew reflects the successful conflation of the categories of nation and language.

If language scholars point to Modern Hebrew as the language revitalization success story of modern times (Hinton, 2003), this message was not necessarily seen in the same way by Jews in the diaspora.

The exception was a small group of highly educated European Jews who arrived in the US in the early 1900s and saw Modern Hebrew as a potent vehicle for the cultural revival of the Jewish people and a means of retaining their distinctiveness in their new home. Identifying Yiddish with working-class radicalism and immigrant ghettos (Krasner, 2009), they believed that a Jewish future in North America would be ensured only if the bonds of community were reinforced through the creation of a local Hebrew-speaking American Jewish community. By the 1930s, the American Hebraists, as they came to be known, had founded popular monthly Hebrew newspapers, created Hebrew literature, founded the first national organization of Hebrew culture in America, created afterschool programs using language immersive methodologies, and established Hebrew-speaking summer residential camps throughout North America (Mintz, 1993). Nonetheless, their achievements were short-lived. By the 1950s, their mission of creating a local Hebrew-speaking Jewish community began to crumble due to a host of sociological and historical dynamics. These included the shift of global Judaism to the newly established state of Israel, the brute force of Americanization on immigrant communities to adopt English, and the embourgeoisement of Jews and their subsequent movement to the suburbs. This demographic shift led to the ascendency of the synagogue as the prime site of Jewish communal life and its focus on teaching liturgical Hebrew for religious ritual participation (i.e. bar/bat mitzvah) – a trend that continues today.

If Modern Hebrew provided an ideological force to achieve Jewish nationhood in Israel, its success doomed its necessity in the American diaspora. Today American Jews do not embrace Modern Hebrew as a language of American Jewish life. As the influential Pew Center's 2013 *Portrait of Jewish Americans* discovered, while half of American Jews (52%) reported knowing the Hebrew alphabet (that is, could decode sacred texts), only 13% said they could understand most or all of the words they read in Hebrew. Interestingly, the survey did not even ask any questions about producing or understanding spoken Modern Hebrew. For many communal leaders concerned with the growing divide between the Israeli and American Jewish communities, American Jews' Modern Hebrew illiteracy is yet another manifestation of this gap. Camp Hebraized English, however, directly challenges this notion that American Jews 'live outside the Hebrew language' (Loeffler, 2019). Rather, the camp register reflects a rich Hebrew presence. As a form of language crossing (Rampton, 2014), campers and staff members not only mobilize Hebrew for their own local needs, but in doing so, cast aside fears that the language does not belong to them.

Camp Hebraized English is full of blends (the combining of Hebrew and English in the same lexical item). Camp Newman, for example, schedules for *p-nik*, a word that mixes the first letter of the word personal with part of the word *nikayon* (cleaning) to signify time for personal hygiene and showering. Campers can also participate in *frolfillah*, which is a blending of frisbee golf and *tefillah* (prayers). Division names of groups also prominently feature blends. *Hevracados* is a mix of *hevra* (community) and avocados and the division *Avodah* (work) called their female campers *avodolls* (avodah mixed with dolls). Camp Alonim uses many blends involving the 'Alo' portion of the camp's (Hebrew) name, such as *Alo-options* (optional activities). These types of blends are ubiquitous at many camps, and often become part of the camp's linguistic landscape, as seen in the photo in Figure 16.1 taken at Camp Eden Village. *Hitbotabooth* mixes the Hebrew word *hitbodadot* (to be alone) with the English word booth to signify a small room equipped with an old-time pay phone where campers can use the phone to practice the Jewish tradition of being alone and talking out loud to God.

Camps also blended Hebrew words to create lexical items to signify camp-specific events or activities. For example, Camp Solomon Schechter has *Yom Tevanut*, which combines *yom* (day) with *teva* (nature) *and omanut* (art) to create Nature and Art Day, Camp Ramah has *zimrikudia*, which mixes *zimriya* (a song festival) with *rikudiya* (a dance festival) to create a word for the camp's song and dance festival

Figure 16.1 Camp Eden Village (photograph by author)

and Greene Family Camp has *motzev*, a mix of *moadon* (lounge) and *tzevet* (staff) for the place that staff can hang out away from the campers. At Camp Gilboa, campers are assigned *tobo* a mix of *toranut* (rotation) and *boker* (morning) to indicate morning duty for setup in the dining room. Words like these, made up of blends between two Hebrew words, reveal that translanguaging occurs not only between Hebrew and English words but also between varieties of the same language.

Translanguaging manifested in a wide array of linguistic processes including clipping, backformation, and conversion. Some of the most common clippings include *chadar* for *chadar ochel* (dining hall), *Birkat* for *Birkat Hamazon* (Grace After Meals), *mo* for *moadon* (clubhouse), *mir, meerp, mirp* or *marp* for *mirpaa* (infirmary), *sif* for *sifriya* (library). Campers refer to *shmeers* for counselors doing *shmira* (guard duty at night), convert the noun *ashpa* (garbage) to a verb meaning cleaning up around camp and convert the noun *toranut* (rotation) to refer to the person doing the job, typically helping to set up the dining room or serve food, as in the sentence, '*Toranut*s, stay after lunch to help clean up'. Camps also made use of figures of speech, including synecdoche; *degel* (flag), for example, became synonymous with the ceremony around the flag at one camp. Camps created English acronyms for Hebrew words, such as B.K. (*beit keneset* – synagogue) or changed the pronunciation of words in Modern Hebrew, as in *cheder misrakim* rather than *cheder mischakim* (game room), conflating the [ch] and [r] sounds, which are articulated in the same part of the mouth in Hebrew. Finally, Camp Hebraized English also changed rules of Modern Hebrew grammar, particularly with the use of smichut (the construct state), when campers said *shalosh mitnadvim* (three volunteers) instead of *shlosha mitnadvim*, or *peula shichva* (divisional activity) instead of *peulot shichva*.

Camp Hebraized English problematizes the idea that languages are bounded, separate codes and captures the contingent and dynamic translanguaging practices at summer camps. What also stands out is the ordinariness and unmarked nature by which these expressions are used for everyday activities. Campers do not bat an eye when using this register; in fact, saying dining room instead of *chadar* would most likely elicit a reaction and mark the user as an outsider. For American campers and staff members, the majority of whom have little to no competency in Modern Hebrew, whether these are made-up camp jargon or the actual words or expressions used in Israel is beside the point; rather, this localized way of using language is part and parcel of what makes the camp experience distinctive. García's analytic framing of translanguaging as a dance – an embodied practice that goes beyond the linguistic – captures the fluidity of the camp linguistic phenomenon (García & Otheguy, 2019). Translanguaging at camp is not a 'simple coda to a code' – something supplemental to another language; rather it 'dynamizes the code, engages it in a dance of moving back and forth and turning upside-down, cracking its bubble and opening up a translanguaging space of different possibilities' (García, 2019: 373).

However, it is a different story for the Israeli staff working at camps, for whom Camp Hebraized English is a site of contestation that challenges claims of Hebrew authenticity and legitimacy. Since the late 1960s, the Jewish Agency for Israel, a para-state Israeli organization, has recruited, trained, and dispatched thousands of Israeli *shlichim* (emissaries) to American Jewish day and overnight summer camps to promote Israel and Israeli culture. Since the early 1990s, the numbers have exponentially grown, reaching over 1200 *shlichim* in 2017. With a J-1 visa, intended for temporary cultural work exchange programs, *shlichim* – typically in their early twenties and often fresh out of mandatory military service in Israel – work in a range of roles, including bunk counselors, lifeguards, activity specialists, and support staff. Unlike their American counterparts, they do not earn a salary, but do receive round-trip airfare.

Shlichim's engagement with and understanding of the role of translanguaging in action brings into stark relief the 'difference within similarity, and similarity within difference' that characterize the American and Israeli Jewish communities (Kelner, 2012: 27). Upon their arrival at camps, *shlichim* quickly recognize there is a camp register that utilizes aspects of Modern Hebrew, but is not 'their' Hebrew used in Israel. Their desire to fit into the local camp culture requires phonological, semantic, syntactic, and pragmatic shifts, as they calibrate their language use in order to establish meaningful relationships with campers and other staff members. Nonetheless, there is a metalinguistic tug-of-war over Camp Hebraized English and its legitimacy and authenticity, with *shlichim* often using the local register, but mocking it among themselves as Hebrish, or an inferior or bastardized form of Israeli Hebrew. Devaluing the local register and positioning themselves as the rightful owners and guardians of Modern Hebrew, Israelis at camp defend this status and reject campers' appropriation of Hebrew by questioning the local register's legitimation. While one Israeli staff member captured this rejection by saying 'some parts [of the camp language] lose all trace of actual Hebrew', another pointed out 'I'll say with respect...the Hebrew of Camp Ramah is not necessarily *Ivrit* (Hebrew)' but rather 'a language that ... is not understood by Hebrew speakers'. This dismissal was also achieved through comments that assert their status as a reflection of their nativeness and linguistic competency and Americans' semi-speaker status as those who do not have full command of the language. This was reflected in one director's telling of a conversation he had with an Israeli staff member, 'it just seems so strange to them (*shlichim*)' he recalled hearing 'that these American kids can sing all the stuff and yet they can't say, "I have to go to the bathroom"'. This discomfort may explain that while *shlichim* at the end of the summer take back to Israel a great deal of English slang, idiomatic language and a sense of confidence in their English mastery, the same cannot be said for Camp Hebraized English. It has not, up to this point, had any discernable effect on Israeli Hebrew usage, though one Israeli staff member did recount being at a reunion with other *shlichim* in Israel and allowing themselves to use the camp register for the event.

Collectively, these responses reflect an unresolved tension between American campers and staff and Israeli *shlichim*, with the latter unwilling to let go of the distinctness of Hebrew, lest it lose its authenticity and rootedness to Israel. Hence, Modern Hebrew and Camp Hebraized English must be understood in relation to nationalistic perceptions through which Israelis' Hebrew language practices are positioned as inherently legitimate and campers' practices are perceived as inherently deficient. While translanguaging, on one hand, affords campers the possibility for linguistic creativity which serves as an indigenous cultural production of American Judaism – with little regard to its use among native speakers in Israel – it cannot fully escape the dynamics of dichotomizing discourses of legitimacy/illegitimacy. When an Israeli counselor says to a camper, 'we have to dumb down our language for you', being American and being a Hebrew speaker are represented as mutually exclusive and oppositional identities. In Israelis' reactions, translanguaging enters into the contested politics of individual, group, national, and transnational identities, and their corresponding fields of difference.

Conclusion

American Jewish summer camps offer the opportunity to see 'the enaction of language practices that use different features that had previously moved independently constrained by different histories, but that now are experienced against each other in speakers' interactions as one new whole' (García & Li, 2014: 21). This chapter positions summer camps as a translanguaging thirdspace to better understand how hybridized language practices give license to an American Jewishness idiom that draws from Modern Hebrew but is not beholden to its geographic boundaries or ideological attachments. While the screeds go unabated that American Jews have given up their linguistic inheritance and have forsaken Hebrew at their own peril (Wieseltier, 2011), anyone who cares to visit an American Jewish overnight camp will find that Hebrew is alive and well on American soil. What would also be evident is that campers are not trying to pass as Hebrew speakers; rather, they are too busy 'speaking locally' (Pennycook, 2012) making use all the linguistic resources available to them in the liminal context of Jewish summer camping.

Camp Hebraized English represents a distinctive form of translanguaging that pushes back against traditional understandings of language boundaries, language mastery, and language ownership. If the bivalency inherent in Word of the Day skits epitomize the blurring of boundaries such that languages can only be understood *vis-à-vis* each other, then campers' linguistic creativity reflect the mobilization of language resources that break away from the shackles of native speakers' hold on legitimacy and authenticity. In this translanguaging thirdspace, language practices are not seen through the restrictive lens of linguistic competence but rather as a performance of American Jewish identity. As Blommaert's rejoinder reminds us, multilingualism 'should not be seen as a collection of 'languages' that a speaker controls, but rather as a complex of specific semiotic resources' – the acceptance of using bits and pieces of a language to accomplish specific social functions without having full competency (Blommaert, 2010: 102).

Nevertheless, translanguaging thirdspaces in ostensibly fun and informal settings like swimming at the pool, doing lanyard or competing in color war are never neutral or entirely free of broader political and cultural currents. Rather, it is at these most quotidian and trivial moments when unresolved and contentious issues (re)surface as language users compete over claims to legitimacy and authenticity. Examining translanguaging at American Jewish camps therefore offers a unique look into the reshuffling of dichotomizing discourses of *ours* and *theirs* and demonstrates the potential of multilingualism to reimagine the connections among place, people, and language. However, translanguaging is not without its complexities; ideologies of native speaker-ness, along with deeply rooted claims to legitimacy and authenticity, penetrate the boundaries of localness and bring with it a host of unresolved tensions caught up in defining center and peripheries, or in this case, nationalism and diasporism. What may be seen or heard at camp as merely youthful summer frolic and silliness, is in fact, as García argues throughout her unparalleled oeuvre of scholarship, a site of potentially transformative and political identification and realignment.

Post-Reading Discussion Questions

(1) How do American Jewish summer camps act as translanguaging thirdspaces? How do camp translanguaging practices challenge notions of local and national Jewish identities?

(2) How can analyzing translanguaging practices in non-classroom environments open up new avenues of inquiry in the field of bilingual education and multilingualism?

Notes

(1) All Modern Hebrew words are written in italics followed with an English translation in parenthesis. Camp Hebraized English words are written in italics and underlined.

(2) For more about the link between masculinity, Judaism and Zionism, see Mayer (2005).

References

Benor, S., Krasner, J. and Avni, S. (2020) *Hebrew Infusion: Language and Community at American Jewish Summer Camps*. New Brunswick, NJ: Rutgers University Press.

Blommaert, J. (2010) *The Sociolinguistics of Globalization*. New York, NY: Cambridge University Press.

García, O. (2019) Translanguaging: a coda to the code? *Classroom Discourse* 10 (3–4), 369–373.

García, O. and Li, W. (2014) Language, bilingualism and education. In O. García and L. Wei (eds) *Translanguaging: Language, Bilingualism and Education* (pp. 46–62). London: Palgrave Macmillan.

García, O. and Otheguy, R. (2019) Plurilingualism and translanguaging: Commonalities and divergences. *International Journal of Bilingual Education and Bilingualism* 10, 1080.

Halperin, L. (2015) *Babel in Zion: Jews, Nationalism, and Language Diversity in Palestine, 1920–1948*. New Haven, CT: Yale University Press.

Hinton, L. (2003) Language revitalization. *Annual Review of Applied Linguistics* 23, 44–57.

Jaffe, A. (2000) Comic performance and the articulation of hybrid identity. *Pragmatics* 10 (1), 39–59.

Kelner, S. (2012) *Tours that Bind: Diaspora, Pilgrimage, and Israeli Birthright Tourism*. New York, NY: NYU Press.

Krasner, J. (2009) The limits of cultural Zionism in America: The case of Hebrew in the New York City public schools, 1930–1960. *American Jewish History* 95 (4), 349–372.

Loeffler, J. (2019) Should American Jews speak Hebrew *Tablet* July 30.

Mayer, T. (2005) From zero to hero: Masculinity in Jewish nationalism. In E. Fuchs (ed.) *Israeli Women's Studies: A Reader* (pp. 97–120). New Brunswick, NJ: Rutgers University Press.

Mintz, A. (1993) *Hebrew in America: Perspectives and Prospects*. Detroit, MI: Wayne State University Press.

Ochs, E. and Schieffelin, B.B. (1984) Language acquisition and socialization: Three developmental stories. In R. Shweder and R. LeVine (eds) *Culture Theory: Essays on Mind, Self and Emotion* (pp. 276–320). New York, NY: Cambridge University Press.

Paris, L. (2008) *Children's Nature: The Rise of the American Summer Camp*. New York, NY: NYU Press.

Pennycook, A. (2012) *Language and Mobility: Unexpected Places*. Bristol: Multilingual Matters.

Pew Research Center (2013) A Portrait of Jewish Americans: Findings from a Pew Research Center Survey of American Jews. See https://www.pewforum.org/2013/10/01/jewish-american-beliefs-attitudes-culture-survey/ (accessed August 2020).

Pieterse, J. (1993) Aesthetics of power: Time and body politics. *Third Text* 7 (22), 33–42.

Pianko, N. (2015) *Jewish Peoplehood*. New Brunswick, NJ: Rutgers University Press.

Prell, R.E. (2007) Summer camp, postwar American Jewish youth and the redemption of Judaism. *Jewish Role in American Life: An Annual Review* 5, 77–208.

Rampton, B. (2014) *Crossing: Language and Ethnicity among Adolescents*. Oxford: Routledge.

Sales, A. and Saxe, L. (2004) *'How Goodly are Thy Tents': Summer Camps as Jewish Socializing Experiences*. Lebanon, NH: University Press of New England.

Sarna, J. (2006) The crucial decade in Jewish camping. In G. Kaye, M. Zeldin, J. Sarna, J. Cohen, H. Gamoran and D. Splansky (eds) *A Place of Our Own: The Rise of Reform Jewish Camping* (pp. 27–51). Tuscaloosa, AL: University of Alabama Press.

Sherzer, J. (2010) *Speech Play and Verbal Art*. Austin, TX: University of Texas Press.

Soja, E. (1996) *Thirdspace: Journeys to Los Angeles and Other Real and Imagined Places*. Oxford: Blackwell Publishing.

Spolsky, B. and Shohamy, E. (1999) *The Languages of Israel: Policy, Ideology and Practice.* Clevedon: Multilingual Matters.

Wieseltier, L. (2011) Language, identity, and the scandal of American Jewry. *Journal of Jewish Communal Service 8612,* 14–22.

Woolard, K. (1998) Simultaneity and bivalency as strategies in bilingualism. *Journal of Linguistic Anthropology* 8 (1), 3–29.

Zerubavel, Y. (1995) *Recovered Roots: Collective Memory and the Making of Israeli National Tradition.* Chicago, IL: University of Chicago Press.

Part 5: Epilogue

Afterword: A Brief History of Work and Play with Ofelia García

Mentors can have a powerful influence on one's life. My own MA mentor, Shirley Raines, and PhD mentor, Muriel Saville-Troike, are wonderful examples. When I learned that Ofelia García's mentor was Joshua A. Fishman, with whom she worked as a Post-Doctoral Fellow at Yeshiva University and for years thereafter, I began to understand something about Ofelia. You see, back in the 80s, when I was a doctoral student in bilingual education at the University of Illinois, I was brash enough to write a letter to Professor Fishman to ask for a copy of his yet unpublished edited volume, *The Rise and Fall of the Ethnic Revival: Perspectives on Language and Ethnicity* (1985). Within a few weeks, I, a total stranger, received a large package in the mail – the manuscript. That gesture was emblematic of Fishman's warmth and generosity towards his students and others, as attested by many who worked closely with him (e.g. Hornberger, 2017). To be clear, Ofelia's generosity of spirit comes from within; she never required a model, but she is undeniably a shining example continuing this tradition. You can see it in her collaborative scholarship with colleagues and students, her efforts to build institutional synergies, her support of emergent bilinguals and their educators and her selfless devotion to friends.

I want to highlight a few of my own experiences as observer and participant in Ofelia's orb as testimonial to this quality of character. My earliest contact with Ofelia was as a freshly minted PhD graduate. Muriel and I were invited by Ofelia and Ricardo to co-author a chapter about children's interactions in Midwest multilingual classrooms for their 1989 edited volume, *English Across Cultures, Cultures Across English: A Reader in Cross-Cultural Communication*. The opportunity for more frequent contact with Ofelia came when I moved to New York City to join the faculty at Teachers College. At that time, Ofelia was

Dean of the School of Education at Long Island University's Brooklyn campus, where she provided enrichment for her faculty and students by inviting guest speakers to share their research. She opened her arms to junior faculty like me who were focusing on language-minoritized populations, and asked me to talk about my ethnographic research on multilingual workers in a Silicon Valley circuit-board assembly plant.

But it was during her time as a fellow faculty member at Columbia University's Teachers College (hereafter, TC) where I experienced her collegiality and friendship up close. Ofelia joined our faculty in 2002, and the College benefited greatly from her leadership, intellect, energy, warmth. We were honored to have her as our colleague in the Department of International and Transcultural Studies, where she was program coordinator of Bilingual/Bicultural Education. During this period, Ofelia and I collaborated on teaching, research, and service initiatives; the experience became for me an educative partnership – a mentorship. Along the way, she offered encouragement and support for my professional advancement, just as she has done for others. We conducted a joint doctoral seminar in linguistics, literacy, and bilingual education and worked together to guide graduate students' dissertation projects; our students and I were inspired by Ofelia's original thinking and energizing presence.

Ofelia is known for her collaboration on scholarly publications, and this was true of her work with department colleagues and students, with whom she co-authored books, book chapters, and journal articles. Working with Ofelia on research and writing projects has brought me both intellectual stimulation and greater purpose in my scholarship. She invited me and Lesley Bartlett to collaborate on a book chapter with her on pluriliteracies (2007), and she and I wrote a chapter on equity and excellence in educating emergent bilinguals (2011). When Ofelia was on the advisory board of TC's Campaign for Educational Equity, she asked me and doctoral student Lorraine Falchi to join her in producing a report in 2008, a monograph on the dissonance between what research tells us about educating emergent bilinguals and actual school policies and practices.

One of Ofelia's most important contributions to TC as an institution was to broaden the College community's awareness about the education of emergent bilinguals through her engagement with the leadership, interviews published on TC's website, and College-wide brown bag seminars. Her efforts bore fruit: She and I were founding members and co-directors of the Center for Multiple Languages and Literacies, established in 2004 at TC to conduct and disseminate research projects on the uses of different languages and literacies throughout the world and to organize symposia and guest lectures in multilingualism, linguistics and literacy.

Ofelia eventually left TC to join the City University of New York (CUNY) Graduate Center, yet our connection has remained constant, and we have continued to collaborate on several writing projects. The monograph we had written in 2008 became a springboard for our co-authored book on educating emergent bilinguals in 2010, with a second edition in 2018. More recently, we co-authored an invited paper on translanguaging and literacies for *Reading Research Quarterly* (2020). Writing with her has meant working alongside a mentor who spurred my evolution in thinking about emergent bilinguals' translanguaging and inspired my own work on their trans-semiotic practices.

But Ofelia's generosity goes beyond the professional, as those who know her can testify. My own story is just one example of how she made a place for me in her all-embracing heart, a heart that makes room for so many. Aside from the pleasures of email check-ins (e.g. her news of a daughter's wedding, another daughter making her a grandmother, a daughter-in-law with another on the way) and informal get-togethers, including lunch dates in city restaurants and gatherings for evening meals at home with Ricardo and John, our respective 'novios', Ofelia has come to my side in more difficult moments. When John was diagnosed with cancer in 2013, she sent me a note sharing her favorite prayer: ('la letrilla de Santa Teresa de Avila … I write it now to say it with you: "Nada te turbe …"'). Then, as soon as she learned that I was diagnosed with lymphoma in 2016, she postponed the submission deadline of our book ('The most important thing is for you not to have any pressure at this time'). She brought me home after treatments, offered soup, and kept me company until I could get back on my feet. And, more recently, when the pandemic limited close contact with loved ones, she suggested that we meet in Central Park for updates on our lives and families amidst trying times. Her compassion and contagious laughter during periods of illness and isolation turned out to be just what the doctor ordered.

Mentors can come along at any stage in one's academic career; by following in their footsteps, we strive to pass on these values to our own students and colleagues. If the term *mentor* entails being a counsellor with wisdom and experience, a generous and inspirational collaborator, and a loyal and empathetic friend, then Ofelia García is *mentor par excellence*.

Jo Anne Kleifgen,
Columbia University Teachers College, Professor Emeritus

References

Fishman, J.A., Gertner, M., Lowy, E. and Milán, W. (1985) *The Rise and Fall of the Ethnic Revival: Perspectives on Language and Ethnicity.* Berlin: Mouton.

García, O. and Kleifgen, J. (2020) Translanguaging and literacies. Invited Article. *Reading Research Quarterly* 55 (4), 553–571.

García, O. and Kleifgen, J. (2018) *Educating Emergent Bilinguals: Policies, Programs, and Practices for English Learners* (2nd edn). New York, NY: Teachers College Press.

García, O. and Kleifgen, J. (2011) Equity and excellence in the education of Emergent Bilinguals. In K. van den Branden, P. van Avermaet and M. van Houtte (eds) *Equity and Excellence in Education* (pp. 166–189). New York, NY: Routledge.

García, O. and Kleifgen, J. (2010) *Educating Emergent Bilinguals: Policies, Programs, and Practices for English Language Learners*. New York, NY: Teachers College Press.

García, O. and Otheguy, R. (eds) (1989) *English Across Cultures, Cultures Across English: A Reader in Cross-Cultural Communication*. The Hague: Mouton.

García, O., Kleifgen, J. and Falchi, L. (2008) *From English Language Learners to Emergent Bilinguals*. Research Review Series Monograph, Campaign for Educational Equity, Teachers College, Columbia University.

García, O., Bartlett, L. and Kleifgen, J. (2007) From biliteracy to pluriliteracies. In P. Auer and L. Wei (eds) *Handbook of Multilingualism and Multilingual Communication* (pp. 207–228). New York, NY: Mouton.

Hornberger, N. (2017) Joshua A. Fishman: A scholar of unfathomable influence. *International Journal of the Sociology of Language* 243, 17–28.

Saville-Troike, M. and Kleifgen, J. (1989) Culture and language in classroom communication. In O. García and R. Otheguy (eds) *English Across Cultures, Cultures Across English: A Reader in Cross-Cultural Communication* (pp. 59–68). The Hague: Mouton.

Appendix: Ofelia García's Publications with Multilingual Matters

Bahar Otcu-Grillman

This list has been compiled from Ofelia García's publications in her curriculum vitae on her personal website. In the interest of space, word limits and relevance to the publisher of this volume, only her publications with Multilingual Matters are included. For a comprehensive list of Ofelia García's lifetime publications (about 15-pages long), please see her personal website at: https://ofeliagarciadotorg.wordpress.com/

Books

García, O., Zakharia, Z. and Otcu, B. (2013) *Bilingual Community Education and Multilingualism: Beyond Heritage Languages in a Global City.* Bristol: Multilingual Matters.

García, O. and Baker, C. (eds) (2007) *Bilingual Education: An Introductory Reader.* Clevedon: Multilingual Matters.

García, O., Skutnabb-Kangas, T. and Torres-Guzmán, M. (eds) (2006) *Imagining Multilingual Schools: Languages in Education and Globalization.* Clevedon: Multilingual Matters. [Reprinted for the Asian market by Orient BlackSwan, Andhra Pradesh, India, 2009].

García, O., Peltz, R. and Schiffman, H.F. (eds) (2006) *Language Loyalty, Continuity and Change: Joshua A. Fishman's Contributions to International Sociolinguistics.* Clevedon: Multilingual Matters.

García, O. and Baker, C. (eds) (1995) *Policy and Practice in Bilingual Education: A Reader Extending the Foundations.* Clevedon: Multilingual Matters.

Articles and Chapters

Blommaert, J., García, O., Kress, G. and Larsen-Freeman, D. (2019) Communicating beyond diversity: A bricolage of ideas. In A. Sherris and E. Adami (eds) *Making Signs, Translanguaging Ethnographies: Exploring Urban, Rural and Educational Spaces* (pp. 9–35). Bristol: Multilingual Matters.

Flores, N. and García, O. (2014) Linguistic third spaces in education: Teachers' translanguaging across the bilingual continuum. In D. Little, C. Leung and P. Van Avermaet (eds) *Managing Diversity in Education: Languages, Policies, Pedagogies* (pp. 243–256). Bristol: Multilingual Matters.

García, O., Menken, K., Velasco, P. and Vogel, S. (2018) Dual language bilingual education in NYC: A potential unfulfilled. In M.B. Arias and M. Fee (eds) *Profiles of Dual Language Education in the 21st Century* (pp. 38–55). Washington, D.C. and Bristol: Center for Applied Linguistics and Multilingual Matters.

García, O. (2014) Countering the dual: Transglossia, dynamic bilingualism and translanguaging in education. In R. Rubdy and L. Alsagoff (eds) *The Global-Local Interface and Hybridity* (pp. 100–118). Bristol: Multilingual Matters.

García, O. and Kano, N. (2014) Translanguaging as process and pedagogy: Developing the English writing of Japanese students in the US. In J. Conteh and G. Meier (eds) *The Multilingual Turn in Languages Education: Opportunities and Challenges* (pp. 258–277). Bristol: Multilingual Matters.

García, O. (2013) From disglossia to transglossia: Bilingual and multilingual classrooms in the 21st century. In C. Abello-Contesse, P.M. Chandler, M.D. López-Jiménez and R. Chacón-Beltrán (eds) *Bilingual and Multilingual Education in the 21st Century: Building on Experience* (pp. 155–175). Bristol: Multilingual Matters.

García, O., Pujol-Ferran, M. and Reddy, P. (2013) Educating international and immigrant students in U.S. higher education: Opportunities and challenges. In A. Doiz, D. Lasagabaster and J.M. Sierra (eds) *English-Medium Instruction at Universities: Global Challenges* (pp. 174–195). Bristol: Multilingual Matters.

García, O. (2012) Bilingual community education: Beyond heritage language education and bilingual education in New York. In O. García, Z. Zakharia and B. Otcu (eds) *Bilingual Community Education and Multilingualism: Beyond Heritage Languages in a Global City* (pp. 3–42). Bristol: Multilingual Matters.

García, O. (2009) Livin' and Teachin' la lengua loca: Glocalizing US Spanish ideologies and practices. In R. Salaberry (ed.) *Language Allegiances and Bilingualism in the United States* (pp. 151–171). Bristol: Multilingual Matters.

García, O. and Mason, L. (2009) Where in the world is US Spanish? Creating a space of opportunity for US Latinos. In W. Harbert, S. McConnell-Ginet, A. Miller and J. Whitman (eds) *Language and Poverty* (pp. 78–101). Bristol: Multilingual Matters.

García, O. (2008) Teaching Spanish and Spanish in teaching in the US: Integrating bilingual perspectives. In C. Hélot and A.M. de Mejía (eds) *Forging Multilingual Spaces: Integrated Perspectives on Majority and Minority Bilingual Education* (pp. 31–57). Bristol: Multilingual Matters.

García, O. and Schiffman, H.F., with Zakharia, Z. (2006) Fishmanian Sociolinguistics: 1949 to the present. In O. García, R. Peltz and H. Schiffman (eds) *Language Loyalty, Continuity and Change: Joshua A. Fishman's Contributions to International Sociolinguistics* (pp. 3–68). Clevedon: Multilingual Matters.

García, O., Skutnabb-Kangas, T. and Torres-Guzmán, M. (2006) Weaving spaces and de(constructing ways for multilingual schools: The actual and the imagined. In O. García, T. Skutnabb-Kangas and M. Torres-Guzmán (eds) *Imagining Multilingual Schools: Languages in Education and Glocalization* (pp. 3–47). Clevedon: Multilingual Matters.

García, O., Morín, J.L. and Rivera, K. (2001) How threatened is the Spanish of New York Puerto Ricans? Language shift with vaivén. In J.A. Fishman (ed.) *Can Threatened Languages be Saved?* (pp. 44–73). Clevedon: Multilingual Matters.

Reports, Forewords

García, O. (2007) Foreword. In S. Makoni and A. Pennycook (eds) *Disinventing and Reconstituting Languages* (pp. xi–xv). Clevedon: Multilingual Matters.

García, O. (1993) Foreword. In C. Baker (ed.) *Foundations of Bilingual Education and Bilingual Education* (pp. vii–ix). Clevedon: Multilingual Matters.

Academic Consultancy

García, O. (1993 and 1996) Academic Consultant for C. Baker's *Foundations of Bilingual Education and Bilingualism*, 1st and 2nd edition. Clevedon: Multilingual Matters.

Index

additive bilingualism 8, 12, 25, 113, 123
adolescent xiii, xiv, 10, 13, 46, 47, 195, 198, 225
advocacy 3, 10, 19, 20, 37, 81, 88, 160, 172, 176, 177, 178
after-school programs 13, 88, 195, 196, 199, 205, 206, 208, 209
agglutinative 155
all-terrain vehicle 37
Arabic 71, 79, 100, 102, 104, 160, 161
Australia xv, 68, 71, 72, 73, 74, 77, 78, 79, 191

bilingual community education viii, xv, xxiii, xxvi, 10, 12, 14, 31, 36, 127, 141, 142, 151, 152, 153, 155, 156, 157, 163, 194, 233, 234
bilingual education viii, xiii, xiv, xv, xvi, xvii, xx, xxiii, xxiv, 6, 7, 8, 10, 12, 14, 19, 20, 21, 22, 23, 24, 25, 29, 30, 31, 32, 35, 37, 38, 44, 45, 64, 78, 79, 81, 82, 91, 92, 93, 97, 98, 110, 111, 112, 104, 107, 124, 125, 126, 129, 140, 142, 155, 156, 158, 160, 161, 162, 163, 177, 194, 210, 211, 224, 225, 229, 230, 233, 234, 235
bilingualism xiv, xv, xvi, xvii, xx, 3, 4, 7, 8, 10, 11, 12, 13, 14, 19, 20, 21, 22, 23, 24, 25, 26, 29, 30, 31, 34, 44, 48, 51, 61, 62, 78, 79, 81, 85, 87, 93, 98, 99, 101, 107, 111, 112, 113, 122, 123, 124, 125, 126, 129, 131, 140, 142, 146, 147, 156, 158, 161, 167, 168, 169, 195, 196, 211, 225, 226, 234, 235
bilingual revolution xiv, 12, 158, 163
bilingual speech xviii
biliteracy 19, 20, 24, 27, 28, 29, 31, 71, 78, 79, 158, 232
Britain 12, 14, 129, 130, 131, 135, 137, 139, 140, 156

Canada xiv, xv, 37, 77, 191
China 135, 136, 137, 138, 139

Chinese 140, 156, 160, 161, 172, 176, 177, 185, 194
Chinese language schools 130, 131, 132, 133, 137, 138, 139, 140
clustering 69
code switching xviii, 20, 68, 105, 140, 145
colonial xix, xx, 26, 31, 92, 113, 124, 125, 177, 178, 197, 212
colonial internalization 113
communicative repertoire 26, 27, 28
community based 36, 82, 143, 154, 155, 157
community language schools 71, 131, 139
complementary schools 133, 134, 136, 138, 139, 140, 142, 156, 167
content xvi, 26, 27, 28, 47, 51, 62, 80, 85, 87, 89, 90, 92, 99, 106, 107, 175, 184, 187, 190, 193, 194, 208
content and language integrated learning xiv, 71, 73, 79
content continua of biliteracy 26, 27, 28
context continua of biliteracy 26, 27, 28
continua of biliteracy vii, xiii, 19, 21, 23, 24, 26, 27, 28, 29, 31
creativity 140, 151, 152, 154, 155, 169, 212, 213, 218, 223, 224
criticality 93, 151, 154, 155, 179
Cuba 1, 5, 6, 13, 20, 21, 25, 30, 31, 32, 186, 194
CUNY xi, xii, xiii, xvi, xxiv, 11, 14, 20, 23, 33, 81, 97, 98, 99, 108, 156, 230

decolonial pedagogy 28, 29
development continua of biliteracy
diasporic plural networks 143, 153, 155
differentiation viii, 11, 66, 67, 68, 69, 70, 73, 77
dilemma 110, 111, 116, 168, 169, 171, 172, 178
discourse analysis xxiii, 12, 126, 141, 144, 156
dual correspondence theory 9

dual language 13, 28, 79, 81, 92, 93, 125, 159, 161, 162, 163, 195, 198, 205, 233
dual-language programs xiv, 44, 200, 205
dynamic bilingualism 8, 13, 14, 25, 34, 87, 99, 125, 142, 195, 196, 234

emergent bilinguals viii, xiii, xvi, xxiv, 9, 10, 11, 14, 33, 43, 44, 45, 47, 48, 50, 51, 52, 53, 55, 57, 59, 61, 62, 63, 64, 65, 81, 85, 93, 97, 98, 109, 229, 230, 231, 232
England xv, 2, 131, 142, 172
English classroom 68, 93
English education xvi, xxvi, 182, 183, 184, 185, 189, 190, 192, 193
English language learners xix, 10, 14, 33, 44, 45, 64, 65, 77, 81, 93, 98, 100, 109, 232
English learners 44, 64, 65, 78, 231
English teaching 191, 192
ethnolinguistic 3, 7, 12, 141, 142, 143, 158, 160

families xv, xxiv, xxv, 3, 20, 23, 28, 29, 81, 84, 85, 89, 92, 94, 97, 98, 99, 100, 101, 103, 104, 106, 112, 116, 129, 131, 144, 159, 160, 161, 162, 163, 192, 207, 231
Fishman, Joshua A. xvii, xviii, xix, xx, 2, 4, 6, 9, 20, 21, 22, 23, 30, 31, 35, 36, 37, 44, 64, 142, 156, 158. 159, 163, 194, 229, 231, 232, 233, 234
Fishmanian xvii, 6, 21, 30, 142, 234
flexible bilingualism 146, 167
French xiii, xxv, 68, 71, 78, 104, 158, 159, 160, 161, 163

German 2, 21, 71, 160, 161
global English 157, 183
globalization xii, xxv, 1, 2, 4, 6, 180, 194, 225, 233
global reform packages 190

Hebrew, modern 212, 213, 214, 217, 218, 219, 221, 222, 223, 224
Hebrew speaking 217, 219
heritage language xv, xvi, xxvi, 14, 31, 86, 129, 130, 139, 141, 142, 155, 156, 157, 159, 163, 167, 168, 169, 170, 172, 194, 233, 234
heteroglossic hybridity 77
hybridity 2, 67, 76, 77, 212, 234

Identity xv, xx, 10, 12, 20, 34, 51, 74, 92, 95, 107, 112, 116, 123, 133, 138, 141, 145, 146, 147, 148, 149, 151, 154, 156, 157, 158, 161, 162, 163, 170, 197, 206, 209, 217, 218, 224, 225, 226

identity-related 145, 146, 148, 151, 154
ideological viii, xi, xix, xx, 23, 99, 143, 156, 167, 168, 169, 170, 171, 172, 173, 175, 176, 177, 178, 190, 213, 214, 215, 216, 217, 218, 219, 223
idiolect 66, 70, 76, 83, 145, 152, 154
imagination 3, 19, 23, 24, 78, 178, 218
Iran viii, xii, xxvi, 13, 36, 180, 182–194
Italian xxv, 71, 73, 160, 161

Japanese 71, 72, 73, 79, 160, 161, 234
Jewish viii, xi, 13, 14, 21, 36, 212, 213, 214, 215, 217, 218, 219, 220, 221, 222, 223, 224, 225, 226
Judaism 213, 214, 219, 223, 224, 225

knowledge economy 188, 189, 192, 193

language education xii, xv, xvii, 11, 14, 24, 25, 28, 29, 30, 31, 34, 44, 79, 80, 85, 90, 91, 112, 123, 124, 125, 156, 161, 162, 168, 169, 177, 179, 180, 183, 187, 233, 234
language identity 157, 206, 226
language ideology 133, 143, 157, 168
language maintenance xv, 141, 142, 156
language policy viii, xiv, xv, xx, 10, 12, 13, 24, 26, 30, 35, 64, 122, 136, 140, 151, 165, 180, 187, 194, 195, 196, 202, 203, 205, 206, 207, 208, 209, 210, 211
language practices 4, 9, 13, 32, 44, 49, 62, 67, 68, 69, 70, 71, 72, 74, 76, 77, 89, 91, 98, 99, 100, 101, 102, 104, 105, 106, 108, 109, 113, 167, 177, 195, 196, 197, 198, 199, 200, 201, 202, 205, 207, 208, 209, 210, 211, 213, 214, 215, 223
language repertoire xviii, xix, 10, 56, 102
languaging viii, xviii, xx, xxv, 5, 6, 8, 9, 25, 26, 28, 69, 97, 105, 106, 107, 111, 112, 114, 116, 118, 122, 124, 142, 153, 155, 196, 197, 198, 212
languaging, mono 197
languaging, pluri 197
languaging, sustainable 142, 153, 155, 156
Latin Americans xi, xviii, xix, 20, 25
Latinx xiii, xiv, xix, 20, 11, 13, 20, 21, 24, 26, 28, 29, 30, 37, 38, 43, 44, 47, 50, 90, 92, 195
linguistic communities xiv, 7, 12, 142, 158, 160, 161, 162
linguistic features 11, 67, 198, 202

linguistic repertoire ii, xviii, xx, 5, 8, 9, 11, 12, 67, 68, 70, 71, 72, 73, 74, 79, 82, 85, 87, 89, 98, 99, 105, 106, 107, 110, 114, 122, 124, 145, 149, 152, 154, 155, 198, 200, 202, 207, 208, 215, 216, 218

Manhattan 114, 143, 167
media continua of biliteracy 26, 27, 28
mediation 169
middle school xiii, 44, 47, 195, 205
minoritized parents' voices 140
monoglossia 67, 113
mono languaging 197
monolinguals xxv, 8, 67, 68, 70, 209, 211
multilingualism v, vii, xii, xiv, xv, xvi, xx, xxiii, xiv, xxiv, xxv, xxvi, 1–12, 14, 17, 19, 20, 22–31, 35, 36, 37, 46, 64, 79, 83, 86, 91, 92, 93, 99, 123, 124, 131, 140, 141, 156, 157, 161, 163, 170, 194, 210, 218, 224, 230, 232, 233, 234
multiliteracy 161

named languages xviii, xix, xxiv, 5, 8, 11, 15, 51, 66, 67, 70, 71, 77, 79, 87, 93, 107, 112, 113, 123, 124, 125, 126
national forces 183, 185, 187, 190, 191, 192, 193
New York City xv, 2, 5, 7, 11, 12, 19, 20, 21, 30, 33, 47, 53, 81, 92, 97, 111, 112, 125, 156, 159, 195, 225, 229
NYCDOE 33, 112
NYSED 34, 98
NYSIEB xiii, xxiv, 11, 14, 33, 97, 98, 99, 108, 156

othering 118
Ottawa 37
overlappings 69, 70, 73, 76

parental voices viii, 12, 129, 132, 139
parents viii, xiv, 6, 12, 45, 50, 51, 73, 84, 88, 98, 103, 108, 112, 129–140, 143, 144, 145, 150, 152, 153, 155, 158-163, 170, 200, 202
Persian xxv, 183, 184
pluri languaging 197
poetic inquiry viii, 110, 111, 113, 114, 115, 117, 119, 121, 123, 125, 126
policy actors 13, 111, 183
policy borrowing xxviii, 186, 187, 188, 190, 192, 193, 194
policy emulation 183, 188
Polish 160, 161
Positioning 11, 67, 73, 77, 78, 79, 93, 145, 156, 222

privatization 185, 186, 187, 188, 192, 193
public schools 26, 159, 187, 188, 191, 193, 225

race 58, 60, 93, 112, 113, 117, 126, 136, 179, 195
racialization 113, 177
raciolinguistically minoritized students/ learners xiii, 19, 20, 28, 29
raciolinguistic ideologies 29, 90, 92, 99, 113, 118, 124, 125
Russian 46, 65, 71, 160, 161

semiotic repertoire 47, 67, 76
semiotic resources/modes ii, 43, 45, 46, 48, 52, 56, 63, 224
social justice viii, xiii, xvii, xx, 11, 13, 35, 80, 81, 83, 84, 88, 90, 91, 93, 111, 122, 125, 171, 176, 177, 178
social semiotics 46
Spanish xvii, xviii, xix, xx, xxv, 3, 7, 8, 20, 21, 28, 30, 31, 47–62, 71, 79, 100, 101, 103, 104, 112, 114, 116–121, 125, 160, 161, 196–209, 234
stakeholders xxi, 111, 129, 140, 145, 151–155, 183
sub-national forces 183, 185, 187, 190, 191, 192, 193
subtractive bilingualism 12
supplementary schools 142
supra-national forces 183, 185, 193
sustainable languaging 142, 153, 155, 156

TC 230
Teachers College xiii, xiv, xv, xxiii, xxvi, 14, 15, 23, 31, 32, 35, 38, 44, 45, 63, 64, 65, 93, 109, 111, 141, 156, 180, 194, 229, 230, 231, 232
teacher dispositions 11, 91
teacher education viii, xii, xv, 10, 11, 41, 77, 78, 80, 81, 84, 89, 90, 91, 92, 93
transculturation 25
transfeaturing viii, 11, 66–78
translanguaging corriente 99, 101, 106, 108, 109
translanguaging pedagogy viii, 11, 28, 70, 74, 76, 97, 98, 99, 107, 108, 132, 136
translanguaging stance 66, 80, 88, 124, 125
translanguaging space 12, 14, 146, 152, 154, 156, 222
translingualism 32, 33, 34
transnational communities 130, 135

trans-semiotic practices viii, 11, 43, 47, 49, 52, 62, 63, 231
Turkish xv, xxv, 12, 141–157, 169

UK xi, xvi, xxi, 13, 79, 130, 131, 167, 178, 186, 190
UN 188
United Kingdom 130, 131, 136, 137, 167, 169, 177, 187
United Nations 143, 188, 194
University of Pennsylvania xii, xiii, xxvi, 6, 36

USA xii, xiii, 64, 156, 186, 215, 217
U-turn viii, 12, 158, 160, 161, 162, 163

World Bank 186, 187, 188, 194

youth viii, xiii, 13, 14, 38, 53, 156, 157, 184, 191, 195–203, 205, 207–211, 213, 214, 224, 225
youths' lived realities 13

Zionism 224, 225